PERSPECTIVES ON
RISK-BASED CAPITAL

A Guide to the New Risk-Based Capital Adequacy Rules

by
Raj Bhala

Bank Administration Institute
Rolling Meadows, Illinois

Bank Administration Institute

BAI is a unique professional services organization that offers research, information services, and professional development opportunities to bankers worldwide. The Institute's independent, not-for-profit status enables it to serve bankers objectively—as both adviser and analyst.

BAI is a creative partnership, blending the policy-level experience of bankers worldwide with the specialized expertise of its professional staff. These bankers serve on the Institute's board of directors, technical commissions, and advisory groups, ensuring that BAI meets changing needs with relevant programs and services.

The Institute presents information across a wide range of critically important areas, including management and administration; strategic planning; accounting, finance and control; audit and tax; corporate financial services; consumer financial services; and operations and technology. This information is conveyed through methods well suited to the varying needs of banking professionals — ranging from research, technical conferences and educational programs to a broad and growing array of publications.

Library of Congress Catalog Card Number: 89-61342

Copyright © 1989 by Bank Administration Institute, Rolling Meadows, Illinois. All rights reserved. This book or any parts of it may not be reproduced in any form without written permission from the publisher.

Printed in the United States of America.

No. 605 ISBN: 1-55520-117-2

Contents

List of Figures ix

List of Tables xi

Foreword xiii

Preface xix
A. Apologies, Omissions, and Vince Lombardi xix
B. The Structure of This Book xxvi
C. Acknowledgments xxviii
Commonly Used Abbreviations xxxi

Introduction: Why You Need This Book 1

1. Preliminary Matters 5
A. Some Background Information and the Ground Rules 5
B. A Little Legal Philosophy: Applying the Substance-Form Distinction to the Basle Agreement 12
C. Chapter Summary 15

2. Why Worry About Bank Capital? 17
A. Isn't the Capital Structure of a Bank Irrelevant? 17
B. The Answer: No 18
C. Why Not Market-Determined Capital? 20
D. The Answer: The Market Is Imperfect 24
E. Substantive Functions of Regulatory-Determined Capital 25
   (1) Absorbing Losses 27
   (2) Enhancing Public Confidence 29
   (3) Preventing Bank Failures 32
   (4) Restraining Asset Growth 35

	(5) Helping the FDIC	36
	(6) Generating Earnings	39
F.	Chapter Summary	40

3. Substance, Form, and the Constituents of Capital   43
A. The Ability to Absorb Losses Is What Matters   43
   (1) Tier One: Core Capital   44
      (a) Equity Capital in Tier One   45
      (b) Disclosed Reserves in Tier One   49
      (c) Adjustments to Equity Capital and Disclosed Reserves   49
         (i) Goodwill   49
         (ii) Cumulative Perpetual Preferred Stock   56
   (2) Tier Two: Supplementary Capital   57
      (a) Undisclosed Reserves   58
      (b) Revaluation Reserves   59
      (c) General Provisions and General Loan Loss Reserves   60
      (d) Hybrid Instruments   61
      (e) Subordinated Term Debt   63
   (3) Calculating Total Capital   64
B. Some Strange Financial Instruments   66
   (1) It's Tough to Keep Up!   66
   (2) Guaranteed Preferred Shares   67
   (3) Floating-Rate Preferred Stock   68
   (4) Upstream Convertibles   69
   (5) Unbundled Stock   70
C. Chapter Summary   76

4. The Risk-Weighting System   79
A. They Said It Couldn't Be Done: Credit Risk Is What Matters   79

CONTENTS

B.	The Five Risk Categories for On-Balance-Sheet Assets	83
C.	Some Weighty Matters: Risk Weights for Treasuries, Mortgage-Backeds, CMOs, and Strips	86
	(1) Treasury Securities: Should Interest Rate Risk Be Considered?	86
	(2) Mortgage-Backed Securities: Look at the Obligor	88
	(3) Collateralized Mortgage Obligations: How About a 20 Percent Risk Weight?	94
	(4) Stripped Mortgage-Backed Securities: These Are Really Risky!	96
D.	Calculating the Credit Equivalent Amount for Off-Balance-Sheet Items	98
E.	A Gearing Ratio: Does This Capture Interest Rate Risk?	99
F.	Chapter Summary	101
5.	**The ABCs of Swaps**	**103**
A.	An Exchange of Obligations	103
B.	The Swap Market and the ISDA	107
C.	Substantive Functions of Swaps	109
	(1) Hedging Interest Rate and Currency Risk	109
	(2) Cost Reduction	110
	(3) Brokerage	111
	(4) Speculation	111
D.	Illustrations of Hedging and Cost Reduction Functions	112
	(1) Anatomy of a Plain Vanilla Swap	113
	(a) Eliminating a Mismatch	113
	(b) Lowering the Cost of Funds	115
	(2) Anatomy of a Basis Swap	120
	(a) Eliminating a Mismatch	120
	(b) Lowering the Cost of Funds	122

	(3) Anatomy of a Currency Swap	124
	(a) Eliminating a Mismatch	124
	(b) Lowering the Cost of Funds	125
	(4) Anatomy of a Cross-Currency Interest Rate Swap	128
	(a) Eliminating Two Mismatches	128
	(b) Lowering the Cost of Funds	129
E.	Chapter Summary	132

6. Substance, Form, and the Treatment of Swaps — 133

- A. Swaps, Irony, and Overinclusion — 133
  - (1) Complexity — 135
  - (2) Irony and Overinclusion — 136
- B. But Can You Differentiate Among the Substantive Functions? — 138
  - (1) Proposed Regulations of the Federal Financial Institutions Examination Council — 138
  - (2) Section 988 of the Internal Revenue Code — 142
- C. Interest Rate and Currency Risk Arising from Swaps — 144
- D. Swap Credit Risk, Take No. 1: The Effect of Counterparty Default Where the Counterparty Does Not Go Bankrupt — 147
  - (1) Reasons for Counterparty Default — 147
  - (2) Counterparty Default and Restoration of the Status Quo Ante — 149
- E. Swap Credit Risk, Take No. 2: The Effect of Counterparty Default Where the Counterparty Does Go Bankrupt — 152
  - (1) Banks as Creditors Under the Bankruptcy Code — 153
  - (2) No Grabbing! — 154
  - (3) Executory Contracts and Financial Accommodations — 155
  - (4) The Trustee's Power of Assumption or Rejection and the Risk of "Cherry Picking" — 157

(5) Adequate Protection and the Risk of Delay Costs	160
(6) The Case of a Counterparty Not Subject to the Bankruptcy Code	173
F. Contractual Mechanisms to Minimize Swap Credit Risk	163
(1) The ISDA's Master Agreements	163
(2) Netting	168
(3) Credit Enhancements	171
G. What Exactly Does the Basle Agreement Say About Swaps?	171
(1) The Concept of Replacement Cost	171
(2) Calculating the Capital Support Required for Swaps	177
H. The Turgid Miasma of Detail: The ISDA's Comment Letter	181
I. Chapter Summary	186
Conclusion: The Building Blocks of Risk-Based Capital	189
Appendix The Basle Agreement on Risk-Based Capital	193
Glossary	237
Bibliography	247
Index	265
About the Author	271

List of Figures

Figure 1	Traditional Corporate Finance Model for Determining Optimal Capital Structure	22
Figure 2	Flowchart of Hypothetical Interest Rate Swap Between Manufacturers Hanover and GMAC (No Intermediary)	116
Figure 3	Flowchart of Hypothetical Interest Rate Swap Between Manufacturers Hanover and GMAC (with Intermediary)	117
Figure 4	Flowchart of Hypothetical Basis Swap Between Manufacturers Hanover and GMAC	123
Figure 5	Flowchart of Hypothetical Currency Swap Between Natwest and Procter & Gamble	126
Figure 6	Flowchart of Hypothetical Cross-Currency Interest Rate Swap Between Bankers Trust and British Petroleum	130

List of Tables

Table 1   Risk-Weight Categories for On-Balance-
          Sheet Assets   83

Table 2   Credit Conversion Factors for Off-Balance-
          Sheet Items Other than Swaps   100

Table 3   Cash Flow Analysis of Hypothetical Interest
          Rate Swap Between Marine Midland and
          Ford   120

Table 4   Percentage of Notional Principal Amount Used
          to Calculate Potential Future Exposure   179

Foreword

Perspectives on Risk-Based Capital by Raj Bhala is a remarkable combination of perspectives. It does not merely focus on the many practical aspects of the implementation of the Basle Agreement, but also asks fundamental questions about the importance of capital adequacy to the safety and soundness of banks. It combines a financial and jurisprudential approach to reviewing the Basle Agreement and its implementation by the Federal Reserve Board. Bhala's analysis of the application of capital rules to swaps demonstrates the difficulty of applying a risk-based approach to new financial instruments. And all of this by a young lawyer at the beginning of his career at the Federal Reserve Bank of New York. An amazing accomplishment.

The Basle Agreement is important for several reasons. First, it demonstrates the commitment of bank regulators to capital adequacy as the centerpiece of safety and soundness regulation. Second, it deals with the moral hazard issue by making risk takers pay a price in the form of increased capital costs. Third, it demonstrates that the definition of capital and the quantification of risk for regulatory purposes is extremely difficult and somewhat arbitrary. Fourth, it recognizes that capital and other forms of bank regulation must be coordinated on an international level because of the increasing growth of international banking combined with the competitive impact of regulation. Finally, it suggests that a tool designed for one purpose, controlling risk, may be converted easily, and some would say misused, for another purpose, credit allocation. Some comments on each of these points follow.

As Bhala's book clearly points out, capital adequacy is central to safety and soundness regulation. Potential losses to the safety net provided by the insurance and lender of last resort system are minimized when adequate capital is initially available to absorb them. More capital means there is a bigger buffer and gives the regulatory agencies more time to detect serious problems and take corrective action. More capital, of course, means less return on capital for banks, which compared with many other industrial and financial firms have not been highly profitable. Stiffer requirements may cause a shakeout, and lead to more mergers and restructurings. But this may be beneficial in the longer term. In any event, if banks are to benefit from a federal safety net, the providers of the net are entitled to protect themselves against loss, and adequate capital is an important part of that protection.

Many analysts have pointed out that the federal safety net creates a moral hazard. Since bank creditors are protected against losses, in part in a liquidation or in whole in many cases of open bank assistance or engineered purchase and assumption transactions, managers are not subject to the usual discipline from creditors.

Risk-based capital is an attempt to impose additional costs on bank shareholders from taking risk, with the hope that this will cause the shareholders, of which management is often an important part, to take more care. In this regard it is the kissing cousin of risk-based insurance premium proposals that have been considered by the Federal Deposit Insurance Corporation. The two approaches principally differ in the method of assessing the cost, cost of capital versus cost of insurance premiums. The cost of the capital increase is essentially the loss of the opportunity to benefit from net interest margins produced by leverage.

Limitations on leverage will reduce returns on capital. This does not mean we do not need both—obviously the collection of premiums by the FDIC is essential for providing the resources to meet their insurance obligations, and increased capital costs result in no direct transfer of funds to the government. But we must also be careful not to over-deter risk taking through the cumulative costs that these two programs might impose.

FOREWORD

Bhala provides an insightful and exhaustive analysis of the problems one confronts in defining capital and in quantifying risk. Both are key components of the Basle proposal. As to the definition of capital, there are three principal concerns. First, one must make sure that one only includes items which are actually a buffer, i.e., funds available to support losses. If reserves are already associated with known losses rather than possible losses, they should not be included. If goodwill value is incapable of being realized, at least at the value it is assigned on the balance sheet, its inclusion in capital should similarly be curtailed. Second, there are significant accounting questions that go to the valuation assigned to items to be included in capital. The issue of allowing revaluation reserves, whether associated with fixed assets or the securities portfolio, fit into this category. While historical cost may under represent the value of the assets, current market value will not reflect market risk or liquidation costs. Third, there is the problem of whether a given security is debt or equity. Capital should only include claims that are subordinate to those of creditors, including the FDIC or the Fed. This issue comes up in the treatment of hybrid instruments, such as perpetual preferred stock and subordinated term debt.

The quantification of risk is one of the most problematic areas in the Basle framework. The ability to discriminate between the risk associated with different types of assets is greatly limited, if not impossible. Indeed, this concern is behind many of the "narrow" bank proposals under which banks would only be able to hold assets that are valued in a secondary market. While it is clear that Treasury bills are less risky than commercial loans, how much less risky is another matter. And the fact that all commercial loans are now considered of equal risk under the risk-based framework demonstrates the extent to which the framework significantly departs from reality. But it is still true that something is probably better than nothing; that is, some risk weighting, although highly imperfect, is better than none.

PERSPECTIVES ON RISK-BASED CAPITAL

The fact that the Basle framework is internationally agreed upon by bank regulators recognizes that leverage has an important competitive effect. More highly leveraged institutions can charge lower prices, through less of a required spread, and earn the same return on capital as less highly leveraged institutions. The amount of leverage permitted by the debt market depends on the terms and conditions of country safety nets and banking structure. The value of Japan's and West Germany's safety net to creditors of a significant bank may be higher than that of the United States. Internationally agreed upon capital requirements seek to limit the leverage advantage. Further, international agreement is essential to permitting cross-border operations of banks. Host countries are naturally concerned that foreign banks taking liabilities from their residents be adequately capitalized, particularly where there is doubt that the home country safety net will cover host country debtholders in the event of a bank failure.

There are some concerns about the legal nature of the international agreement. In the United States, it has been entered into by bank regulators, pursuant to existing statutory authority to regulate banks. It is not in any sense a treaty or agreement approved by Congress. The same is true for other countries which are party to the agreement. This means that bank regulators in this country or abroad are not required by domestic law to live up to the agreement. One assumes central bankers will honor their commitments, and one must recognize that even statutes passed by Congress or parliaments may be later changed. But the level of firm commitment represented by a "gentleman's agreement" among central bankers may be less than that of a treaty formerly enacted into law. This is not to say a treaty would have been preferable—like any statute it would have been more frozen in time, and regulation of capital will have to be continually fine tuned, a job more properly left to the regulators. Perhaps it would be preferable to combine an agreement in principle enacted into law with delegation of implementation authority to the regulators. This would increase political commitment without strait jacketing the on-going process.

The most intriguing aspect of the agreement is whether it presages agreements in other areas of bank regulation, such as bank powers. These issues are already being addressed in the GATT round on trade and services, albeit a forum completely different than represented by the central bankers who meet under the auspices of the Bank of International Settlements. Agreement on other issues is given some impetus by increasing demands for reciprocity emanating from the European Economic Community, and questions of powers certainly affect safety and soundness and competition among banks from different countries. It is entirely possible that the Basle Agreement on capital represents a first step in a broader harmonization of bank regulatory regimes.

Finally, one must be aware that the risk-based capital framework can be used to achieve objectives other than safety and soundness and an even playing field. The movement of collateralized mortgage obligations from the 100 percent category of loans to a 20 percent risk weight decreased the capital cost of making mortgage loans. Political pressures connected with the desire to foster this kind of lending played an important role in this change. There is a danger that once the risk-based framework is established, the temptation will be unavoidable to use the framework for credit allocation. One virtue of making risk-based capital an international agreement is that domestic pressures of this kind can be resisted on the grounds that change, particularly in the form of less onerous standards, requires the agreement of other countries.

Professor Hal S. Scott
Harvard Law School

Preface

A. Apologies, Omissions, and Vince Lombardi

This study represents a rather different book from what I had initially conceived. I had planned to treat the Basle Agreement in a broader fashion, touching upon a range of issues. For example, what are the likely competitive effects of the agreement? One of the stated purposes is to "level the playing field" on which international banks compete. (The other frequently mentioned purpose is to strengthen the soundness and stability of the international banking system.)[1] Will "money-center" banks be disadvantaged relative to the "super-regionals"? Many commentators have pointed out that the super-regionals already meet the ratio of 8 percent capital/risk-weighted assets, whereas the money-center banks (with the exception of Morgan Guaranty, Bankers Trust, and Citicorp) will require substantial additional capital to meet the ratio.[2] Will American

---

[1] *See* Committee on Banking Regulations and Supervisory Practices, *International Convergence of Capital Measurement and Capital Standards*, July 1988 (Bank for International Settlements, Basle, Switzerland), 2. *See also* B. Orr, "The Fed Drops the Other Shoe," ABA *Banking Journal* 127 (October 1988); "Capital Ratio Is Set by Banks of 12 Nations," *Wall Street Journal*, July 12, 1988, at 3. For an argument that the guidelines may not level the playing field to the extent hoped, *see* M. Malloy, "U.S. International Banking and the New Capital Adequacy Requirements: New, Old and Unexpected," 7 *Annual Review of Banking Law* 75 (1988). Malloy argues, *inter alia*, that differential capital requirements are but one source of international competitive inequality. *Id.* at 80.

[2] *See, e.g.*, "Large U.S. Banks Should Easily Meet Fed's New Capital Rules, Analysts Say," *Wall Street Journal*, August 5, 1988, at 20; "Bank Capital Rule Expected to Slow the Pace of Lending," *New York Times*, July 13, 1988, at D1; C. Friesen, "Capital Guidelines and Global Markets," 4 *The Review of Financial Services Regulation* 123, 127, 129 (July 1988); and "Hard Times for Three Big Banks," *New York Times*, April 10, 1988, at Section 3, 1.

banks be disadvantaged relative to the Japanese banks? There is no dearth of commentary on this incarnation of the general "America versus Japan" issue. Some Federal Reserve officials insist that Japanese banks will have to raise more capital than American banks.[3] Alternatively, the fact that Japanese banks will be entitled to count 45 percent of unrealized capital gains as core capital, while U.S. banks will not, is thought by some to be unfair.[4] Will the Basle Agreement hinder the competitiveness of banks relative to other financial institutions? Some bankers argue that banks will become less able to compete with investment banks and insurance companies as sources of funds for strong corporate clients.[5]

Similarly, I generally neglect the many questions concerning adjustment. How will the banks meet the required capital/risk-weighted assets ratio of 7.25 percent by the end of 1990 and 8 percent by the end of 1992? However, because these questions are interesting, particularly for those who (like me) enjoy planning, I cannot help but comment on them here. There are three ways to meet a capital/asset ratio: raise capital through external financing, raise capital through retaining earnings, or lower assets. Flammia summarizes these as follows:

> Banks adjust to higher required capital-to-asset ratios with three basic techniques. First, the bank may *issue more*

---

[3]*See e.g.*, "Fed Clears Minimum Capital Standards, Forcing Some Banks to Raise $15 Billion," *Wall Street Journal,* August 4, 1988, at 6; "Capital Ratio Is Set by Banks of 12 Nations," *Wall Street Journal,* July 12, 1988, at 3; and "Agreement on Banks' Capital Set," *New York Times,* July 12, 1988, at D1.

[4]For a highly critical account asserting that the risk-based guidelines will help Japanese banks and weaken U.S. banks, *see* N. Osborn and G. Evans, "Cooke's Medicine: Kill or Cure?," *Euromoney* 34 (July 1988).

[5]*See, e.g.*, "Banks' New Minimum Capital Rules Add to International Bankers' Worries," *Wall Street Journal,* July 12, 1988, at 35.

stock. The cash paid by the buyers of the stock can be held as capital. However, there is a limit to this source of bank capital. If so much stock is issued that it floods the market, the market value of the stock will drop. Notably, the recent rash of bank failures has created an overall decline in the value of most banks' stock. Since stock ownership represents ownership of the bank, selling stock at a low price, in essence, further liquidates ownership of the bank. Thus, banks must also utilize the other two methods of raising capital-to-asset ratios.

Second, the bank may *retain earnings*. Profits that are not paid to stockholders nor reinvested in loans can be held by the bank as capital. Third, the bank may *sell assets*. Reducing the number of assets reduces the amount of capital needed to meet the required ratio.[6]

The fundamental question with respect to adjustment is not so much how to meet the ratio but how much to rely on each of the three mechanisms. My own forecast is that securitization of assets will play a large role in meeting the required ratio.[7] In principle, almost any group of bank assets can be securitized. Mortgage loans, computer leases, automobile receivables, credit card receivables, consumer loans, manufactured housing loans, and boat receivables have all been securitized.[8] Currently, attempts are being made to securitize junk bonds and Third World debt.[9]

---

[6]M. Flammia, "Bank Capital Requirements: Placebo or Cure?," 7 *Annual Review of Banking Law* 485, 486-487 (1988) (emphasis supplied).

[7]For an argument that securitization is a useful technique to meet the required ratio, *see* J. Rosenthal and J. Ocampo, *Securitization of Credit* 17-20, 220 (1988). *See also* "Asset-backed Securities," *International Financing Review* 1921 (June 18, 1988). *See generally* E. Gardener, "Securitization: The Challenge for World Banking," 7 *The World of Banking* 3 (Jan./Feb. 1988).

[8]"Asset-backed Securities," *International Financing Review* 1921 (June 18, 1988).

[9]*Id*. at 1922.

PERSPECTIVES ON RISK-BASED CAPITAL

Securitizing assets can help a bank comply with risk-based capital regulations in two ways: it can boost the numerator of the capital/risk-weighted assets ratio, and it can reduce the denominator. A bank that pools relatively similar assets and sells them receives cash proceeds from the sale. Such proceeds will increase the cash account on the left-hand side of the bank's balance sheet and one of the capital accounts (*e.g.*, a surplus account such as earned surplus) on the right-hand side of the balance sheet. The bank's capital position is thereby strengthened. As long as the sale complies with generally accepted accounting principles (GAAP) and regulatory accounting principles (RAP) regarding recourse (specifically, as long as there is no recourse against the selling bank in the event that any of the assets sold becomes nonperforming), then the assets may be removed from the bank's balance sheet.[10] A decrease in an asset account will be matched by a decrease in one of the capital accounts. Capital will no longer be needed to support the sold assets.

A third issue I regret to omit concerns the place of the Basle Agreement in the general scheme of capital regulation of financial institutions. How does the agreement compare with the net equity rules prescribed by the Securities and Exchange Commission (SEC) for securities brokers and dealers?[11] If and when the wall of the Glass-Steagall Act is removed by Congress (or as it increasingly resembles Swiss cheese because of administrative and judicial fiat), will the

---

[10]*See* J. Rosenthal and J. Ocampo, *Securitization of Credit* 67-73 (1988).

[11]SEC Rule 15(c) (3), 15 C.F.R. § 240.15c3-1. For a stimulating comparison of capital requirements for commercial and investment banks, *see* G. Haberman, "Capital Requirements of Commercial and Investment Banks: Contrasts in Regulation," Federal Reserve Bank of New York *Quarterly Review* 1 (Autumn 1987). I must note that I am awed by an author who grasps the mechanics of capital regulation for both commercial and investment banks.

same capital requirements exist for the securities and banking subsidiaries of the same bank holding company? Section 20 of the Glass-Steagall Act (12 U.S.C. § 377) states that "no member bank shall be affiliated ... with any corporation ... engaged principally in the issue, flotation, underwriting, public sale, or distribution ... of stocks, notes, or other securities...."

In 1986, acting upon a Citicorp application to engage in securities activities, the Federal Reserve took the position that a securities affiliate of a bank may underwrite and deal in types of securities that are otherwise off-limits to such affiliates so long as no more than 5 percent of that affiliate's revenue is derived from underwriting and dealing in the securities. The remaining 95 percent of the affiliate's revenues must come from underwriting and dealing in federal, state, and certain local instruments all of which are permissible activities under section 16 of the Glass-Steagall Act (12 U.S.C. §§ 24, 335, and 378).

Banks have attacked the section 20 limitation in two ways. First, they have sought sweeping legislative changes. The most recent attempt to modify or eliminate the section 20 limitation, which was sponsored by Senator William Proxmire, failed to win approval of both houses of Congress.[12] Second, banks have sought judicial and regulatory approval to include a greater array of instruments within the 5 percent limitation and have also sought an increase in this percentage limit.[13] The relation of all of this to risk-based

---

[12]The Financial Modernization Act of 1988, S. 1886, 100th Cong., 2nd Sess.

[13]The U.S. Supreme Court recently denied a writ of certiorari on a Second Circuit decision that granted banks the authority to underwrite commercial paper, mortgage-backed securities, and securities backed by consumer loans. *See Securities Industry Association v. Board of Governors of the Federal Reserve System,* 839 F.2d 47 (2nd Cir. 1988), *cert. denied,* 108 S.Ct. 2830 (1988). Also, following the failure of Congress to enact Sena-

capital is the logic of different capital requirements for different subsidiaries held by the same parent holding company. The Federal Reserve has reserved the discretion to rule, on a case-by-case basis, that risk-based capital regulations do not apply to securities dealers and other nonbank affiliates of banks.[14] The Federal Reserve will so rule if adequate "firewalls" exist to separate the affiliate and the bank.[15]

All of the foregoing is simply "issue-spotting." I am sorry to say that I have not offered any insight into these issues in this book. Rather, I have focused on a few issues in some depth. This focus is deliberate. The more I studied risk-based capital, the more convinced I became that a thorough understanding of the building blocks of the topic was needed. To understand risk-based capital, one must understand its basic elements: *capital* and *risk*. What is capital?

---

tor Proxmire's bill, Citicorp, Chase Manhattan, Morgan Guaranty, and Bankers Trust applied to the Federal Reserve to underwrite and deal in corporate issues. These banks seek to underwrite and deal in corporate debt and preferred stock. Bankers Trust applied for permission to underwrite and deal in corporate stock as well. Similar applications are expected from Manufacturers Hanover and Chemical Bank. See "Four Banks Ask Fed for Broad Powers to Underwrite, Deal in Corporate Issues," *Wall Street Journal*, October 26, 1988, at A3.

[14]54 Fed. Reg. 4186, 4195 (January 27, 1989). This citation is to the Federal Reserve Board's final risk-based capital regulations. It is explained further in Chapter 1. *See also* the following two Federal Reserve Board memorandua: (1) Federal Reserve Board Staff Memorandum Re: Risk-Based Capital Guidelines, December 14, 1988 (Taylor, Spillenkothen, Cole, Pugh, O'Rourke, and Barger [Board]; and Spindler and Bardos [New York]) (mimeo), 10-12, 142-143, 149-152, 213, and 216-219 (for state member banks), 314 and 317-322 (for bank holding companies), and (2) Federal Reserve Board Staff Memorandum Re: Risk-Based Capital, August 1, 1988 (Taylor, Spillenkothen, Cornyn, O'Rourke, and Barger [Board]; and Spindler [New York]) (mimeo), 18, 57-58. Hereinafter, I refer to and cite the first memorandum as the "December 14, 1988, Board Staff Memorandum." The second memorandum is hereinafter referred to and cited as the "August 1, 1988, Board Staff Memorandum."

[15]*Id.*

PREFACE

Why do banks need capital? Why do federal regulators have to tell banks how much capital is adequate? And what is risk? What risks threaten the solvency of banks? What techniques do banks employ to reduce risks?

Thus, this is not an encyclopedic study of the implications of every provision in the Basle Agreement. Nor is it an aggressive critique of the agreement. My own view is that risk-based capital regulations are a sensible way for regulators to improve the safety and soundness of the commercial banking system. The capital a bank maintains should be tied to the riskiness of its asset portfolio. Also, the Basle Agreement is a major negotiating triumph. International convergence remains an elusive goal in many fields of commercial regulation—tariff reduction and insider trading, for example.

I must also confess an academic affection for the Basle Agreement: I believe it is a superb pedagogical tool for learning about other concepts. To study the agreement, it is not only possible but necessary to study the business of banking in general and cutting-edge financial transactions in particular. The lengthy discussion of swap transactions is an example—the rules on swaps are meaningless unless swaps are understood. Furthermore, a study of the Basle Agreement is a study of the heart of banking regulation: How can the safety and soundness of the financial system be improved? The events of October 19, 1987, make safety and soundness even more important goals. Are the values of certain assets in the portfolios of banks now more volatile? Are securities activities of banks more risky than before the crash? Has the credit risk associated with bank loans to securities brokers and dealers changed?[16] It is the banking

---

[16]*See* L. Pemberton (Governor, Bank of England), "Convergence of Capital Standards and the Lessons of the Market Crash," 28 *Bank of England Quarterly Bulletin* 220-221, 223 (May 1988). For an interesting

regulators' concern with safety and soundness that underlies questions about the nature and functions of capital.

My purpose is to examine, in an entertaining as well as edifying manner, the two building blocks of the Basle Agreement, capital and risk. No model of the atom is possible without an understanding of electrons, neutrons, protons, and other subatomic particles. No model of the macroeconomy is possible without an understanding of the workings of consumption, saving and investment, government spending and taxation, and imports and exports. Similarly, the Basle Agreement could not have been proposed and adopted, and it cannot be interpreted, without a thorough grasp of the underlying concepts of capital and risk. To put it simply, I am adopting a Vince Lombardi approach to the Basle Agreement: focus on the fundamentals.

B. The Structure of This Book

Banking regulators from the major industrial countries recently negotiated the Basle Agreement, a common set of standards concerning the capital adequacy of commercial banks. Under the agreement, capital support is a function of the risk profile of a bank's asset portfolio; a riskier portfolio requires additional capital. By the end of 1992, commercial banks are expected to maintain a ratio of capital/risk-weighted assets of 8 percent.

Capital and risk are the building blocks of the Basle Agreement. This book approaches the concept of capital by studying the *constituents of capital*. The functions of bank capital are reviewed, and the constituents that count under

---

article on the effect of the October 19 stock market crash on the payment system, *see* "The Day the Nation's Cash Pipeline Almost Ran Dry," *New York Times*, Oct. 2, 1988. *See also* "A Crisis Manager Takes on the Mechanics of the Market" and "One Year After, the Market Lives but Matters Less." *Id.*

PREFACE

the Basle Agreement are studied. It is seen that the key function of capital stressed in the agreement is the *ability to absorb losses*.

To survey the concept of risk, the book examines a particular type of off-balance-sheet transaction, *swaps*. How do interest rate, currency, and cross-currency interest rate swaps work? Why do parties enter into swap transactions? How are swaps treated under the Basle Agreement? It is seen that the focus of the Basle Agreement is on the *credit risk* associated with both on- and off-balance-sheet activities of banks. However, it is also seen that considerations of interest and foreign exchange rate risk "creep in." Capital constituents therefore may be called upon to absorb losses arising from risks other than pure credit risk.

An attempt is made to differentiate form from substance. The form capital constituents take is compared with the substantive functions capital fulfills. The substantive functions that swaps fulfill are explored. It is argued that while substance triumphs over form with respect to capital constituents, form triumphs over substance with respect to the treatment of swaps.

The triumph of substance with respect to capital constituents helps to ensure that *new financial instruments* banks might issue in the future can be dealt with under the Basle Agreement. This is because the agreement will "look through" the form any new instrument takes and instead focus on whether the instrument is able to perform the substantive function of absorbing losses.

The triumph of form with respect to swaps is ironic, because swaps are used to hedge against interest and foreign exchange rate risk. Stated differently, the guidelines are *overinclusive* in requiring capital support for swaps used to hedge interest rate or currency risk. The irony is heightened when the credit risk on swap contracts is explored. So long as bankruptcy law is inoperative, the effect of *counterparty default* on a swap used by the nondefaulting party to hedge interest rate or currency risk is merely to reinstate the *status quo ante, i.e.*, the initial unhedged position. However, if default occurs because of counterparty bankruptcy, and bankruptcy law is triggered, the nondefaulting party is potentially worse off than before it entered into the swap contract.

C. Acknowledgments

There are several individuals to whom I am greatly indebted, and there is one individual to whom this book is dedicated.

My friend and classmate, John Vlahoplus, must be thanked for his patience. John kindly tolerated my lengthy monologues on risk-based capital for almost a year. (I trust the monologues were not a factor in his decision to begin practicing tax instead of banking law.) I am grateful to Hal Scott, professor at Harvard Law School, for the many helpful comments he provided on earlier drafts of this book. He was also gentle in administering the dreaded Socratic teaching method to me in class, perhaps knowing full well that the night before I had read about risk-based capital instead of doing my homework.

Andrew Spindler and Thomas Baxter, vice presidents of the Federal Reserve Bank of New York, provided some much-appreciated encouragement and prudential supervision throughout the writing of this book. Of course, nothing in this book represents the official view of the Federal Reserve Bank of New York or any other part of the Federal Reserve System.

My best friend and fiancee, Kara Tan, offered her loving patience. She understood when I was too busy to go apartment-hunting in New York or watch cartoons. Finally, for my father, Dr. Ram Bhala, this book undoubtedly represents the culmination of a nine-year vicarious journey

PREFACE

through higher education. All of the successes during the journey, including this book, are directly attributable to Dad.

I would like to dedicate this book to my late grandfather, P. G. Aiyappa, a 1928 graduate of the Madras University Law School, Madras, India. The stories of his legal practice, as told to me by him and others, have been and will continue to be a source of guidance.

Commonly Used Abbreviations

August 1, 1988, Board Staff Memorandum	Memorandum Re: Risk-Based Capital from Federal Reserve Board to Board of Governors of the Federal Reserve System, dated August 1, 1988.
Bank Board	Federal Home Loan Bank Board.
Basle Agreement	Basle Agreement on Risk-Based Capital Adequacy Standards, July 1988.
Basle Committee or Cooke Committee	Committee on Banking Supervision of the Bank for International Settlements.
Basle Proposal	Basle Proposal on Risk-Based Capital Adequacy Standards, December 1987.
BHCs	Bank holding companies.
BIS	Bank for International Settlements.
BYB	Base-year bond.
Board (or Federal Reserve)	Federal Reserve Board.
Call reports	Reports of Condition and Income.
CD	Certificate of deposit.
C.F.R.	Code of Federal Regulations.
CMOs	Collateralized mortgage obligations.
December 14, 1988, Board Staff Memorandum	Memorandum Re: Risk-Based Capital Guidelines from Federal Reserve Staff to Board of Governors of the Federal Reserve System, dated December 14, 1988.

EAC	Equity appreciation certificate.
Fannie Maes	Mortgage-backed securities issued or guaranteed by FNMA.
FDIC	Federal Deposit Insurance Corporation.
Fed Funds rate	Federal Funds rate.
Fed. Reg.	*Federal Register.*
FFIEC	Federal Financial Institutions Examination Council.
FHLMC	Federal Home Loan Mortgage Corporation.
Final regulations	Final risk-based capital regulations adopted by the Federal Reserve Board on January 27, 1989.
FNMA	Federal National Mortgage Association.
Freddie Macs	Mortgage-backed securities issued or guaranteed by the FHLMC.
FRN	Floating-rate note.
FSLIC	Federal Savings and Loan Insurance Corporation.
G-10	Group of Ten countries.
GAAP	Generally accepted accounting principles.
Ginnie Maes	Mortgage-backed securities issued or guaranteed by GNMA.
GNMA	Government National Mortgage Association.
IDP	Incremental dividend preferred share.
ISDA	International Swap Dealers Association.
LIBOR	London Inter-Bank Offered Rate.
Master Rate Agreement	ISDA's standard interest rate swap contract.

ABBREVIATIONS

Master Rate and Currency Agreement	ISDA's standard interest rate and currency exchange swap contract.
May 28, 1987, ISDA Comment Letter	Letter from ISDA chairman to Federal Reserve Board and Bank of England.
Mortgage-backeds	Mortgage-backed securities.
1986 Swaps Code	ISDA's Code of Standard Wording, Assumptions and Provisions for Swaps.
OECD	Organization for Economic Cooperation and Development.
OCC	Office of the Comptroller of the Currency.
Prime	Prime interest rate.
RAP	Regulatory accounting principles.
Repo	Repurchase agreement
S&L	Savings and loan association.
SEC	Securities and Exchange Commission.
SPV	Special payment vehicle.
Strips	Stripped mortgage-backed securities.
T-notes	Treasury notes.
T-bills	Treasury bills.
T-bonds	Treasury bonds.
Technical Working Paper	Federal Reserve Board paper on potential future credit exposure on swap contracts, dated 1987.
Treasuries	Treasury securities.
Trustee	Trustee in bankruptcy.
U.S.C.	United States Code.
U.S.-U.K. Joint Proposal	Proposal on Risk-Based Capital Adequacy Standards agreed to by the Federal Reserve and the Bank of England.

Introduction
Why You Need This Book

Perspectives on Risk-Based Capital is an accurate, up-to-date guide to the new risk-based capital adequacy regulations for commercial banks. It is the first book of its kind on these important new laws. It provides a thorough, practical foundation for understanding and working with the new regulations. Here are just a few of the specific benefits of *Perspectives on Risk-Based Capital:*

- It explains complicated legal provisions in nontechnical language.

  The risk-based capital regulations are written in "legalese." This book is written in simple, commonsense prose.

- It teaches you the theoretical basis of the risk-based capital regulations.

  More important than merely memorizing the numerous intricate regulatory provisions is knowing how they fit together in an orderly scheme. Only then can you make sense of the maze of detail. By focusing on the building blocks — capital and risk — this book gives you a conceptual framework for comprehending and critiquing the regulations.

- It helps you comply with the new risk-based capital regulations.

  Understanding the details of the risk-based capital regulations is a key to meeting them. This book provides essential information for proper compliance.

- It suggests how you might raise new capital by taking advantage of certain provisions in the risk-based capital regulations.

PERSPECTIVES ON RISK-BASED CAPITAL

New financial instruments are constantly being developed. This book offers insights into how some of the new instruments might help your bank raise more capital by explaining how they might be treated under the new regulations.

- It shows you the effects of the risk-based regulations on holdings of various assets and off-balance-sheet activities.

This book tells you how practically everything from mortgage-backeds to plain vanilla swaps are treated under the new regulations.

- It provides you with helpful reference tools.

Each chapter begins with a list of key concepts to be encountered and concludes with a capsule summary of the main points. You will find a handy glossary of risk-based capital terminology at the end of the book, as well as a bibliography of the up-to-date sources used to compile this text.

In addition, *Perspectives on Risk-Based Capital* provides a comprehensive review of:

- The functions of bank capital.
- Risks incurred in the banking business.
- How interest rate, currency, and cross-currency interest rate swaps work.
- The operation of bankruptcy law in the context of swap transactions.

Perspectives on Risk-Based Capital will appeal to all those practicing or planning a career in the financial services industry. It is particularly appropriate for banking managers, lawyers, regulators, consultants, and analysts.

This book is also ideal as a supplementary textbook for graduate and professional students of banking and finance

INTRODUCTION

as well as for students enrolled in in-house training programs at financial institutions.

In sum, *Perspectives on Risk-Based Capital* is a unique, invaluable guide to the far-reaching risk-based capital regulations. Whether you are a seasoned or budding banking practitioner, you will need this convenient map to steer your way through the new regulations.

1
Preliminary Matters

Key Concepts	
Basle Agreement	Substance-form distinction
Capital	Loss absorption
Risk	Credit risk
Capital/risk-weighted assets ratio	Interest rate risk
	Currency (foreign
Bank holding company	exchange) risk

A. Some Background Information and the Ground Rules

The basis for this study is the Basle Agreement. This agreement was signed at the Bank for International Settlements (BIS) in Basle, Switzerland, in July 1988 by central bank representatives from the Group of Ten (G-10) countries and from Luxembourg. The G-10 countries are Belgium, Canada, France, Germany, Italy, Japan, the Netherlands, Sweden, Switzerland, the United Kingdom, and the United States.[17] Vice chairman of the Federal Reserve Manuel Johnson signed the agreement on behalf of the Federal Reserve System.[18] The BIS Committee on Banking Regulations and Supervisory Practices drafted the agreement. This committee is sometimes referred to as the Cooke Committee, after its chairman, Peter Cooke, who is an associate director of the Bank of England. It is also sometimes referred to as the Basle Committee, after the city in which it meets.[19] The committee consists of representa-

---

[17] Basle Agreement, note 1 at 1.
[18] "Agreement on Banks' Capital Set," *New York Times*, July 12, 1988, at D1.
[19] J. Bardos, "The Risk-Based Capital Agreement: A Further Step Towards Policy Convergence," 12 Federal Reserve Bank of New York *Quarterly Review* 26, note 3 at 28 (Winter 1987-88).

PERSPECTIVES ON RISK-BASED CAPITAL

tives from the central banks of each of the G-10 countries and Luxembourg.[20]

Pursuant to a recommendation by the Board staff in the August 1, 1988, Memorandum, the Governors of the Federal Reserve System approved the Basle Agreement by a vote of 5 to 1 on August 3, 1988.[21] Governor Martha Seger voted against the agreement, apparently for at least three reasons. She felt that it would damage the international competitive position of U.S. banks, that the 8 percent capital/risk-weighted assets ratio should not be applied to bank holding companies (BHCs), and that the favorable risk-weight for mortgages is an arbitrary incentive in favor of mortgage lending.[22]

A draft of the Federal Reserve Board's final regulations became available in mid-December 1988.[23] The draft was approved on December 16, 1988, at an open meeting of the Federal Reserve's Board of Governors by a unanimous vote (Governor Martha Seger was not present at the meeting).[24] These approved regulations were issued in the January 27, 1989, edition of the *Federal Register*.[25] They took effect on March 15, 1989.[26] The Board's final regulations are based on the Basle Agreement. Nothing in them materially alters any points made in this book.

---

[20]*Id.*

[21]"Fed Clears Minimum Capital Standards, Forcing Some Banks to Raise $15 Billion," *Wall Street Journal*, August 4, 1988, at 6.

[22]*See* "Fed Clears Minimum Capital Standards, Forcing Some Banks to Raise $15 Billion," *Wall Street Journal*, August 4, 1988, at 6, and "Fed Approves Rules Requiring More Capital at All Banks," *New York Times*, August 4, 1988, at D2.

[23]December 14, 1988, Board Staff Memorandum.

[24]"Fed Adopts Risk-Based Capital Guidelines; Will Also Propose Minimum Leverage Ratios," 52 *BNA Banking Report* 4 (January 2, 1989).

[25]54 Fed. Reg. 4186 (January 27, 1989) (to be codified for state member banks at Regulation H, 12 C.F.R. part 208, and for BHCs at Regulation Y, 12 C.F.R. part 225).

[26]*Id.*

The Office of the Comptroller of the Currency (OCC) also issued regulations pursuant to the Basle Agreement in the *Federal Register* (January 27, 1989).[27] These regulations will apply to all nationally chartered banks and are almost identical to the Board's regulations. The Federal Deposit Insurance Corporation (FDIC) issued risk-based capital regulations pursuant to the Basle Agreement in the *Federal Register* (March 21, 1989).[27A] These will apply to state-chartered banks that are not members of the Federal Reserve System and are similar to the Board's final regulations.

Finally, banking regulators from countries that signed the Basle Agreement have already or will soon pass regulations pursuant to the agreement. To the extent that activities of banking regulators are discussed in this book, the focus is on the Federal Reserve Board, not the OCC, the FDIC, or regulators in other countries.

Technically, the Basle Agreement applies only to international banks.[28] Application to purely domestic banks or to bank holding companies is left to the discretion of national regulators.[29] The Board has indicated that its final regulations will apply to state banks that are members of the Federal Reserve System regardless of whether they participate in international transactions, and to BHCs.

Indeed, two sets of regulations are adopted: one for all state member banks, and the other for BHCs whose con-

---

[27]*Id.* at 4186 (to be codified at 12 C.F.R. part 3).

[27A]54 Fed. Reg. 11500 (March 21, 1989); (to be codified at 12 C.F.R. part 325).

[28]Basle Agreement, 1. *See also* 54 Fed. Reg. 4186, 4187, 4193-4194 (January 27, 1989); December 14, 1988, Board Staff Memorandum, 137; and August 1, 1988, Board Staff Memorandum, 51. The term "international banks" is not defined in the agreement, final regulations, or memoranda.

[29]Basle Agreement, 1.

solidated assets exceed $150 million.[30] (Hereinafter, "state member banks" are referred to simply as "banks.") While much of the same material appears in both sets of regulations, the Board staff states in its December 14, 1988, Memorandum that publishing two sets is justified "to accommodate functional regulation and the prudent expansion of bank powers through the recognition of firewalls and the deduction of certain investments in subsidiaries from the holding company's consolidated capital position."[31] The Board staff also points out that final regulations for BHCs "provide for a somewhat more flexible definition of capital than contained in the bank guidelines."[32] As discussed below, the additional flexibility is based on the differential treatment of cumulative preferred stock and goodwill.

Thus, pursuant to the Basle Agreement, the Board's final regulations specify that banks will have to meet the 8 percent ratio.[33] In addition, BHCs will have to meet the 8 percent capital/risk-weighted assets ratio at the holding company level on a consolidated basis, even if the subsidiary banks are regulated by the OCC (because they are national banks) or by the FDIC (because they are state nonmember banks).[33] Both the Basle Agreement and the Board's final regulations require banks and BHCs to meet the 8 percent ratio by December 31, 1992.[34] Of this 8 percent, at least 4

---

[30]54 Fed. Reg. 4186, 4187, (January 27, 1989). The risk-based capital regulations applicable to state member banks will become part of Regulation H, 12 C.F.R. part 208, which is the supervisory provision covering these institutions. The regulations for BHCs will become part of Regulation Y, 12 C.F.R. part 225, which is the supervisory provision for these organizations. The exemption for BHCs whose consolidated assets are less than $150 million is discussed at 54 Fed. Reg. 4186, 4197, 4209 (January 27, 1989).

[31]December 14, 1988, Board Staff Memorandum, 12.

[32]*Id.*

[33]54 Fed. Reg. 4186, 4187 (January 27, 1989); *Id.* at 4209, 4218.

percent must consist of Tier One capital.[34] The final regulations, but not the Basle Agreement, establish an interim target ratio of 7.25 percent.[35] Of this 7.25 percent, at least 3.25 percent must be Tier One capital.[35] This must be met by December 31, 1990.[35] In addition, the final regulations state that the ratio should be calculated based on period-end data, not average figures.[35]

The American Bankers Association (ABA) opposed the application of risk-based capital regulations at the holding company level. The ABA contended that such application was not necessary to insure safety and soundness and would be overinclusive, since nonbanking activities of bank holding companies would be covered.[36] More specifically, the Board staff summarized the criticisms of application at the holding company level as follows:

> 1) Consolidated capital ratios are unnecessary if nonbank subsidiaries are functionally regulated and subject to firewalls designed to protect affiliated banks; 2) the holding company structure is unique to the United States and, therefore, consolidated risk-based capital requirements would constitute a competitive disadvantage for U.S banking organizations; 3) such requirements could induce increased holding company risk-taking; and 4) applying capital standards to holding companies could imply an undesirable extension of the federal safety net to parent companies and nonbank affiliates.[37]

In response to these arguments, the Federal Reserve in effect chose to focus on substance over form. The basic

---

[34]Basle Agreement, 16. 54 Fed. Reg. 4186, 4187, 4206 (for banks), 4218 (for BHCs); (January 27, 1989); *Id.*

[35]54 Fed. Reg. 4186, 4187, 4206 (for banks), 4218 (for BHCs); (January 27, 1989); *Id.; See also* Basle Agreement at 16; *Id.* at 4193.

[36]B. Orr, "The Fed Drops the Other Shoe," *ABA Banking Journal* 127, 130-131 (October 1988).

[37]54 Fed. Reg. 4186, 4195 (January 27, 1989).

premise of the Federal Reserve's position is that a BHC should be a source of strength and support for its subsidiaries.[38] The formalistic corporate divisions in a holding company structure are neglected; what matters is the underlying safety and soundness, as measured by capital adequacy, of the entire corporate group. As the Board staff said in its August 1, 1988, Memorandum, "The U.S. banking system is strengthened when companies that own banks have adequate capital."[39] This premise is stated in the Basle Agreement itself: "The [Basle] Committee will be concerned to ensure that ownership structures should not be such as to weaken the capital position of the bank or expose it to risks stemming from other parts of the group."[40]

Practical considerations also motivated the Federal Reserve to choose to apply risk-based capital regulations at the holding company level. It was felt that strong firewalls do not yet exist between banks and their nonbank (particularly securities) affiliates. Consequently, weaknesses of a nonbank subsidiary could be transmitted to a banking subsidiary, necessitating support from the parent holding company.[41]

Further, some BHCs have borrowed money to fund equity investments in banking subsidiaries, a technique called "double leveraging" or "double gearing."[42] The Board staff pointed out that "For such companies, the actual capital available to absorb losses at the consolidated level is less than the reported capital that appears on the balance sheets of the subsidiaries on a separate entity basis."[43]

---

[38]*Id.* at 4194-4195.
[39]August 1, 1988, Board Staff Memorandum, 8, 51-53.
[40]Basle Agreement, 4.
[41]54 Fed. Reg. 4186 4194 (January 27, 1989). August 1, 1988, Board Staff Memorandum, 8, 53.
[42]*Id.*
[43]August 1, 1988, Board Staff Memorandum, 8.

However, the Federal Reserve may designate certain nonbank subsidiaries of a BHC to be excluded from the consolidated risk-based capital requirements if strong firewalls do exist.[44] The theory for such exclusion is functional regulation based on clearly delineated and separated financial activities.[45]

Throughout this book, reference is made to the December 1987 Basle Proposal and earlier versions of the Board's regulations.[46] The first proposed risk-based capital regulations were issued by the Board in January 1986.[47] Discussions were later held with the Bank of England, and in February 1987, a U.S.-U.K. Joint Proposal on capital adequacy standards was reached. The Board issued new proposed regulations pursuant to this agreement.[48] This was followed in March 1987 by a U.S.-U.K. agreement on the treatment of interest rate and foreign exchange contracts. The Board also issued proposed regulations pursuant to this agreement.[49]

At this point, further bilateral action was suspended as it became clear that other major industrial countries were interested in reaching a multilateral agreement on capital adequacy for commercial banks. The first Basle agreement, a draft, was reached in December 1987.[50] This was followed

---

[44] 54 Fed. Reg. 4186, 4195 (January 27, 1989). *See also* August 1, 1988, Board Staff Memorandum, 18.

[45] *Id. See also* August 1, 1988, Board Staff Memorandum, 8.

[46] A description of the negotiation process is found in J. Bardos, "The Risk-Based Capital Agreement: A Further Step Towards Policy Convergence," 12 Federal Reserve Bank of New York *Quarterly Review* 26 (Winter 1987-88).

[47] 51 Fed. Reg. 3976 (1986) (proposed January 31, 1986).

[48] 52 Fed. Reg. 5119 (1987) (proposed February 19, 1987).

[49] 52 Fed. Reg. 9304 (1987) (proposed March 24, 1987).

[50] Committee on Banking Regulations and Supervisory Practices, *Proposals for International Convergence of Capital Measurement and Capital Standards*, December 1987 (Bank for International Settlements, Basle, Switzerland).

by a revised set of proposed Board regulations in March 1988.[51] These were based on the December 1987 Basle Proposal, just as the Board's final regulations are based on the Basle Agreement of July 1988.

B. A Little Legal Philosophy: Applying the Substance-Form Distinction to the Basle Agreement

The recognition of certain items as capital indicates an emphasis on substance over form with respect to the concept of "capital." The substantive feature is this ability to absorb losses; the form of the item is not especially relevant. This emphasis is prudent. Rigid formalisms are either over- or underinclusive (or both). Wall Street investment bankers and lawyers will always be able to invent financial products that outpace formalistic rules developed by banking regulators. Indeed, as discussed as follows, financial instruments already exist that straddle the risk-weight categories of the Basle Agreement.

By contrast, the requirement that capital support be offered for swap contracts implies an emphasis on form over substance with respect to the concept of "risk." Even if the underlying substantive function of a swap transaction is to hedge against interest rate or currency risk, the form—the fact that the bank has entered into a swap contract to accomplish this hedging—is what matters. There is an irony here. Banks commonly use swaps to lower interest rate or currency risk. Yet the Basle Agreement charges them for doing so by requiring additional capital support. This irony is heightened when the credit risk on a swap contract is closely examined. Such examination reveals that, where

---

[51] 53 Fed. Reg. 50 (1988) (proposed March 15, 1988).

PRELIMINARY MATTERS

bankruptcy law is inapplicable, counterparty default does not leave the nondefaulting party any worse off than before it entered into the swap transaction.

In sum, the Basle Agreement looks to whether the substantive function of loss absorption can be performed in establishing what counts as capital. But in requiring capital support for all swap transactions, the Basle Agreement does not look to the substantive function each swap fulfills.

This insight is just that—an insight, *not* a criticism. The argument is not that the emphasis on substance with respect to deciding what counts as capital and the emphasis on form with respect to whether swaps require capital support is an indefensible inconsistency. Indeed, there are sound reasons for the shift in emphasis. For example, swaps might involve some credit risk (though, as discussed later in this text, this depends on how the *status quo ante* is defined and whether bankruptcy law is applicable). Moreover, the function a swap fulfills may not be readily apparent to a bank examiner (although this may be an open issue). Finally, it must be remembered that the Basle Agreement is a political compromise among the world's major industrialized countries, not an academic exercise in regulatory symmetry.

Common law reasoning based on distinctions that rely on absolute, formal concepts and categories is a favorite target for critical legal studies or deconstructionist analysis.[52] Whether the substance-form distinction is meaningless be-

---

[52] A recent defense of formalism is found in E. Weinrib, "Legal Formalism: On the Immanent Rationality of Law," 97 *Yale Law Journal* 949 (May 1988). A classic article on form and substance is Duncan Kennedy's "Form and Substance in Private Law Adjudication," 89 *Harvard Law Review* 1685 (1976). Additional sources on this distinction include P. Schlag, "Rules and Standards," 33 *UCLA Law Review* 379 (1985) and J. Wilson, "The Morality of Formalism," 33 *UCLA Law Review* 431 (1985). A summary of deconstructionist theory is found in J. Balkin, "Deconstructive Practice and Legal Theory," 96 *Yale Law Journal* 743 (March 1987).

cause of the inseparability of substance and form is an interesting issue in legal philosophy. Perhaps this distinction is based on categories that are not immutable. Perhaps it could be argued, for example, that the recognition of nonfinancial instruments as Tier Two rather than Tier One capital indicates an emphasis on form. Similarly, the requirement of capital support for swaps could be seen as a triumph of the substantive policy concern about credit risk over the form of the swap transaction.

Nevertheless, lawyering is something like the children's television show "Sesame Street." The legal issue is often "Which one of these things is not like the other?" Lawyers are paid to make distinctions and to break down distinctions. The substance-form distinction is a commonly used one, whatever its merits. For example, it is a crucial mode of argumentation in tax law. Whether a corporate merger is taxable under the Internal Revenue Code turns sometimes on the underlying substance of the merger transaction and sometimes on the form used to accomplish the merger.[53] It is also important in corporate law, where the determination of remedies for minority shareholders in freeze-out mergers turns in part on the form of the transaction and in part on the substantive fairness of the deal.

In the end, what matters is not that a particular application of the substance-form distinction be accepted as correct. Rather, what matters is that the act of applying the distinction generates thought as to what the Basle Agreement is all about and what it is intended to accomplish.

The substance-form distinction is insightful because it highlights the concepts of "capital" and "risk" on which the Basle Agreement rests. It allows for a separation of the substantive requirement for qualification of capital from the many forms used to raise capital in the securities mar-

---

[53]26 U.S.C. § 368.

kets. An examination of capital constituents reveals that capital must be able to absorb losses, regardless of its form. It is as if the bank examiner said to a bank officer: "Even though this item is not in the form of common stock or something similar, any losses can be written off against this item, so it counts as capital."

The distinction also allows for an inquiry into the substantive functions of off-balance-sheet transactions, whatever their form. An examination of the treatment of interest rate and currency swaps shows that the formality of entering into a swap contract is deemed to result in increased credit risk, regardless of any risk-hedging function the swap transaction may serve. It is as if the bank examiner said to the bank officer: "While the underlying substantive function your swap transaction fulfills is to hedge against interest rate or currency risk, swap contracts are a form of off-balance-sheet item that we recognize as resulting in further credit risk. Thus, capital support is required."

C. Chapter Summary

Capital and risk are the building blocks of the Basle Agreement on risk-based capital. The agreement was signed in July 1988 at the Bank for International Settlements in Basle, Switzerland, by central banking authorities from the United States, Western Europe, and Japan. These authorities have or will soon take steps to implement the agreement. In the United States, the Federal Reserve Board adopted final risk-based capital regulations on January 27, 1989. These took effect on March 15, 1989. The regulations are applicable to all American banks and all American bank holding companies whose assets exceed $150 million.

By the end of 1992, banks and bank holding companies must meet two capital/asset ratios: (1) Total capital must equal or exceed 8 percent of risk-weighted assets, and (2)

PERSPECTIVES ON RISK-BASED CAPITAL

Tier One capital must equal or exceed 4 percent of risk-weighted assets. By the end of 1990, two interim targets must be met: (1) Total capital must equal or exceed 7.25 percent of risk-weighted assets, and (2) Tier One capital must equal or exceed 3.25 percent of risk-weighted assets.

To say that the building blocks of the Basle Agreement (and the implementing regulations) are capital and risk is to say that no risk-based capital rules would be possible without an underlying concept of the purposes of bank capital. What criteria determine whether an item counts as capital? Given such criteria, exactly which items count? What sorts of risk arise from a bank's on-balance-sheet assets and from its off-balance-sheet activities? Which of these risks are regulated through capital/asset rules?

Loss absorption is the underlying concept of bank capital in the Basle Agreement and in the Federal Reserve Board's final regulations. An item counts as capital if it is freely available to absorb losses arising from a bank's on- or off-balance-sheet items. The label attached to the item and the "looks" of the item are immaterial. What matters is substance, not form. If the substantive function of loss absorption can be fulfilled, then the item counts as capital regardless of its form.

Credit risk, not interest rate or currency risk, is the type of risk to be managed through the required capital/asset ratio. Credit risk is the risk of default by the counterparty, the other obligor, in its obligations. Thus, with respect to swaps, what matters is the risk of default by the counterparty on its swap payments. In reality, swaps are commonly used to hedge against interest rate and currency risk, and credit risk is quite low. But in the Basle Agreement and the Federal Reserve's final regulations, capital support must be provided for a swap contract regardless of the function of the swap. Form, not substance, matters here. If a swap contract is signed, credit risk is deemed to arise. The substantive function of the swap—hedging—is immaterial; the form—the contract—is what matters.

2

Why Worry About Bank Capital?

Key Concepts

Market-determined capital
Traditional corporate finance model
Modigliani-Miller model
Regulatory-determined capital
Loss absorption
Public confidence
Bank failure
Asset growth
FDIC
Earnings generation

A. Isn't the Capital Structure of a Bank Irrelevant?

It would seem that any legal regulation of bank capital presupposes that the capital structure of a bank—in particular, the debt/equity ratio—matters. Why worry about a capital/asset ratio if the debt/equity ratio is irrelevant? The irrelevance of the debt/equity mix, and thereby the nonexistence of an "optimal" capital structure, was first asserted by Modigliani and Miller.[1] They argued that the value of a corporation is the discounted value of its expected earnings stream. How the claims on this stream are divided up (i.e., whether more debt is issued relative to equity, or vice versa), does not matter. Put simply, how the pie is sliced up will not alter its size.

---

[1] F. Modigliani and M. Miller. The Cost of Capital, Corporation Finance and the Theory of Investment, 48 *American Economic Review* 261 (June 1958).

This logic has been applied in the context of bank capital in a discussion of adjustment by banks and bank holding companies to the guidelines.[2] Friesen points out that whether the target capital/risk-weighted assets ratio is set at 5 percent or 8 percent (as in the Basle Agreement) may not matter.[3] The issue is this: From the Modigliani-Miller proposition that the debt/equity ratio is irrelevant to the value of a corporation, can it be inferred that the capital/asset ratio is irrelevant?

B. The Answer: No

There are at least four problems with extending the Modigliani-Miller proposition to capital/risk-weighted assets ratios. First, as a technical matter, Modigliani and Miller address the effect of debt and equity (i.e., of different types of claims on a corporation's earnings stream) on the value of the corporation. The proposition is that the present discounted value of a corporation's earnings stream, not the mix of debt and equity in its capital structure, is the key determinant of its value. Valuation is not necessarily the prime concern of banking regulators who worry about capital/asset ratios. There is no need to claim that the value of a corporation and its capital/asset ratio are wholly divorced; it suffices to point out that Modigliani and Miller did not argue they are divorced. The irrelevance of the capital/asset ratio is not an obvious inference to be drawn from the proposition that the debt/equity ratio is irrelevant.

Second, as a practical matter, creditors and financial analysts use the two ratios for entirely different purposes. The debt/equity ratio is a financial leverage ratio — that is, a

---

[2]C. Friesen, "Capital Guidelines and Global Markets," 4 *The Review of Financial Services Regulation* 123 (July 1988).
[3]*Id.* at 125.

measure of the extent to which debt financing is used by a corporation. Prospective creditors and security analysts use financial leverage ratios to assess the ability of a prospective borrower to meet new debt-servicing obligations in light of the existing debt burden and earnings forecasts. A capital/asset ratio is used as a proxy for the strength or solvency of a corporation. Solvency here is measured by the balance sheet—the extent to which assets exceed liabilities (i.e., the extent to which net worth is positive). Again, debt/equity and capital/asset ratios are different animals, and to assert that one is harmless does not mean the other is also harmless.

Third, also as a practical matter, it is unlikely that officers and directors of banks and bank holding companies believe the capital/asset ratio is irrelevant. Would an officer or director really be indifferent to having to meet an 8 percent capital/risk-weighted assets ratio rather than a 5 percent ratio? The higher the ratio, the more resources have to be devoted to meeting it, and the greater the likelihood of a lower return on equity because of foregone earnings opportunities. Stockholders and the investment community care about return on equity, so bank officers and directors do too.

Finally, even if the debt/equity and capital/asset ratios were the same animal (or at least the same species), the Modigliani-Miller proposition would be seriously flawed because of certain assumptions on which it rests.[4] One assumption is that there are no corporate taxes. Obviously, such taxes do exist. Indeed, federal tax laws favor the issuance of debt over equity because interest payments on debt, but not dividend payments on stock, are deducted

---

[4]A more comprehensive analysis of the assumptions may be found in E. Brigham and L. Gapenski, *Intermediate Financial Management* 180-220 (1985). This discussion is based on their analysis.

from a corporation's gross income when taxable income is calculated.

Modigliani and Miller also assume away bankruptcy costs. These costs include the sale of assets at below-market prices in liquidation sales, legal and administrative expenses associated with bankruptcy proceedings, delay costs that arise because of the duration of bankruptcy proceedings, and the loss of employment experienced by workers of the bankrupt entity. In reality, the risk of bankruptcy, and thereby the risk of incurring bankruptcy costs, increases with leverage. As Brigham and Gapenski state:

> [T]he greater the use of debt financing, and the larger the fixed interest charges, the greater the probability that a decline in earnings will lead to bankruptcy, and hence the higher the probability of a bankruptcy-related loss of value.[5]

Still another problematic assumption is that individuals can borrow at the same rate as corporations. This assumption is critical to the proof of the Modigliani-Miller proposition. In reality, few individuals are able to borrow at rates as favorable as those available to creditworthy corporations.

In sum, an argument that risk-based capital ratios are not important is suspect insofar as it is based on the Modigliani-Miller proposition.

C. Why Not Market-Determined Capital?

It is not obvious that capital must be subject to regulation. As Dince and Fortson point out, the capital base of nonfinancial corporations is market-determined:

> The question of capital adequacy is primarily linked to regulated financial institutions. For example, the capital adequacy of airlines, pipelines, or retail stores is an unexplored and unregulated area left to the workings of the free capital

---

[5]*Id.* at 195.

market. Too much capital is reflected in low return on equity and low valuation of common stock; too little capital is evidenced by a market perception of high risk and resulting low valuation in common stock. Only in the case of financial institutions does capital adequacy emerge as an issue.[6]

But why should capital adequacy be an issue in the case of financial institutions? Any banking regulation must be compared not only with possible less restrictive regulations, but also with solutions established by the free market. Would not market forces determine the optimal level of bank capital? And would not such a market-determined outcome be arrived at more efficiently than one that requires numerous bank examinations and legal analyses? P. C. Jackson, a former member of the Board of Governors of the Federal Reserve System, stated in 1978 that:

> I think the industry as a whole has become overregulated by the way its supervisors set standards for a bank's capital and assets. We need to stop treating banks like public utilities and allow the marketplace by its own risk analysis to make a determination between the successful and the unsuccessful bank. No government official, regardless of how competent or well intentioned, can manage an individual bank or the industry as a whole as well as the collective efforts of bank stockholders, directors and officers.[7]

The traditional corporate finance model for determining the optimal capital structure of a corporation can be applied to the problem of how much capital a bank should maintain. Assume a bank has two sources of funds: equity and debt. The latter source can be taken to include all categories of

---

[6]R. Dince and J. Fortson, "Bank Examination, Capital Adequacy and Risk," 163 *The Bankers Magazine* 49 (May/June 1980).

[7]P. C. Jackson, Member of the Board of Governors of the Federal Reserve System, May 11, 1978 *quoted in* J. Sinkey, Jr., "Regulatory Attitudes Toward Risk," in *Handbook for Banking Strategy* 347 (R. Aspinwall and R. Eisenbeis, eds., 1985).

debt (short- and long-term, fixed and floating rate, etc.), as well as depositors' funds. The optimal debt/equity ratio is defined as the ratio at which the bank's overall cost of funds (specifically, its weighted cost of capital) is minimized. This optimal ratio is represented as the minimum point of the U-shaped curve in Figure 1.

**Figure 1
Traditional Corporate Finance Model for
Determining Optimal Capital Structure**

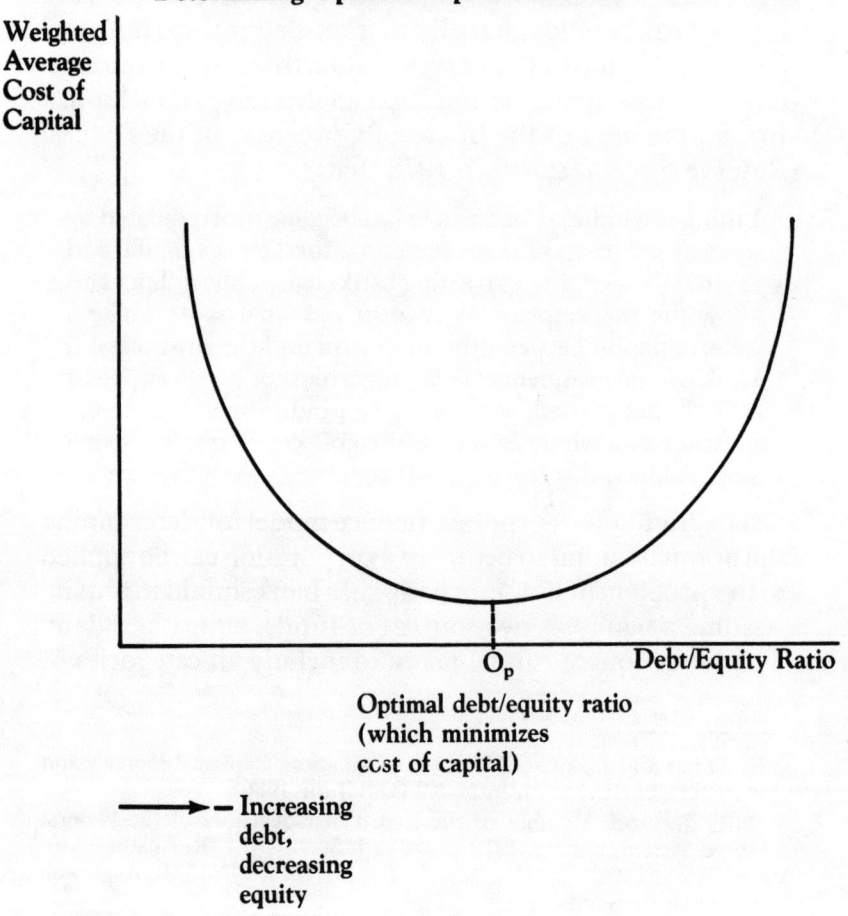

O_p

Optimal debt/equity ratio
(which minimizes
cost of capital)

⟶ — Increasing debt, decreasing equity

At very low levels of debt, the risk of default on debt payments is quite low. Dividend payments to equity holders are not legal obligations of the bank. The bank and the stockholder are not in a debtor-creditor relationship. There is no risk of default from failure to pay dividends. As the bank begins to issue some debt, the rate charged by creditors (purchasers of the debt) is low because of the low default risk.

At some point, depicted as point O_p in Figure 1, the optimal combination of equity and debt is reached. The weighted average of the cost of debt and equity is minimized. That is, the sum of interest payments on debt and dividend payments on equity, weighted by the proportion of debt and equity in the capital structure, respectively, is minimized. If the bank continues to issue debt beyond point O_p, it will have to pay creditors a higher default risk premium to induce them to purchase additional debt. Since the bank is becoming more highly leveraged, the probability of the bank's earnings being insufficient to meet its legal obligations to its creditors increases. Sinkey summarizes the traditional theory as follows:

> It is assumed that the bank wants to maximize the market value of its debt plus equity. This objective is achieved at the optimal debt ratio (*i.e.*, where the difference between the present value of the tax shield from debt and the present value of the costs of financial distress is maximized). The theory goes like this. As a bank increases its leverage, its market value increases up to a point (the optimum), and then it declines. What happens is that the market penalizes banks for excessive leverage (i.e., "inadequate capital"). The discipline, which comes from existing or would-be equity shareholders and uninsured creditors, is manifested in the form of higher cost of funds (e.g., CDs) or inability to raise funds.[8]

---

[8] J. Sinkey, Jr. "Regulatory Attitudes Toward Risk" in *Handbook for Banking Strategy* 347, 365-366 (R. Aspinwall and R. Eisenbeis, eds., 1985).

D. The Answer: The Market Is Imperfect

Allowing the market to determine the level of a bank's capital creates at least two problems. The first is imperfect information.[9] Dispersed public depositors lack sufficient and timely information about the general condition of a bank, and about the state of a bank's assets in particular. No informed decision about the optimal capital level can be made with incomplete information. This fact is compounded by the existence of federal deposit insurance. Since depositors believe that the FDIC will protect them in the event of a bank failure, they are likely to underestimate the importance of capital as a source of payment of claims against a failed bank.[10] Admittedly, one response to this might be that what depositors think is immaterial, because the real creditors of a bank are the FDIC and the Federal Reserve.

The second problem with allowing the market to determine the level of bank capital relates to the first. The market is likely to underestimate systematically the impact of a bank failure on the banking system. Bank failure may be contagious. Depositors of a healthy bank, upon learning of the failure of a different bank, may (perhaps irrationally) develop fears about the solvency of their own bank. This argument is debated in the literature on bank failures, and particular attention is given to the differences between insured depositors (those with accounts of less than $100,000) and uninsured depositors (those whose accounts exceed $100,000). Benston contends that the effect of a single bank failure is overstated and therefore prevention

---

[9] *See* W. Isaac, "Capital Adequacy and Deposit Insurance," 1 *Annual Review of Banking* 59, 61 (1982).

[10] *Id. See also* J. Sinkey, Jr., "Regulatory Attitudes Toward Risk," in *Handbook for Banking Strategy,* 347, 365-366 (R. Aspinwall and R. Eisenbeis, eds., 1985).

of bank failure should not be used to justify banking regulation.[11] Benston implicitly assumes that because of their faith in the FDIC insurance system, insured depositors will act rationally and will not cause a run on an otherwise solvent bank.[12]

E. Substantive Functions of Regulatory-Determined Capital

The Basle Agreement "looks through" the form of items that count as capital and instead focuses on whether such items perform a certain substantive function. This substantive function is the *ability to absorb losses*. Yet there are other roles that bank capital can play. Indeed, one point developed in this book is that *many* substantive functions are ascribed to bank capital.

A second point developed here is that whether bank capital can actually perform a role ascribed to it is a matter that deserves some thought. For example, the statement that capital is a cushion against losses is not particularly insightful unless further information is provided. What sort of losses can be absorbed? What amount of losses can be absorbed? How much capital is adequate to absorb losses? There is nothing magical about bank capital. It is a legal concept, a regulatory concept, that lawyers and regulators have developed and to which they have attached certain meanings.

Various roles of capital are mentioned in the January 1986 version of the Board's proposed regulations:

> [A] limited risk-adjusted measure of capital adequacy would provide the Board with a supplemental means of assessing

---

[11] G. Benston, "Why Continue to Regulate Banks?: An Historical Assessment of Federal Banking Regulation," 5 *Midland Corporate Finance Journal* 67 (Fall 1987).
[12] *Id.* at 75-76.

whether the capital level of individual banks and bank holding companies is fully adequate to serve the key functions of capital, namely to provide a *buffer to absorb losses* in times of poor performance, to *promote the safety of depositors' funds*, to help *maintain public confidence* in banking organizations, and to *support the reasonable growth* of such organizations.[13]

Similarly, a review of the literature on bank capital reveals various purposes:

Capital performs several important functions in banking institutions. It *absorbs fluctuations in income* so that banking institutions can continue to operate in periods when losses are being sustained. It also *provides a measure of assurance to the public* that an institution will continue to provide financial services, thereby helping to maintain confidence in individual entities and the banking system as a whole. It serves to support growth yet *restrains unjustified or imprudent expansion of assets*. Capital also *provides protection to depositors* in the event of a threatened insolvency.[14]

Absorbing fluctuations in income provides a buffer against losses. This is also known as the cushion function. Assuring the public that a bank is financially strong is related to this function. Whether either of these functions can actually be performed if need be is, as discussed later in the text, a debatable matter. Restraining asset growth may be achieved not by capital, but by capital ratios. (This point is also discussed later.) Protecting depositors is a curious function insofar as the FDIC insures deposits. The real substantive function here may be to protect the FDIC.

---

[13]51 Fed. Reg. 3976, 3977 (proposed January 31, 1986); (emphasis supplied).

[14]FDIC Final Rule on Capital Maintenance, 44 Wash. Fin. Rep. (BNA) 4892 (Mar. 18, 1985) *quoted in* M. Flammia, "Bank Capital Requirements: Placebo or Cure?," 7 *Annual Review of Banking Law* 485, 486 (1988); (emphasis supplied).

(1) Absorbing Losses

The first function in both passages just quoted is cushioning: losses are absorbed by capital. This function is often mentioned.[15] For instance, a *New York Times* article on the Basle Agreement states that:

> The banking industry has experienced several crises in recent years, including huge problem loans to the developing world and difficulties stemming from the depressed farm, energy and real estate sectors, while the Government has shifted toward less regulation. In response, regulators have suggested that banks need more capital as a cushion.[16]

What is usually not well explained in the literature is the mechanism by which capital absorbs losses. If a bank is forced to write off or write down an asset, the accounting principle of double-entry bookkeeping means that it must also enter a corresponding reduction on the liability side of its balance sheet. Yet liabilities, by definition, are items the bank owes to its creditors; these items cannot be used to offset losses on assets. As William Isaac, the former chairman of the FDIC, put it, "Debt is not able to fulfill the principle function of capital; that is, it's not available to absorb losses in a 'going concern' and thereby prevent insolvency.[17] Thus, a bank must turn to the capital account on its balance sheet.

Typically, the capital account actually consists of several

---

[15]*See, e.g.*, W. Roberts and R. Rosholt. "Risk-Adjusted Capital: How Can Banks Cope?,"/*Bank Accounting and Finance* 29, 39 (Summer 1988); G. Zavvos, "1992: One Market," 7 *International Financial Law Review* 7, 10 (March 1988); E. Gardener. "A British View of Bank Capital Adequacy in Europe," 9 *Issues in Bank Regulation* 21, 32, 37 (Spring 1986).

[16]"Fed Approves Rules Requiring More Capital at All Banks," *New York Times*, August 4, 1988, at D2.

[17]W. Isaac, "Capital Adequacy and Deposit Insurance," 1 *Annual Review of Banking Law,* 59, 62 (1982).

accounts: paid-in capital at par value, capital surplus (paid-in capital in excess of par value), and earned surplus (retained earnings or undivided profits). Losses on the left-hand side of the balance sheet are written against the earned surplus account on the right-hand side. The losses that arise may result from various forms of risk, not just credit risk. Nagel and Petersen write that aside from being used as a funding source:

> Capital is a firm's cushion against adversity. Corporations may from time to time experience losses resulting from specific problems like poor management and defalcation, or from business risks gone awry. Risk-taking is a vital component of financial intermediation and is the chief contributor to the profitability of financial institutions. Mismatching the durations of assets and liabilities, thus exposing the firm to the risks of changing interest rates, is one common form of risk. Making unsecured or undercollateralized loans is another. Regardless of the cause, when losses do occur, capital protects the firm from insolvency. Because capital funds need not be repaid, they can absorb these losses. A firm can experience losses of up to 100 percent of its net worth, while meeting its obligations and continuing to operate. Conversely, debt must be repaid and cannot absorb a firm's losses.[18]

One specific role of capital is to absorb *unexpected* losses. The attractiveness of this alternative is twofold. First, prudent bank managers should provide for anticipated losses—for example, loan losses on Third World debt—by setting up reserve accounts out of retained earnings. Second, the distinction between expected and unexpected losses leads naturally to the issue of how much loss can be absorbed. Much of the literature on bank capital espouses the view

---

[18]R. Nagel and B. Petersen. "Capitalization Problems in Perspective" in *Handbook for Banking Strategy* 293, 294 (R. Aspinwall and R. Eisenbeis, eds., 1985).

that the function of absorbing losses is illusory, that no amount of capital can absorb large losses. As Danielsson explains:

> Capital in a bank is particularly necessary to absorb unexpected losses. I say "unexpected losses" because where losses are foreseen and cannot be avoided they should be provided for as soon as they become apparent.

It is not surprising that a bank will from time to time suffer losses, for it is after all an essential part of a banker's business to take carefully assessed risks. But it is the mark of a well-managed bank that these risks are controlled as part of a well-diversified portfolio of assets and are not disproportionate to the resources available to meet any losses that arise. Against these losses a bank has two lines of defense. The first is its current earnings. If a bank earns a return on its assets which is commensurate with the risks involved in its activities, then, with due attention to costs, its earnings should more than cover any losses that arise in the normal course of business. If a bank has exceptional losses, however, which impair its earnings for a year, then it has to fall back on its second line of defense — its capital and accumulated reserves. This capital will either allow it to absorb the losses and continue trading or, if they are so heavy as to leave the bank insolvent, its capital will at least reduce the losses suffered by depositors.[19]

(2) Enhancing Public Confidence

A second function of capital concerns public confidence.[20] The argument is that the existence of a strong

---

[19]S. Danielsson. "A Supervisory View of the Role of Capital and Capital Adequacy," 9 *Issues in Bank Regulation* 11, 12 (Spring 1986). *See also* R. Roberts and R. Rosholt, "Risk-Adjusted Capital: How Can Banks Cope?" 1 *Bank Accounting and Finance* 29 (Summer 1988).

[20]*See generally* J. Sinkey, Jr. "Regulatory Attitudes Toward Risk," *Handbook for Banking Strategy* 347, 348-350 (R. Aspinwall and R. Eisenbeis, eds., 1985).

capital base assures depositors that their bank will have funds available to meet withdrawals. Depositors' assurance that their bank is liquid helps prevent a run on the bank.

The irony is that unless a bank is 100 percent capitalized—that is, unless every dollar in assets is not leveraged but supported by a dollar in capital—it will not be possible to pay off all depositors and other claimants on demand. The public may be correct in viewing a strong capital position as indicative of a healthy bank insofar as this position is available to absorb losses, but it is an illusion that this position alone will protect all claimants for the full value of their claims.

Moreover, as a practical matter, it is not capital that assures liquidity. Banks meet withdrawals out of cash on hand and, if that is insufficient, through cashing short-term assets such as Treasury bills. A bank's capital/asset ratio is not really a measure of liquidity. Rather, the ratio of short-term assets to total assets, and the current ratio (the ratio of current assets to current liabilities) are measures of liquidity.

The question is whether the function of enhancing public confidence is substantively different from that of absorbing losses. Perhaps the two are indistinguishable in substance. Public confidence is enhanced precisely because assets can be written down or written off against one of the capital accounts. The link between these two functions has been noted in the literature. For instance, Danielsson argues that:

> [t]he role of capital in absorbing losses is essential in maintaining the confidence of depositors. It demonstrates commitment by the shareholders. The knowledge that adequate capital is available to protect them from losses reassures depositors and so increases their confidence in the bank. This question of confidence is crucial. It is the fear of insolvency which leads depositors to rush to withdraw funds. Capital by itself cannot provide the liquidity needed in such

circumstances, but by being demonstrably sufficient to safeguard the bank's solvency it preserves the confidence of depositors and makes the bank less likely to suffer a run on deposits.... What is true of the individual bank is also true of the banking system as a whole. The capital positions of the banks making up the system must be seen to be adequate in order to ensure that depositors continue to have confidence in the soundness of the system.[21]

Noonan and Fetner argue that public confidence is maintained through the expectation that capital will be able to absorb losses. They review the various sources of loss and mention the limits on the ability of capital to absorb losses:

> Perhaps the most important function bank capital plays is maintaining confidence. Uninsured depositors must be confident that their money is safe, and borrowers must be confident that the bank will be in a position to give genuine consideration to their credit needs in bad times as well as good. Because banks operate in a protected environment, maintaining the confidence of the bank supervisor is essential to the bank's continued existence.
>
> .... How do we expect capital to maintain that confidence? We expect that bank capital will be available to absorb temporary and unexpected losses resulting from one or a combination of the following:
>
> (1) Credit risk—possible deterioration in the quality of the loan portfolio as evidenced by borrowers defaulting and the resulting increased collection costs.
>
> (2) Investment risk — result of rising interest rates and disintermediation. Includes the possibility of default on securities.

---

[21]S. Danielsson. "A Supervisory View of the Role of Capital and Capital Adequacy," 9 *Issues in Bank Regulation* 12 (Spring 1986) 11, 12.

(3) Liquidity risk—poor match in the term structure of assets and liabilities and the possibilities of massive deposit withdrawals.

(4) Operating risk—operating inefficiencies and management errors.

(5) Fraud risk—embezzlement and other fraudulent activities that could produce uninsured losses.

(6) Other risks—exchange, transaction, trust department, and the like.

These losses are either charged to an appropriate reserve account or deducted from net earnings and, if earnings are inadequate, from retained earnings. This role of absorbing losses is instrumental in avoiding failure, adding to the confidence in a bank's continuing viability. But "temporary" and "unexpected" losses are just what their names imply. No reasonable amount of capital will sustain a bank that incurs losses for an extended period of time.[22]

Similarly, Ehlen writes:

Capital, or more specifically equity and reserves in a banking context, plays a rather singular role of demonstrating financial strength and stability. Basically, capital stands ready to absorb adverse financial developments that could impair the viability or continuity of a bank's business. It is a vital component of the ongoing confidence necessary to a depository institution.[23]

(3) Preventing Bank Failures

It is often thought that a key role of capital is to prevent bank failure. This is debatable on three grounds. First, if failure is defined as balance-sheet insolvency (an excess of

---

[22] J. Noonan and S. Fetner. "Capital and Capital Standards," 68 Federal Reserve Bank of Atlanta *Economic Review* 50, 51 (November 1983).
[23] J. Ehlen. "A Review of Bank Capital and Its Adequacy," 68 Federal Reserve Bank of Atlanta *Economic Review* 54, 55 (November 1983).

liabilities over assets, or negative net worth), then the more capital a bank has, the less likely it is to fail because it is better able to absorb losses. Capital does not "prevent" failure; it merely absorbs losses.

Second, it is conceivable that increases in capital requirements may weaken banks, and perhaps even help cause rather than prevent failure. This argument is made forcefully by Flammia:

> [B]ank capital levels are neither the cause of, nor the cure for, the recent rash of troubled banks. Bank failures are caused by the banks' poor performance in loan and deposit markets, nonperforming loans, fraud, mismanagement, and negative interest rate spreads. Increasing capital requirements is an inappropriate and damaging response to the bank failure problem. High capital requirements are making it more difficult for the banks to compete and remain profitable. The proposed risk-based capital-to-asset ratios are not likely to reduce the present capital requirements, and may even increase the required level. In short, the regulators' response to the bank failures has made, and continues to make, matters worse.[24]

Third, empirical studies reveal that there is little if any correlation between the level of capital and the probability of insolvency.[25] Inadequate capital is not a cause of bank failure, nor is adequate capital a cure for the problems faced by troubled banks.

As discussed later in the text, the purpose of capital emphasized in the Basle Agreement is not the prevention of bank failures. Regulators are well aware of the poor correla-

---

[24] M. Flammia. "Bank Capital Requirements: Placebo or Cure?," 7 *Annual Review of Banking Law* 485 (1988).

[25] It is not, however, unanimously agreed that capital ratios do not predict bank failures. *See* J. Marino. "Comparison of Failed and Healthy Bank Capital Ratios: An Update," Federal Deposit Insurance Corporation *Economic Outlook* 26-28 (November 1985).

tion between levels of capital and the probability of failure. Rather, the emphasis is on the ability to absorb losses. Flammia is incorrect in asserting that risk-based capital guidelines are a response to bank failures. Ehlen is correct in arguing that inadequate bank capital is a consequence rather than a cause of bank failure:

> The point is often made that banks do not fail due to inadequate capital. Such a statement is true as far as it goes. Lack of capital does not cause a failure. Failures are more often due to massive real or prospective losses on earning assets or the loss of liquidity, which itself is usually related to the perception of prospective losses. However, if the equity were sufficient to absorb the prospective losses, liquidity would likely not be threatened. After a bank failure, there is seldom residual equity available for distribution to common stockholders. Thus, while inadequate equity does not precipitate failure, it is the inevitable result of a failure. Accordingly, we conclude that a bank would not fail if capital were in fact adequate. To take this to an extreme: would a bank with 100 percent equity ever fail?[26]

Similarly, a recent study by the OCC concludes that the leading cause of bank failure is poor management.[27] While poor asset quality leads to erosion of a bank's capital, and this in turn may lead to failure, the initial cause of poor asset quality is typically deficiencies in a bank's board of directors and managers.[27] Such deficiencies range from incompetence to insider abuse and fraud.

---

[26] J. Ehlen. "A Review of Bank Capital Adequacy," 68 Federal Reserve Bank of Atlanta *Economic Review* 54, 55 (November 1983).

[27] F. Graham and J. Horner, "Bank Failure," 12 *Issues in Bank Regulation* 8 (Fall 1988). *See also* J. Macey and G. Miller, "Bank Failures, Risk Monitoring, and the Market for Bank Control," 88 *Columbia Law Review* 1153, 1165-1169 (October 1988). *Id.* at 9-10.

(4) Restraining Asset Growth

Federal deposit insurance also prevents runs on banks, yet such insurance creates a moral hazard problem and leads to a third function of capital. Under federal law, each depositor's account is insured up to $100,000 by the FDIC. Unlike life, health, or automobile insurance premiums paid by individuals, the insurance premium paid by a bank to the FDIC is not tied to any measure of the bank's riskiness. This creates a moral hazard problem in that bank managers have no incentive to invest in low-risk assets. Because depositors are protected in the event of failure, the managers may as well invest in high-risk assets in order to maximize returns to the bank's shareholders (many of whom are likely to be managers). Sinkey writes:

> Since deposit insurance was instituted in 1933, banks have been substituting deposit insurance for bank capital. In addition, BHCs [bank holding companies] have used the technique of double leverage (i.e., parent company debt downstreamed as bank equity capital) to increase further their effective degree of leverage. Although bank capital serves as a cushion or buffer to absorb realized losses, the ability of banks to pass a major portion of their portfolio risk on to the deposit insurer encourages them to seek riskier assets and additional leverage.[28]

Capital ratios help to restrain the rapid acquisition of high-risk assets by forcing managers to provide capital support for assets. The theory of risk-based capital regulations is that more capital support should be provided for riskier assets. Young explains the function of restraining asset growth by distinguishing capital per se from the capital ratio:

---

[28]J. Sinkey, Jr. "Regulatory Attitudes Toward Risk," in *Handbook for Banking Strategy* 347, 355-356 (R. Aspinwall and R. Eisenbeis, eds., 1985) (citation omitted).

> [T]he purpose of *capital* is to absorb losses—and perhaps to induce confidence in the bank's ability to do so. The purpose of capital *ratios* is to control growth. There is no question of regulators (or anyone) knowing what *amount* of capital is adequate. In a sense, the phrase "capital adequacy" is misleading. No amount of capital is adequate if the bank's credit culture goes wrong. No amount is sufficient to weather a liquidity crisis. But if, for one reason or another, a bank has to maintain a certain capital *ratio*, it will only be able to grow so fast. And rapid growth *is* what gets banks in trouble. One of the most illuminating facts about Continental Illinois is that between year-end 1979 and year-end 1981, its domestic commercial and industrial loan portfolio increased 56 percent. Although banks from time to time have grown at comparable rates without mishap, many knowledgeable observers would argue that the reason Continental Illinois was able to do so was that other banks wouldn't make those loans.[29]

The problem with Young's argument is that, if taken too seriously, it can imply a conscious intent on the part of regulators to inhibit bank growth. It would seem that regulators would seek to restrain only imprudent growth. This is precisely why the Basle Agreement requires additional capital support for the acquisition of risky assets.

(5) Helping the FDIC

When capital serves to absorb losses or enhance confidence in the banking system, banks and their creditors are the most prominent beneficiaries. But they are not the only parties who benefit from the existence of bank capital. Banking regulators may also be beneficiaries.

It is no secret that in the event of a bank liquidation, capital can be used to pay off creditors of the bank. A strong

---

[29]H. Young. "Bank Regulation Ain't Broke," 64 *Harvard Business Review* 106, 109 (Sept.-Oct. 1986).

capital position lowers the cost to the FDIC of any liquidation. That is, capital serves not only as a cushion against variations in the earnings from a bank's assets, but also as a cushion for insurers. When commenting on the rationale for higher capital requirements, former Federal Reserve Chairman Paul Volcker said, "Added capital would provide an extra cushion of protection against the possibility of loss to depositors *and* the deposit insurance fund."[30]

In the event of a liquidation following insolvency, bank capital is available to be paid out to depositors, along with FDIC insurance funds. In the event of a purchase and assumption "rescue" following insolvency, the more bank capital exists, the less the FDIC must contribute to the reorganized entity. Stanley Silverberg, director of the FDIC's division of research and strategic planning, states this point clearly:

> Because banks operate with substantial leverage, the protective cushion afforded by bank capital has always been important. In an environment where most deposits are federally insured or indirectly backed by federal deposit insurance, a large capital cushion affords more protection to the insurer. If higher capital requirements are enforced, there are likely to be fewer bank failures and smaller losses to the insurer.
>
> In the U.S. system, the presence of deposit insurance is the principal (perhaps the only) reason to single banks out for special supervision and to enforce capital standards. That proposition has important implications for what is included in the capital cushion. It is the bank whose liabilities are protected by insurance and it is bank insolvency that exposes the insurer to potential loss. Thus, it is capital at the bank

---

[30]Paul A. Volcker, statement before the Senate Committee on Banking, Housing, and Urban Affairs, September 11, 1985, quoted in C. Friesen, *International Bank Supervision* 11, note 89 at 92 (1986); (emphasis supplied).

level, as opposed to the holding company, that affords protection to the supervisor and should be of concern to bank supervisors.[31]

A different way of stating the argument that capital serves as a cushion against losses to the FDIC is to consider the role of deposit insurance in the overall banking regulatory framework. Benston argues that there is only one legitimate reason to regulate banks to a greater extent than any nonfinancial business: the presence of deposit insurance.[32] E. Gerald Corrigan, president of the Federal Reserve Bank of New York, also suggests this argument.[33] Since the FDIC charges a flat insurance premium regardless of the risk profile of the assets of an insured bank, a moral hazard problem exists. Banks have no incentive to lower the risk profiles of their asset portfolios, since they are not charged for taking on higher risk. Indeed, insofar as higher returns on assets are earned by higher risk, and the stock prices of banks rise, bank managers have a perverse incentive to take on more risk. Thus, banks must be discouraged from excessive risk-taking at the expense of federal insurers. Risk-based capital regulations are one check on such risk-taking.

---

[31] S. Silverberg. "Regulation of Bank Capital," 9 *Issues in Bank Regulation* 7 (Spring, 1986). James Chessen, Financial Economist in the Division of Research and Strategic Planning at the FDIC, also discusses this point in "Risk-Based Capital Comes to the Fore," 10 *Issues in Bank Regulation* 3 (Spring 1987).

[32] G. Benston. "Why Continue to Regulate Banks?: An Historical Assessment of Federal Banking Regulation," 5 *Midland Corporate Finance Journal* 67, 76 (Fall 1987). I do not agree with Benston's overall conclusion that the supervisory role of the Federal Reserve should be abolished. *See id.* at 68. Rather, I am more comfortable with Gardener's assertion that "[n]o serious student of banking... can argue convincingly that supervision is unnecessary." E. Gardener, "Securitization: The Challenge for World Banking," 7 *The World of Banking* 3, 6 (Jan./Feb. 1988).

[33] E. Gerald Corrigan. "Are Banks Special?," Federal Reserve Bank of Minneapolis *Annual Report 1982*, 2.

(6) Generating Earnings

Implicitly, the perspective of the regulator on the functions of capital has been taken in this discussion. But bankers and shareholders of a bank have quite a different perspective. As Elliot suggests, "Regulators do not view capital the same way bankers do. Regulators are influenced by their primary occupational goal, which is to protect the safety and soundness of the banking system. Bankers, on the other hand, are primarily concerned about earnings, especially earnings on equity."[34] This point is also made by Roussakis:

> Profits in banking, just as in other businesses, have an important determinant of investors' interest in bank stock. Thus, from the stockholders' point of view, the function of bank capital is to achieve a sufficient yield to meet operating costs and net a fair return to its owners. With possible rare exceptions, the suppliers of bank capital are motivated solely by the desire to own a good investment.... They invest in the stock of a bank for the same reasons that they invest in the shares of any other business enterprise: to obtain a competitive return on their funds, with the hope of appreciation in the value of their stock. Unless this return is obtained, they have no reason for wishing to continue to supply capital to the bank. An unprofitable bank is, after all, an unhealthy bank, and cannot survive.[35]

Howcroft discusses the difference in perspective on capital between bank regulators and bankers in his review of the U.S.-U.K. Joint Proposal:

> The regulators were essentially concerned with maintaining a high level of capital for prudential reasons, with emphasis

---

[34]J. Elliot. "Capital Planning for Regulatory Purposes," 9 *Issues in Bank Regulation* 16 (Spring 1986).

[35]E. Roussakis. *Commercial Banking in an Era of Deregulation* 130 (1984).

being placed on the traditional loss-absorption functions of capital. Conversely, bankers were essentially concerned with maintaining the least possible capital base in an endeavour to maximize returns within an acceptable level of risk. These differing opinions manifested themselves in prolonged discussions about the exact definition of bank capital.[36]

F. Chapter Summary

It is not obvious that bank capital should be subject to regulatory supervision. Modigliani and Miller suggest that the debt/equity ratio of a corporation is irrelevant. The value of any corporation, including a bank, is the present discounted value of its expected future earnings stream. How claims on this earnings stream are divided between debt and equity is irrelevant.

This proposition might lead one to think that the capital/asset ratio also is irrelevant. But it is not reasonable to base an inference about the capital/asset ratio on the theoretical irrelevance of the debt/equity ratio. The two ratios are different, and in any case the Modigliani-Miller proposition is itself questionable.

Alternatively, one might infer from the traditional corporate finance model that regulatory-determined capital is unnecessary because market forces will lead to an optimal capital ratio. Under this model, the debt/equity ratio is not irrelevant; rather, the optimal ratio is where the weighted average cost of capital is at a minimum. Again, there is the distinction between a debt/equity ratio and a capital/asset ratio. Moreover, it is possible that the market underestimates the systemic costs of bank losses and bank failure. If so, the need for bank capital will be understated.

Regulatory-determined capital can serve several func-

---

[36]J. Howcroft. "U.K. Bank Capital Adequacy and the Convergent Proposals," 2 *Journal of International Banking* 203 (1987).

tions. One, which is emphasized in the Basle Agreement, is the absorption of losses, particularly of unexpected losses. Such losses arise from a bank's asset portfolio or its off-balance-sheet activities. When a loss is incurred on an asset, the asset account on the left-hand side of the bank's balance sheet must be written down or written off. A corresponding reduction must be made to a capital account on the right-hand side of the balance sheet.

Public confidence may be enhanced by the existence of a strong capital base. This may be related to the loss absorption function—that is, public confidence may be enhanced because depositors know the bank has sufficient capital to absorb unexpected losses. Whether bank capital actually prevents bank failures is questionable. There are many causes of bank failure, including fraud and mismanagement. However, in the event of bank failure, the FDIC benefits from bank capital because it can be used to make payments to insured depositors. The more capital available for such a payout, the less money will need to be drawn from the federal insurance fund.

Bank capital is not itself a constraint on asset growth, though meeting required increases in the capital/asset ratio may act as a constraint. Finally, bank capital is linked to the generation of earnings.

3
Substance, Form, and the Constituents of Capital

Key Concepts

Tier One Capital (core capital)
Equity capital
Disclosed reserves
Goodwill
Noncumulative perpetual preferred stock
Cumulative perpetual preferred stock
Tier Two capital (supplementary capital)
Undisclosed reserves
Revaluation reserves
General loan loss provisions
Hybrid instruments
Subordinated term debt
Guaranteed preferred shares
Floating-rate preferred stock
Upstream convertibles
Unbundled stock

A. The Ability to Absorb Losses Is What Matters

The *ability to absorb losses* is the function of capital emphasized in the Basle Agreement. That is, the rationale offered in the Basle Agreement (as well as in the December 1987 Basle Proposal) for the inclusion of certain items in the capital base, and the exclusion of others, is their ability to absorb losses (or lack thereof). Yet certain newly developed financial instruments do not fit neatly into one of the formal categories of Tier One or Tier Two. Financial instruments exist now and more will doubtless be developed in the future that "fall through the cracks." Consequently, it is fortunate that the Basle Agreement does not simply slot an

43

instrument into a category based on the label attached to the instrument; rather, it looks to whether the instrument can fulfill the substantive function of absorbing losses.

(1) Tier One: Core Capital

Tier One capital, also called "core capital" or "basic equity," contains the only elements of capital on which all countries participating in the Basle negotiations agreed: equity capital and disclosed reserves.[1] It is undisputed that these elements can function as a buffer against losses. For example, the Board's March 1988 proposed regulations stated with respect to equity capital that

> the predominant role afforded common stockholders' equity reflects the fact that this element provides maximum strength and flexibility to a banking organization experiencing losses or other financial pressures. For this reason, international supervisors reached a consensus that a minimum level of common stockholders' equity should serve as the foundation of a bank's capital base.[2]

No creditor has a legal claim to equity capital or reserves, precisely because these are not debt instruments. No shareholder has a legal right to redeem his proportionate interest in equity capital or reserves. Shareholders may sell their stock in the secondary market, but they cannot force the bank or bank holding company whose stock they seek to liquidate to purchase in redemption. Shareholders may be paid dividends on their common stock based on the existence of a capital account, such as earned surplus (retained earnings), but this is at the discretion of the bank or bank holding company that pays the dividends.[3] As Robinson and White explain:

---

[1] Basle Agreement, 4.
[2] 53 Fed. Reg. 8550, 8553 (proposed March 15, 1988).

CAPITAL

Equity is the claim to the residual or net income of the firm, and all other claims take priority over it. The most junior equity is the common share, and that is what finance theory considers to be pure equity. This means that the income from common shares is riskier than the income paid to any other claimant who shares in some way in the firm. Dividends are a discretionary distribution of some or all of that residual claim.

Debt is a defined or nonresidual claim on the firm, and it takes priority over equity. The priority of different issues of debt is determined contractually. Interest is the rent on the principal amount, and it is not discretionary—it must be paid or the creditor gets the right to seize some of the firm's assets. Since debt has priority over equity and interest is not discretionary, the income stream from debt is less risky than that from equity.[4]

In sum, if a bank or bank holding company experiences losses for which it has not set aside a special reserve account, equity capital and disclosed reserves can be reduced to match the corresponding reductions in asset accounts.

(a) **Equity Capital in Tier One.** The definition of equity capital covers several items. "Equity capital" includes common stock and *noncumulative* perpetual preferred stock.[5] For bank holding companies, but not banks, it also includes *cumulative* perpetual preferred stock.[6]

---

[3]The wording "paid dividends out of a reserve account" is deliberately avoided, because dividends are *never* paid out of an account on the right-hand side of the balance sheet. The source of money from which dividends are paid is always an asset account, typically cash. A sufficient balance in a right-hand account (such as earned surplus) may be required under state corporate law in order to pay dividends out of an asset account. *See* B. Manning, *Legal Capital* 33-34 (1981).

[4]C. Robinson and A. White, "Guaranteed Preferred Shares—Debt or Equity," 1 *Banking and Finance Law Review,* 215-216 (1987-88).

[5]Basle Agreement, note 2 at 4.

[6]This differential treatment is discussed later in this section.

Common stock refers to paid-in capital at par value, or stated capital if no par stock is issued. Common stock must be issued and fully paid up—that is, not "watered."[7] Watering involves undercontributions by subscribers to the stock issue; the par value of stock (or stated value of no par stock) given to subscribers is less than the value of the consideration received from the subscribers. The legal issue is the adequacy of consideration given by the original owners of the bank or bank holding company in exchange for the stock.[8]

Noncumulative perpetual preferred stock has three distinct features. First, it is "preferred" in that holders have some sort of preference to dividend distributions or distributions in liquidation ahead of common stockholders. Second, it is "perpetual" in that it has no maturity date and cannot be redeemed at the option of the holder. Third, it is "noncumulative" in that unpaid dividends do not accrue. Noncumulative perpetual preferred stock was not included in the December 1987 Basle Proposal.[9] The Federal Reserve was criticized for this exclusion:

> The exclusion of preferred which is widely used in the U.S. but not by banks in other countries from the early [i.e., December 1987] BIS draft regulation caused much anger among bank chairmen in Manhattan. We were very poorly represented by the New York Fed at the BIS. They sent a boy who we hadn't even met.[10]

In its August 1, 1988, Memorandum the Board staff took

---

[7]*Id.*

[8]How to measure the quantity of watering is a matter of some legal dispute. An in-depth discussion of the dispute is found in V. Brudney and M. Chirelstein, *Corporate Finance* 317-334 (3d ed. 1987). *See also* B. Manning, *Legal Capital* 17-26 (1981).

[9]August 1, 1988, Board Staff Memorandum, 15.

[10]N. Osborn and G. Evans, "Cooke's Medicine: Kill or Cure?," *Euromoney* 34 (July 1988).

note of this criticism and agreed to the inclusion of noncumulative perpetual preferred stock in Tier One. The reason for this inclusion is the similarity of such stock to common shares, in spite of the three features noted above.

A large number of organizations argued that perpetual preferred stock should count as Tier 1 capital. These organizations noted that perpetual preferred stock serves as a nearly perfect substitute for common equity because it is permanent, it is subordinate to deposits and general debt obligations, and preferred dividends can be deferred without triggering an act of default.

The Basle Accord has been modified to include *noncumulative* perpetual preferred stock in Tier 1 capital with no limitations. The noncumulative feature makes this type of preferred stock a closer substitute for common stock than cumulative preferred stock since any dividend payments that have been waived do not represent a contingent claim on the issuer.[11]

However, the Board's final regulations impose some limit on the inclusion of perpetual preferred stock. For banks, the final regulations state that "overreliance" on preferred stock should be avoided.[12] For bank holding companies, the total amount of perpetual preferred stock, both noncumulative and cumulative, included in Tier One may not exceed 25 percent of Tier One capital.[13] Any excess over 25 percent may count to an unlimited extent in Tier Two.[14]

While noncumulative perpetual preferred stock is akin to

---

[11] August 1, 1988, Board Staff Memorandum, 19-20. Similarly, the final regulations state, "Perpetual preferred stock that has a noncumulative feature is a closer substitute for common stock than cumulative preferred stock since any dividend payments that have been waived do not represent a contingent claim on the issuer." 54 Fed. Reg. 4186, 4188 (January 27, 1989).
[12] 54 Fed. Reg. 4186, 4188, 4199 (January 27, 1989).
[13] *Id.* at note 5 at 4188, 4195, 4210.
[14] *Id.* at 4195, 4210-4211.

common stock for the reasons indicated above, it is not obvious that it is more akin to common than to cumulative perpetual preferred stock. As a matter of corporate law, dividend payments on noncumulative perpetual preferred stock that have been waived may indeed be a contingent claim on the issuer. There is some legal controversy as to the precise meaning of "noncumulative."

One view, found in *Guttmann* v. *Illinois Central R.R. Co.*, is that it bars accruals in all cases — once unpaid, forever extinguished.[15] An alternative view, the "New Jersey rule" found in *Sanders* v. *Cuba Railroad Co.*, is that it means accruals are barred only if the payor corporation does not have earnings.[16] If earnings are sufficient to pay the dividends on the noncumulative perpetual preferred stock, yet such dividends are not paid, then the dividends do accrue.

The Board's final regulations indicate that banks and bank holding companies will be allowed to include floating-rate (or adjustable-rate) preferred stock in Tier One.[17] This is preferred stock whose yield varies with a certain index; for the stock to be eligible for inclusion, the index must be some market interest rate, not a measure of the issuer's credit standing or financial condition.[18] For instance, neither banks nor bank holding companies will be allowed to include auction-rate perpetual preferred stock in Tier One.[19] Such stock has a dividend that is "reset periodically based to some degree upon the banking organization's current credit rating."[20] The rationale here is:

> [i]f sufficient buyers are not interested in holding the stock at the maximum rate at which is can be offered, the auction is

---

[15] 189 F.2d 927 (2d Cir. 1951), *cert. denied*, 342 U.S. 867, 72 S.Ct. 107.
[16] 21 N.J. 78, 120 A.2d 849 (1956).
[17] 54 Fed. Reg. 4186, 4188 (January 27, 1989).
[18] *Id.*
[19] *Id.* at 4188, 4199 (for banks), 4210 (for BHCs).
[20] *Id.* at 4195.

said to have failed. This ... can raise questions about the issuer's financial standing and subject the issuer to pressure from unhappy or unwilling investors to repurchase the outstanding stock. In addition, the very fact that the preferred stock dividend yield can rise when a banking organization's financial condition or credit rating is deteriorating can exacerbate the institution's financial difficulties. [This is] ... inconsistent with the notion of Tier 1 instruments as the highest-quality form of capital.[21]

Auction-rate perpetual preferred stock can be counted in Tier Two.[22]

(b) **Disclosed Reserves in Tier One.** Disclosed reserves also encompass more than one item, in this case reserves that are "created or increased by appropriations of retained earnings or other surplus."[23] That is, it includes retained earnings (also called "earned surplus") and paid-in capital in excess of par value (also called "capital surplus," or just "surplus" if no par stock is issued). It also includes minority interests in the equity of subsidiaries that are not wholly owned.[24]

(c) **Adjustments to Equity Capital and Disclosed Reserves.** Total Tier One capital is not simply the sum of equity capital and disclosed reserves. Two adjustments must be made to this sum; the first concerns goodwill and the second concerns cumulative perpetual preferred stock. Both adjustments involve differentiating between a bank and a bank holding company.

(i) **Goodwill.** — Goodwill is defined as "an intangible asset that represents the excess of the purchase price over the fair market value of net assets acquired in acquisitions accounted for under the purchase method of

---

[21]*Id.* at 4196.
[22]*Id.* at 4196, 4199 (for banks), 4210 (for BHCs).
[23]Basle Agreement, Annex 1 at 2.
[24]*Id.*

accounting."[25] The purchase method of accounting is one of two methods of accounting for the merger with or acquisition of another company. It is used when all or part of the consideration paid by the acquiring corporation for the acquired corporation is cash.[26] The other method, pooling accounting, is used if no part of the consideration is cash—for example, in a stock-for-stock acquisition.[27]

Goodwill does not arise in a noncash merger or acquisition (a merger or acquisition where pooling accounting is used). This is because of the treatment of tangible assets under the two methods. Typically, under either method, the financial statements of the acquiring and target corporations are combined.[28] Under purchase accounting, assets of the acquired corporation are written up or down to fair value. The excess of the consideration paid over this

---

[25]53 Fed. Reg. 8550, 8556, 8573 (proposed March 15, 1988). *See also Intangible Assets,* Opinion of the Accounting Principles Board No. 17, p.26 (Am. Inst. of Certified Pub. Accountants 1970); D. Kieso and J. Weygandt, *Intermediate Accounting* (5th ed. 1986) 503; and A. Mosich and E. Larsen, *Intermediate Accounting* (6th ed. 1986) 656-657. As Kieso and Weygandt point out, to be more precise, goodwill is the excess of the purchase price over identifiable net assets (i.e., over tangible assets and identifiable intangible assets). The point is that goodwill is an unidentifiable, intangible asset.

[26]For a quick summary of GAAP regarding business combinations, *see* N. Dauber et al., *The Vest-Pocket CPA* (1988) 151-161.

[27]For a discussion of the advantages and disadvantages of each method in the context of bank mergers and acquisitions, *see* A. Heggestad, "Fundamentals of Mergers and Acquisitions," in *Handbook for Banking Strategy* 703, 712-714 (R. Aspinwall and R. Eisenbeis, eds., 1985).

[28]There are instances in which the acquiror and target corporations may prefer to maintain separate financial statements—for example, if the target operates independently of the acquiror. The two corporations may seek to use "push-down" accounting, which is essentially purchase accounting without combined financial statements. The FDIC, but not the Federal Reserve, allows banks to use push-down accounting in certain circumstances. *See* R. Swegle, "Push-Down Accounting: Its Impact on Bank Capital," 1 *Bank Accounting and Finance* 29 (Winter 1987-88).

CAPITAL

fair value is goodwill.[29] Any goodwill is then amortized over its useful life, but in no case in excess of 40 years.[30] Fair values will be established for the purchased assets based on audits and independent appraisals.[31] As Brudney and Chirelstein explain, under purchase accounting:

> the assets and liabilities of the acquired company are recorded on the books of the acquiring company at their *fair values as of the date of the combination.* Any difference between the total value of the consideration paid by the acquiring company and the fair value of the tangible and identifiable intangible assets of the acquired firm is recorded as goodwill. If goodwill is recognized to have a limited useful life, then, like any other asset whose value disappears over time, its cost is *amortized year-by-year against the income of the combined enterprise.*[32]

By contrast, under pooling accounting, the assets of the target are recorded on the combined entity's financial statements at book vaue. In a stock-for-stock acquisition, the acquiror's stock is given to the target corporation's shareholders in exchange for target stock. The value of the target's stock received is equivalent to the value of the acquiror's stock used as consideration, and no revaluation of the target's assets occurs. Brudney and Chirelstein write that:

> the combination is treated not as a purchase but as a joining or *"marriage"* of two previously separated entities. The amounts (roughly, historical cost) at which assets and liabili-

---

[29]D. Kieso and J. Weygandt, *Intermediate Accounting* (5th ed. 1986) 503-505.

[30]*Intangible Assets,* Opinion of the Accounting Principles Board No. 17, p.10 (Am. Inst. of Certified Pub. Accountants 1970). *See also* D. Kieso and J. Weygandt, *Intermediate Accounting* (5th ed. 1986) 496-497.

[31]D. Kieso and J. Weygandt. *Intermediate Accounting* (5th ed. 1986), 504.

[32]V. Brudney and M. Chirelstein. *Corporate Finance* 594 (3d ed. 1987); (emphasis supplied).

ties are recorded on the books of the acquired company are carried forward *without change* in the accounts of the acquiring company. Neither the fair value of the acquired company's assets nor the value of its goodwill is recognized.[33]

The Basle Agreement sets forth a simple rule on goodwill: It should be deducted from Tier One.[34] The rule on goodwill in the Board's March 1988 proposed regulations with respect to banks is the same: All goodwill must be deducted immediately from Tier One capital (equity capital plus disclosed reserves).[35] This rule is retained in the Board's final regulations.[36] An exception is made for goodwill acquired through supervisory mergers with troubled or failed banks.[37]

The rule in the March 1988 proposed regulations and in the Board's final regulations for bank holding companies is the same as for banks for goodwill booked on the balance sheet after March 12, 1988.[38] (Again, an exception is made for goodwill acquired through supervisory mergers.[39] Goodwill booked before this date need not be deducted from Tier One during the transition period in which the regulations are phased in — that is, until December 31, 1992.[40]

The rules on deducting goodwill raise at least three issues. First, is the reason for immediate or eventual exclusion of goodwill from Tier One that it may be unavailable

---

[33]*Id.* at 595 (emphasis supplied).
[34]Basle Agreement, 8.
[35]53 Fed. Reg. 8550, 8556, 8572, 8574 (proposed March 15, 1988).
[36]54 Fed. Reg. 4186, 4198, 4200 (January 27, 1989).
[37]53 Fed. Reg. 8550, 8556, 8572, 8574 (proposed March 15, 1988) and 54 Fed. Reg. 4186, note 14 at 4200 (January 27, 1989).
[38]53 Fed. Reg. 8556, 8572-8573 (proposed March 15, 1988) and 54 Fed. Reg. 4186, 4196, 4210, 4212 (January 27, 1989).
[39]54 Fed. Reg. 4186, note 15 at 4212 (January 27, 1989).
[40]*Id.*

for loss absorption? The Basle Agreement does not explicitly answer this question. All that is stated in the March 1988 proposed regulations is that "[a]s a general rule, the Board believes that banking organizations should maintain strong tangible core capital in relation to weighted risk assets."[41] The draft of the Board's final regulations suggests this may be the reason, saying, "During periods of financial adversity some intangibles may not provide the degree of support that is normally expected from an organization's assets.[42]

Conservative accounting principles also suggest this is the reason. The excess in purchase price over fair value that goodwill represents reflects the view of the purchaser and seller that there is something to the target corporation beyond hard assets. (Of course, there is a risk that the purchaser will pay too much because it overvalues the target.) The target may have a good reputation in its community and its markets. There may be brand name loyalty to the products its sells. The target may enjoy a monopoly or oligopoly position in certain markets.

All of these advantages may contribute to the return on tangible assets. For example, trade creditors may negotiate more lenient credit terms, and lenders may accept lower interest rates on debt incurred. The higher return on tangible assets may justify a merger or acquisition price that exceeds the book value of the target's assets.

Yet all of these advantages are potentially evanescent. Tangible assets are analogous to solid matter, but goodwill is like gas — it exists, but it may dissipate. Reputation is a matter of perception, and perceptions change, as do brand loyalties. Goods manufactured in Japan did not always en-

---

[41]*Id.* at 8574.
[42]54 Fed. Reg. 4186, 4196 (January 27, 1989).

joy a reputation of high quality; indeed, after World War II "made in Japan" was often taken to be synonymous with "junk."

Monopoly or oligopoly positions may erode over time, or may erode forcibly through antitrust action. The position of money-center banks as a source of short- and intermediate-term credit has been eroded by the commercial paper market sponsored by investment banks.

Most importantly, the time when a bank is most likely to need to draw on goodwill is precisely the time when goodwill is most likely to dissipate. While Texas savings and loan associations may have enjoyed the benefits of substantial goodwill in the mid- and late 1970s, it is difficult to imagine that such goodwill can serve as a cushion for losses from energy and real estate loans in the mid- and late 1980s. Similarly, money-center banks experiencing actual or probable losses on their Third World loan portfolios cannot draw on goodwill. When Citicorp chairman John Reed moved $3 billion into loan loss reserves to cover such possible losses, he did not record a charge to a goodwill account on the left-hand side of Citicorp's balance sheet.[43] Rather, the $3 billion came from retained earnings, a component of disclosed reserves.

A second issue is the treatment of intangible assets other than goodwill. Examples include purchased mortgage servicing rights, leaseholds, and core deposit values. Why not carry through on the accounting philosophy of conservatism and require that all intangible assets be deducted? The answer to this is not clear, but other intangible assets are not deducted. Rather, they are to be monitored by the Federal Reserve's bank examiners.[44]

---

[43]R. Hedges, Jr. "The Loan Loss Reserve Decisions of 1987," 1 *Bank Accounting and Finance* 47, 48 (Winter 1987-88). *See also* "John Reed's Bold Stroke," *Fortune* (June 22, 1987).

[44]53 Fed. Reg. 8550, 8574 (proposed March 15, 1988) and 54 Fed. Reg. 4186, 4200 (for banks), 4212 (for BHCs).

CAPITAL

The impact of excluding goodwill on bank merger activity is a third issue. This is of special relevance given recent and anticipated merger activity among U.S. banks. An often-heard comment is that U.S. banks must be allowed to merge in order to meet competitive challenges from Japanese and other foreign banks. Denial of goodwill in Tier One is a disincentive to use cash as consideration in a merger or acquisition. Osborn and Evans report that:

> the Chemical Bank chairman, Walter Shipley... broadly supports the Cooke initiative but is a harsh critic of the way the BIS proposals treat goodwill. Under the draft regulations, goodwill is assigned no value: the goodwill in a cash acquisition is wiped off a bank's equity, a reversal of previous U.S. practice. This effectively halts acquisitions of regional banks by money centers for cash, and, Shipley argues, "throws a roadblock in the consolidation of America's fractionated banking system." Impeding consolidations, Shipley would argue, robs U.S. banks of the economies of scale involved, for example, in combining back offices and headquarters staff.[45]

The Board staff takes note of this criticism in its December 14, 1988, Memorandum. The staff writes that banking organizations opposed the treatment of goodwill because "the deduction would hamper the process of domestic banking consolidation by effectively eliminating purchase accounting as a viable method of consummating mergers and acquisitions."[46]

The assumption hidden behind this criticism is that bigger banks are more competitive—bank mergers are a good thing because the resultant banking combinations are more competitive. If this assumption is accepted *arguendo*, the issue raised is whether the deduction of goodwill from Tier

---

[45]N. Osborn and G. Evans, "Cooke's Medicine: Kill or Cure?," *Euromoney* 34 (July 1988).
[46]December 14, 1988, Board Staff Memorandum, 147. *See also* 54 Fed. Reg. 4186, 4196 (January 27, 1989).

One capital is merely an artificial incentive to use stock as consideration in bank mergers and acquisitions. Is there some substantive policy justification for discriminating against cash acquisitions?

(ii) **Cumulative Perpetual Preferred Stock.** —The second adjustment to the sum of equity capital and disclosed reserves concerns cumulative perpetual preferred stock. For bank holding companies, but not banks, such stock may be included in Tier One. The most common form of perpetual preferred stock issued by banks is cumulative.[47] It is not readily apparent why only bank holding companies should be allowed to include cumulative perpetual preferred stock. The draft of the Board's final regulations states that:

> bank holding companies also should be allowed to include *cumulative* preferred stock in Tier 1. While cumulative preferred dividends can only be deferred, the deferral can last as long as necessary to enable the organization to regain its financial health. Moreover, supervisors have the authority to prohibit the resumption of preferred, as well as common, dividends until they are satisfied that resumption of such payments is in the best interests of the institution.[48]

The issue is whether this rationale is equally applicable to banks.

Federal regulators are reported to have suggested that banks convert their cumulative stock into noncumulative stock.[49] There is a question whether as a matter of corporate law such a conversion can be effected, particularly if there are dividend arrearages on the cumulative preferred stock that the issuing bank seeks to convert.

---

[47]"Central Banks Approve Risk-Based Capital Rules," *American Banker*, July 18, 1988, at 9.

[48]December 14, 1988, Board Staff Memorandum, 144.

[49]"Central Bankers Approve Risk-Based Capital Plan," *American Banker*, July 12, 1988, at 1.

CAPITAL

To summarize, the formula for Tier One capital for a bank holding company is found in equation 1. The formula for banks is found in equation 2.

Equation 1.
Tier One capital =   Common stock
 + surplus accounts (e.g., paid-in capital in excess par and retained earnings)
 + Noncumulative perpetual preferred stock
 + Cumulative perpetual preferred stock
 − Goodwill booked after March 12, 1988 (after December 31, 1992, all goodwill regardless of when booked)

Equation 2.
Tier One capital =   Common stock
 + Surplus accounts (e.g., paid-in capital in excess of par and retained earnings)
 + Noncumulative perpetual preferred stock
 − Goodwill booked after March 12, 1988 (after December 31, 1992, all goodwill regardless of when booked)

(2) Tier Two: Supplementary Capital

There are five constituents in Tier Two: undisclosed reserves, revaluation reserves, general provisions and general loan loss reserves, hybrid debt/equity instruments, and subordinated term debt.[50] The distinction between Tier

---

[50] Basle Agreement, Annex 1 at 2-4.

One and Tier Two capital elements is one of degree, not of kind. In both tiers, all elements can function as a cushion to absorb losses. In Tier Two, one or a few characteristics of each element could cause the element to be less readily available to absorb losses.

In some cases, the characteristics are legal—namely, the nature of the claimant. Claimants to equity capital and disclosed reserves are owners (shareholders) of the bank or bank holding company. Alternatively, some claimants on Tier Two elements are creditors of the bank holding company or bank. Thus, there is a potential debtor-creditor relationship. In other cases, the characteristic that renders a Tier Two element less readily available to absorb losses is not legal but economic.

(a) **Undisclosed Reserves.** Undisclosed reserves are accumulated after-tax retained profits that regulators in some countries allow to remain undisclosed. In other words, these are retained earnings that are not published on a balance sheet. The Federal Reserve does not allow bank holding companies or banks to maintain undisclosed reserves. The Basle Agreement states that undisclosed reserves "should have the same high quality and character as disclosed capital reserves; as such, [they] should not be encumbered by any provision or other known liability but should be freely and immediately available to meet unforeseen future losses."[51] Hidden reserves must, therefore, be as able to absorb losses as retained earnings that are disclosed.

Yet, if undisclosed reserves are of the same high quality as disclosed retained earnings, why are they not included in Tier One? No answer is given in the Basle Agreement, but possibly it is precisely because they are hidden. The market

---

[51]*Id.* at Annex 1 at 3.

is unaware of the hidden reserves as a potential cushion. In other words, mere ability to function as a cushion against losses is not necessarily sufficient for capital to qualify as Tier One. This ability must be generally known. If depositors, shareholders, financial analysts, and other interested parties are unaware of the existence of reserves that can absorb losses, then the hidden reserves cannot build public confidence. Placing hidden reserves in Tier Two instead of Tier One reflects an incentive to provide the market with full information, and serves as a reminder not to focus exclusively on the loss absorption function of capital.

(b) Revaluation Reserves. Revaluation reserves are reserve accounts on the right-hand side of the balance sheet that are increased whenever an asset on the left-hand side is revalued to reflect market value. Bank regulators in some countries allow fixed assets and/or equity holdings to be written up to fair market value. Increases in reserves to reflect unrealized appreciation in equity holdings are also called "hidden values" or "latent revaluation reserves."[52] This is not permitted in the United States under GAAP or RAP. These conservative accounting rules require that all assets be carried at book values. Moreover, U.S. bank holding companies and banks are prohibited by law from owning more than a small percentage of the outstanding stock of nonbanking corporations.[53]

By contrast, Japanese banking regulators do permit revaluation of bank assets. Under the Basle Agreement, if such revaluation is allowed, the full amount of the unrealized appreciation of fixed assets, such as real estate, can

---

[52] *Id.*
[53] C. Golembe and D. Holland, *Federal Regulation of Banking 1986-87* 168-171 (1986).

count as capital. Forty-five percent of the appreciation in equity capital can be counted in Tier Two.[54]

There are two reasons for discounting latent revaluation reserves. The first is the capital gain that would have to be recognized were the appreciation in equity value to be realized.[55] That is, for each share sold, a capital gains tax (assuming one exists) would have to be paid on the difference between the sale price and the historic book value. Thus, the full difference would not be available to absorb losses. Second, stock market values are volatile. An unrealized capital gain could become an unrealized loss in a few hours. The discount serves as a sort of arbitrary hedge against such depreciation.

(c) **General Provisions and General Loan Loss Reserves.** The word to be stressed when general provisions and general loan loss reserves are considered is "general." As explained in the Basle Agreement, "provisions or loan loss reserves held against future, presently unidentified losses are freely available to meet losses which subsequently materialize and therefore qualify for inclusion within supplementary elements. Provisions ascribed to impairment of particular assets or known liabilities should be excluded."[56]

The task here is to distinguish "general" from "particular." When can provisions or loan loss reserves be labeled "ascribed"? This again suggests that mere availability to absorb losses is not enough. It is necessary that *unexpected* losses be absorbed. Funds in a reserve for losses on loans to Argentina cannot be used to offset unanticipated losses that may occur elsewhere in the asset portfolio. The Board staff made this point in its August 1, 1988, Memorandum:

---

[54] Basle Agreement, Annex 1 at 3.
[55] "Recognition" and "realization" are not synonymous. Income may be realized without being recognized for tax purposes.
[56] Basle Agreement, Annex 1 at 3.

The general thrust of the comments received from U.S. banking organizations on the proposed treatment of loan loss reserves was that general reserves should be included in Tier 1 and that the proposed limits on reserves should be raised or eliminated. On the other hand, commenters from many other countries argued that certain types of reserves, such as those established against loans to less developed countries, are not freely available and such reserves are, indeed, excluded from capital in these countries. Moreover, under generally accepted accounting principles, reserves in U.S. banking organizations take the form of valuation adjustments to the loan portfolio. These adjustments represent losses inherent or anticipated in the existing portfolio but not yet identified. If capital is intended to serve as a buffer against unanticipated losses, then it does not seem inappropriate to relegate such reserves to Tier 2 subject to the limits contained in the Basle Accord.[57]

The Basle Committee hopes to develop a method of distinguishing specific from general provisions and reserves by the end of 1990.[58] If agreement cannot be reached, then a cap on the amount of provisions and reserves that count as Tier Two will be imposed. This cap would equal 1.25 percent (or, in the extreme, 2 percent) of risk-weighted assets.[58]

(d) **Hybrid Instruments.** Hybrid instruments combine features of equity and debt. The Basle Agreement states that "where these instruments have close similarities to equity, in particular when they are able to support losses on an ongoing basis without triggering liquidation, they may be included in supplementary capital."[59]

Mandatory convertible debt instruments are an example of a hybrid instrument that would qualify as Tier Two

---

[57] August 1, 1988, Board Staff Memorandum, 20-21.
[58] Basle Agreement, 7.
[59] *Id.*

capital. Holders of these instruments receive fixed income payments; this is the bond element of the instrument. The equity element is the conversion to equity. Until conversion, the holder is a creditor of the issuer; after conversion, the holder becomes an owner. Upon conversion, the right to fixed payments is surrendered and the holder receives dividends at the discretion of the issuer.[60] As Wood explains:

> A convertible bond allows the holder to exchange his bonds for shares of the company or of the company's parent or subsidiary during a specified period (the *conversion period*) at a specified price per share (the *conversion price*). This price may be the same for the entire conversion period or it may be stepped up at specified intervals. On conversion, no consideration is normally payable: the subscription price is paid by setoff of this price against the principal amount of the bonds which are surrendered for conversion.[61]

The term "mandatory" means that the issuer can force conversion. A holder will not want to convert until the market price far exceeds the conversion price. Indeed, the holder purchases a convertible partly to speculate in the future growth of the issuer as reflected in the share price.[62]

> Investors do not usually convert until the market price is well in excess of the conversion price, for example, because of inertia or because the margin is not sufficient to compensate for the investor's view of the future prospects for the value of

---

[60]W. Klein, "The Convertible Bond: A Peculiar Package," 123 *University of Pennsylvania Law Review* 547, 550-551 (1975). The "watered stock" problem discussed earlier is relevant to the issuance of convertibles. Issuing convertible bonds at a discount that are immediately convertible to equity at par would allow the investor to pay less than par for the share. Consequently, issuing convertibles at a discount is generally impermissible. *See* P. Wood, "International Convertible Bond Issues," 1 *Journal of International Banking Law* 69, 70 (1986).

[61]P. Wood, "International Convertible Bond Issues," 1 *Journal of International Banking Law* 69 (1986).

[62]*Id.*

the shares, or because tax is under the laws of a particular jurisdiction deductible from dividends but not from interest, or because the company has a policy of not distributing all its profits as dividends.[63]

However, the time at which the holder will seek to convert is precisely when the issuer will find conversion least desirable, for the issuer will be obligated to issue equity at below-market prices.[64]

A common reason to issue convertibles is to achieve deferred equity financing.[65] For example, suppose a bank or bank holding company forecasts a *possible* need for increased Tier One equity capital to meet the 4 percent ratio of Tier One capital to risk-weighted assets by the end of 1992. It does not want to issue stock now because it may not need the capital. So it issues convertibles.

If in late 1991 or early 1992 the issuing bank or bank holding company does need equity but the market price of its outstanding shares has not risen far above the conversion price on the convertibles, holders will not voluntarily convert. From the issuer's perspective, this is a desirable time for conversion, because the issuer does not have to issue shares at a below-market price and thereby dilute the value of existing shares. A mandatory redemption provision in the convertibles contract will allow the issuer to require holders to convert. The issuing bank or bank holding company will have achieved deferred Tier One equity financing.

(e) Subordinated Term Debt. The final element in Tier Two listed in the Basle Agreement is subordinated term debt. This category covers debt instruments with a maturity over five years that are subordinated.

---

[63] *Id.* at 70.
[64] *Id.*
[65] *Id.* at 69-70.

PERSPECTIVES ON RISK-BASED CAPITAL

No precise definition of "subordinated" is offered, but the examples of subordinated term debt are revealing. The category includes conventional unsecured subordinated debt (subordinated debentures) and limited life preferred stock. Typically, in liquidation subordinated debenture claimants follow holders of all other financial instruments — including, possibly, common stock. Limited life preferred stock may be superior to subordinated debentures.

The Basle Agreement recognizes that "subordinated term debt instruments have significant deficiencies as constituents of capital in view of their fixed maturity and inability to absorb losses except in liquidation."[66] Consequently, during the final five years to maturity, a 20 percent discount or amortization factor is to be applied to subordinated term debt.[67] Moreover, the total amount of these instruments that may be counted in Tier Two is limited to 50 percent of Tier One.

(3) Calculating Total Capital

Total capital (the numerator of the capital/risk-weighted assets ratio) is the sum of Tier One capital, as adjusted, and Tier Two capital, with one deduction. That deduction, which applies to banks and bank holding companies, is investments in certain unconsolidated subsidiaries.[68] The deduction is made if the subsidiary is engaged in banking and financial activities and the parent company has a direct or indirect ownership stake of 50 percent or more in the subsidiary.[69] If investments in any subsidiary are deducted

---

[66] Basle Agreement, 8.
[67] *Id.* at Annex 2, 4.
[68] *Id.* at 8. 54 Fed. Reg. 4186, 4200-4201 (for banks), 4212 (for BHCs). A third deduction, reciprocal holdings of banking organizations' capital instruments, is specified in the Board's final regulations. *See* 54 Fed. Reg. 4186, 4201 (for banks), 4212-4213 (for BHCs).
[69] 54 Fed. Reg. 4186, note 15 at 4200 (for banks), note 16 at 4212 (for BHCs).

from the parent's capital, then the assets of that subsidiary will be deducted from the parent's assets for purposes of calculating the capital/risk-weighted assets ratio.[70]

Neither the Basle Agreement nor the Board's March 1988 proposed regulations indicates precisely how a parent bank or parent bank holding company is to deduct its investments in unconsolidated subsidiaries. Should the deduction be from Tier One, from Tier Two, or from each tier? The answer is found in the Board's final regulations, which state that (with respect to parent bank holding companies) 50 percent of the investments should be deducted from Tier One and 50 percent from Tier Two.[71] (Presumably, the same rule applies to parent banks.)

The Board staff states its concern that deduction entirely from Tier Two "would provide only minimal firewall protection to banks since their holding companies could replace capital invested in an unconsolidated subsidiary with subordinated debt at the parent level—yet any actual loss sustained on the investment would reduce the holding company's retained earnings and, hence, Tier 1 capital."[72] By "firewall protection" the Board staff means that sufficient capital should be "available at the holding company level to support the company's banking activities without reliance on the resources invested in the unconsolidated subsidiary."[73]

The general formula for total capital is presented in equation 3. (Any limitations applicable to specific elements are not included in the equation. The differential treatment of cumulative preferred stock for banks and bank holding companies is also excluded.)

---

[70]*Id.* at note 13 at 4200 (for banks), note 14 at 4211 (for BHCs).
[71]*Id.* at note 18 at 4212.
[72]December 14, 1988, Board Staff Memorandum, 10.
[73]*Id.* at 11.

Equation 3.
Total Capital = Tier One Capital + Tier Two Capital
= [(Equity Capital + Disclosed Reserves) − Goodwill]
+ [Undisclosed Reserves + Revaluation Reserves + General Provisions and General Loan Loss Reserves + Hybrid Debt/Equity Instruments + Subordinated Term Debt]
− [Investments in Certain Unconsolidated Subsidiaries]

B. Some Strange Financial Instruments

(1) It's Tough to Keep Up!

Not all financial instruments can be easily categorized. Wall Street professionals can usually develop an instrument that defies established legal categories. The Basle Agreement is all the more effective regarding capital constituents because it is flexible. Absolute, rigid thinking is an inviting target for the creative. As banks, particularly money-center banks, struggle to meet the 8 percent capital/risk-weighted assets ratio, regulators should anticipate the introduction of creative financing techniques.

Banks may not want to issue straight equity because of the depressed level of their stock prices. Commercial bankers may ask investment bankers to develop "sexy" products that can be issued at higher prices. Inevitably, this will involve new labels to market the instruments. It may also involve juggling the legal rights of prospective holders. Regulators will be challenged to look past labels and see whether different forms affect the substantive loss-absorption function of the instrument.

(2) Guaranteed Preferred Shares

Consider, for instance, a Canadian instrument called "guaranteed preferred shares." This instrument has three features.[74] First, a fixed-rate dividend is paid. The term is a matter of contract between the issuer and holders. Second, the issuer has a right of redemption and the holder has a right of retraction. These rights usually do not arise for at least five to seven years, or until the shares trade at near par.

Third and most interestingly, the dividend is guaranteed. "A bank provides an irrevocable guaranty to pay all dividends and all principal amounts on retraction, if the issuing corporation fails to do so. If the issuer so fails and the bank makes the payment, then it has recourse against the issuer's assets."[75] In this sense, the instrument looks like debt rather than equity. Equity owners bear the full risk of the failure of the issuer; debt holders do not. This instrument is called "stock," yet the holders have a guarantee against downside risk.

Assume that a bank or bank holding company issues guaranteed preferred shares. The fact that the holder has a right of retraction would preclude such shares from inclusion in Tier One. These shares would be unavailable as a cushion against losses if the holder exercised the retraction right.

Suppose holders had no such right. Should guaranteed preferred shares then be counted in Tier One? Dividends are neither noncumulative nor cumulative; they are guaranteed by a third-party guarantor. The guarantee neither enhances nor detracts from the loss-absorption

---

[74] C. Robinson and A. White. "Guaranteed Preferred Shares—Debt or Equity," 1 *Banking and Financing Law Review* 211 (1987-88).
[75] *Id.* at 213.

function, so guaranteed preferred shares should be placed in Tier One equity capital for banks and bank holding companies.

Alternatively, it could be argued that from the point of view of the issuing bank or bank holding company, guaranteed preferred shares with no retraction right are substantively equivalent to straight debt since they pay a fixed rate for a fixed term and can be redeemed. This argument would result in placement in Tier Two.

(3) Floating-Rate Preferred Stock

Floating-rate preferred stock is another instrument that might be difficult to categorize based on labels. The dividend on this instrument is revised quarterly.[76] The revision "is based on the highest of three rates; the 90-day Treasury bill rate, the 10-year Treasury bond rate, or the 20-year Treasury bond rate."[76] Typically, the dividend is based on a par value of $50. As of 1983, approximately $2 billion of floating-rate preferred stock had been issued by banks, including Chase Manhattan and Manufacturers Hanover.

Should the fact that the dividend floats affect the status of this instrument for risk-based capital purposes? There is no reason to think so, unless, perhaps, the dividend yield is tied to some measure of the credit standing of the issuer. Again, the method of calculating the return to investors is largely immaterial to the issue of loss absorption. Generally speaking, how investor returns are calculated should not affect whether the instrument is counted as a constituent of capital. If the dividend yield is tied to some measure of creditworthiness, the same concerns that exist with auction-rate perpetual preferred stock will arise.

---

[76]J. Woolridge and K. Shuey. "Floating Rate Preferred Stock — An Innovation in Bank Capital," 166 *The Bankers Magazine* 78 (May/June 1983); *Id.* at 79.

(4) Upstream Convertibles

The Basle Agreement is silent on the definition of "conversion." No mention is made of upstream convertibles, junior securities that are convertible to senior securities (i.e., preferred stock or debt).[77] While such instruments may not be issued in New York (under section 519(a)(1) of the New York Business Corporation Law), they may be issued in other states—for example, in Delaware (under section 151(e) of the Delaware General Corporation Law) and New Jersey (under New Jersey Statutes section 14A:7-9(1)).[78]

Insofar as many banks and bank holding companies are incorporated in Delaware or New Jersey or in other jurisdictions that allow upstream convertibles to be issued, it must be asked how such instruments should be treated. Should they, for example, be counted in Tier One as equity capital until conversion into a senior security, at which time they are counted in Tier Two?

Three requirements of the Basle Agreement shed some light on this problem. These requirements must be met if a hybrid instrument is to count in Tier Two. First, the instrument must be unsecured and subordinated. Presumably this means that an upstream convertible that is convertible into nonsubordinated debt cannot count in Tier Two. But what does "subordinated" mean? Does it mean subordinated to all financial elements except common stock? By contrast, presumably an upstream convertible that is convertible into a subordinated debenture does qualify for Tier Two.

Second, the instrument must not be redeemable at the initiative of the holder. The instrument must be available to participate in losses without the bank's being obliged to

---

[77]*See* V. Brudney and M. Chirelstein. *Corporate Finance* note at 286 (3d ed. 1987).
[78]*Id.*

cease trading. This is consistent with the emphasis on loss absorption. Under current Delaware and New Jersey law, conversion is an option of both the issuer and the holder.[79]

Finally, the contract under which the instrument is issued must allow for deferral of payments if the issuer is not profitable enough to support payment of obligations on the instrument. This is permissible under a cumulative perpetual preferred stock contract. Thus, banks may count such stock in Tier Two.

(5) Unbundled Stock

(Note to Reader: The SEC recently decided that unbundled stock units must be included in the total number of shares outstanding when calculating earnings per share. This decision caused Shearson Lehman to withdraw its unbundled stock plan, though the idea of unbundling may materialize in a different form in the future. *See* "Shearson to Withdraw Unbundled Stock Plan," *Wall Street Journal*, March 29, 1989, at C1).

The investment banking firm of Shearson Lehman Hutton recently devised a means for corporations to break up, or "unbundle," a share of outstanding common stock into three units. The first is a bond called a "base-year bond" (BYB), the second is a share of preferred stock called an "incremental dividend preferred share" (IDP), and the third is called an "equity appreciation certificate" (EAC).[80] In exchange for each share of common stock currently held, the holder would receive one BYB, one IDP, and one EAC.

An investor would thus be left with three pieces of paper

---

[79]Delaware General Corporation Law § 151(e), New Jersey Statutes § 14A:7-9(1).

[80]"New Plan to Retire Companies' Equity," *Financial Times*, December 6, 1988, at 27.

CAPITAL

that together amount to the single piece of paper he owned initially.[81] The units would trade separately on the New York Stock Exchange—there would be a market for BYBs, one for IDPs, and one for EACs. In 30 years, the three units would be "rebundled" into one common share. In effect, one share of stock would be separated into a debt/equity hybrid composed of three independent parts, and then it would be rejoined after 30 years.

At least four companies—American Express (Shearson's parent company), Dow Chemical, Pfizer, and Sara Lee—have plans to unbundle a portion of their outstanding common stock, pending approval by the SEC.[82] (Most of each company's outstanding common stock would not be unbundled.) Banks or bank holding companies may want to unbundle some of their common stock, so the capital adequacy considerations are worth exploring.

BYBs will pay a fixed interest rate exactly equivalent to the current dividend rate paid on the issuer's common stock.[83] In the case of American Express, this would be $0.84 in interest annually.[84] The BYBs will mature in 30 years and will be issued at a deep discount to the par value at which they will be redeemed.[85] BYBs resemble interest-paying debentures because they are unsecured. They resemble zero-coupon bonds because they are issued at a discount

---

[81]"British Steel in the Bull's Eye," *Financial Times*, December 6, 1988, at 26.

[82]"Dow Rises by 31.48, to 2,123.76," *New York Times*, December 6, 1988, at D1; "Four Big Companies Set New Stock Unit Plans," *New York Times*, December 6, 1988, at D6.

[83]"Some Big Firms to Break Up Stock into New Securities," *Wall Street Journal*, December 5, 1988, at C1.

[84]"New Tactic of Breaking Up Stocks Alters Landscape for Investors," *Wall Street Journal*, December 7, 1988, at C2.

[85]"New Plan to Retire Companies' Equity," *Financial Times*, December 6, 1988, at 27.

and redeemed at a premium.[86] American Express plans to redeem its BYBs in 2019 at $75 per share.[87]

The IDPs will pay holders dividends equal to any increases in the issuer's dividend on remaining outstanding common stock during the next 30 years.[88] Thus, if American Express were to increase its annual common stock dividend from $0.84 to $1 per share, IDP holders would receive an annual dividend of $0.16 per share ($0.84 + $0.16 = $1). American Express' IDP will have a $2 liquidation value in 2019—that is, holders will receive $2 for each IDP held, regardless of whether the price of American Express' common stock has risen.[89]

The third unit, the EAC, pays no dividends during its 30-year life.[90] Rather, it entitles holders to capture all of the increases in the price of the issuer's common stock beyond the redemption price of the IDP.[91] The EAC is essentially a 30-year call option; for each EAC held, the holder can buy one share of the issuer's common stock at an exercise price just above the BYB redemption value.[92] The holder thereby captures any capital gain in the common stock price beyond the BYB redemption value. For example, holders of the American Express EAC will be able to purchase American Express stock at $77 per share in 2019, which is $2 above the $75 BYB redemption value.[93] In effect, these holders are

---

[86]*Id.*
[87]"New Tactic of Breaking Up Stocks Alters Landscape for Investors," *Wall Street Journal,* December 7, 1988, at C2.
[88]"Some Big Firms to Break Up Stock into New Securities," *Wall Street Journal,* December 5, 1988, at C1.
[89]"New Tactic of Breaking Up Stocks Alters Landscape for Investors," *Wall Street Journal,* December 7, 1988, at C2.
[90]*Id.*
[91]"Some Big Firms to Break Up Stock into New Securities," *Wall Street Journal,* Decembr 5, 1988, at C1.
[92]"New Plan to Retire Companies' Equity," *Financial Times,* December 6, 1988, at 27.

betting that in 2019 the common stock price will be higher than $77.

Why would a bank or bank holding company want to unbundle some of its stock? Like any nonfinancial corporation, it might benefit in four ways. First, when some common shares are replaced by the three units, the number of outstanding common shares is reduced. This raises reported earnings per share (EPS), which by definition is earnings divided by the number of outstanding shares.[94] This would be a formal way to increase EPS, as it follows tautologically and not from any increase in the fundamental value of the issuer.[94] Yet perhaps investors would see through this formal rise and adjust the common stock price downward.

Second, earnings may rise because of tax savings from two sources.[95] Dividend payments on common shares that are unbundled are replaced by interest payments on BYBs. Interest (but not dividend) payments are tax deductible.[95] Further, the annual increases in the value of deep discount bonds are tax deductible.[95]

Unbundling may serve as a defensive tactic against hostile takeovers if it leads to an increase in the price of the issuer's remaining outstanding common stock. If the semistrong form of the efficient markets hypothesis is correct (i.e., if the market price of a corporation's common stock fully reflects all publicly available information about the corporation), then the sum of the prices of the three units should equal the price of one common share.[96] Indeed, one scenario is that the BYB will trade at 50 percent of the price

---

[93]"New Tactic of Breaking Up Stock Alters Landscape for Investors," *Wall Street Journal*, December 7, 1988, at C2.

[94]"Four Big Companies Set New Stock Unit Plans," *New York Times*, December 6, 1988, at D6.

[95]"Concern on 'Unbundled' Stock Units," *New York Times*, December 7, 1988, at D1.

of the issuer's remaining outstanding common stock, the IDP at 25 percent, and the EAC at 25 percent.[96]

However, if the hypothesis is incorrect and the sum of the three units is at a premium over the common stock price, investors may believe they undervalued the common stock and bid up its price.[96] An issuing bank or bank holding company will thereby be a less desirable takeover target, because it will cost an acquiror more to purchase its common stock.[97] This is probably wishful thinking.

If the market is not semistrong efficient (a big "if"), what is more likely to occur is arbitrage activity.[97] Arbitrageurs will purchase the less expensive common stock and sell the more expensive unbundled units until the common stock price equals the sum of the prices of the three units. It cannot be said *a priori* that such arbitrage activity will bid up the stock price. The prices of the unbundled units could fall, or there could be some bidding up of the stock price and some decline in the prices of the units.

Finally, unbundling some common stock allows a corporation to leverage "without taking on the huge debt burdens of a leveraged buyout or a major recapitalization."[98] In one sense, this is not much of an advantage to banks or bank holding companies. They are already among the most highly leveraged institutions. On the other hand, it is no secret that the Federal Reserve is becoming increasingly concerned about loans made to finance leveraged buyouts.[99] Insofar as unbundling stock is a less worrisome form of leveraging, it may be advantageous.

---

[96] "Some Big Firms to Break Up Stock into New Securities," *Wall Street Journal*, December 5, 1988, at C1.

[97] "New Tactic of Breaking Up Stock Alters Landscape for Investors," *Wall Street Journal*, December 7, 1988, at C2.

[98] "Some Big Firms to Break Up Stock into New Securities," *Wall Street Journal*, December 5, 1988, at C1.

CAPITAL

Thus, the only certain benefit of unbundled stock from the perspective of a bank or bank holding company would be the tax savings.[100] The clear disadvantage of unbundling stock is that common shares that count as Tier One equity capital are replaced by three financial instruments, none of which may qualify for inclusion in Tier One.

There are at least three ways to deal with unbundled stock under the Basle Agreement. The first is simply to ignore the unbundling—essentially to view it as a 30-year separation—and thus allow those common shares that are unbundled to count in Tier One. The problem with this approach is that it fails to differentiate among the abilities of the three unbundled units to absorb losses. BYB holders would be creditors of the issuer with a fixed income claim. By contrast, EAC holders would have only a residual claim — that is, a claim to a capital gain in excess of the BYB redemption price. Hence, BYBs would be more likely to be available to absorb losses than would EACs.

A second tactic is to treat the unbundled shares as unbundled. BYBs could be analogized to subordinated term debt, IDPs to limited life preferred stock, and EACs to common stock. Thus, BYBs and IDPs would be placed in Tier Two and EACs in Tier One. One problem is what par value should be ascribed to the EACs. The aggregate par value of the EACs would have to be less than that of the initial block of bundled common shares that was un-

---

[99] *See*, e.g., "Congress Is Moving Closer to Weighing Buyout Curbs," *New York Times*, December 5, 1988, at D1; "Banks May Suffer from LBO Loans, S&P Report Says," *Wall Street Journal*, December 5, 1988, at C1; "Bank Loans for Buyouts to Be Placed Under Tighter Scrutiny by Regulators," *Wall Street Journal*, November 7, 1988, at A3.

[100] For a discussion of the pros and cons to investors, *see* "New Tactic of Breaking Up Stocks Alters Landscape for Investors," *Wall Street Journal*, December 7, 1988, at C2 and "New Plan to Retire Companies' Equity," *Financial Times*, December 6, 1988, at 27.

bundled; otherwise, the unbundling might have little or no effect on the issuer's capital account.

A third approach is to treat the unbundled units as a debt/equity hybrid. As in the first alternative, the three unbundled units are treated as one. But here they are treated as one debt/equity package, not one equity package. If the three units are viewed as a debt/equity hybrid, they will be placed in Tier Two. The rationale might be that BYBs and IDPs are properly regarded as senior securities, and EACs resemble equity. Taken together, the three units resemble a hybrid instrument, such as mandatory convertible debt, because they are rebundled into common stock after 30 years.

C. Chapter Summary

Capital is divided into two tiers in the Basle Agreement. Tier One (core) capital is made up of "pure" capital—that is, of the forms best able to serve the substantive function of loss absorption. Specifically, Tier One consists of equity capital plus disclosed reserves, with two adjustments. Goodwill is deducted from the sum of equity capital and disclosed reserves. Bank holding companies may count both cumulative and noncumulative perpetual preferred stock.

Tier Two (supplementary) capital consists of five elements. Each of these elements can serve the loss-absorption function, though none is as pure a form of capital as equity or disclosed reserves. The five elements are undisclosed reserves, revaluation reserves, general loan loss provisions, hybrid instruments, and subordinated term debt.

The sum of Tier One and Tier Two capital yields the numerator of the capital/risk-weighted assets ratio. Specifically, Tier One capital (as adjusted) plus Tier Two capital, minus any investments in unconsolidated subsidiaries, serves as the numerator.

Since the focus of the Basle Agreement with respect to capital is on the substantive function of loss absorption, it should not be difficult to decide whether new financial instruments might count as capital. While the form of these instruments may be strange, it will also be irrelevant. What will matter is loss-absorption potential. Thus, it is already possible to comment on whether instruments like guaranteed preferred shares, floating-rate preferred stock, upstream convertibles, and unbundled stock might count as capital under the Basle Agreement and, if so, whether they might be placed in Tier One or Tier Two.

4
The Risk-Weighting System

> **Key Concepts**
> Risk weight
> Credit risk
> Interest rate risk
> Currency (foreign exchange rate) risk
> On-balance-sheet assets
> Treasury securities
> Mortgage-backed securities
> Collateralized mortgage obligations
> Stripped mortgage-backed securities
> Gearing (leverage) ratio
> Off-balance-sheet items

A. They Said It Couldn't Be Done: Credit Risk Is What Matters

Some commentators believed that a risk-based capital agreement could not be achieved because of the difficulty of categorizing bank assets by risk. For example, Silverberg wrote as late as 1986:

> Few people would seriously believe they could develop, implement and defend quantifying risk distinctions among categories of performing loans and investments. Such a system would tend to allocate resources toward the favored loan categories... Such a system will never get very far. The more complex, subjective variation may be useful for a bank's analysis, but it is unlikely to prove very useful to the supervision of most banks where quantitative guidelines are necessary.[1]

The very existence of the Basle Agreement casts doubt on such pessimistic forecasts. The primary mode for classifying assets held in the portfolio of a bank or bank holding

---

[1] S. Silverberg. "Regulation of Bank Capital," 9 *Issues in Bank Regulation*," 7, 9 (Spring 1986).

company is *credit* risk. This was also the classification mode for previous incarnations of the Board's regulations.[2] That is, the feature of assets most emphasized in the Basle Agreement is *credit* risk. As is explained in the agreement:

> There are many different kinds of risks against which banks' managements need to guard. For most banks the major risk is *credit risk*, that is to say the risk of counterparty failure, but there are many other kinds of risk — for example, investment risk, interest rate risk, exchange rate risk, concentration risk. The central focus of this framework is credit risk and, as a further aspect of credit risk, country transfer risk. In addition, supervisory authorities have discretion to build in certain other types of risk. Some countries, for example, will wish to retain a weighting for open foreign exchange positions or for some aspects of investment risk. No standardisation has been attempted in the treatment of these other kinds of risk in the framework at the present stage.[3]

Credit risk is defined as the risk that the party with whom a bank has contracted (the counterparty) will default on its obligations to the bank. With respect to a loan contract, the borrower may not meet interest and principal payments. With respect to a certificate of deposit (CD) the bank has purchased, the seller of the CD may fail to make interest payments or to return principal upon maturity.

Some bank assets clearly involve more credit risk than others: It is more likely that an individual borrower will default on loan payments than the U.S. Government will

---

[2] *See, e.g.,* the notice issued by the Bank of England pursuant to the U.S.-U.K. Joint Proposal, "Convergence of Capital Adequacy in the U.K. and the U.S.," 27 Bank of England *Quarterly Bulletin* 85 (February 1987).

[3] Basle Agreement, 10. *See also* 54 Fed. Reg. 4186, 4187, 4198 (for banks), 4209-4210 (for BHCs); (January 27, 1989). 53 Fed. Reg. 8550, 8552 (proposed March 15, 1988), and Fried, Frank, Harris, Shriver, and Jacobson, "Financial Services Update, Capital Requirements of Financial Institutions," 2 (October 1988).

default on the interest payable on Treasury securities. With respect to all bank loans, there is the further issue of the significance of credit enhancements. Should the fact that the bank has fully secured a loan in satisfaction of applicable requirements of Article 9 of the Uniform Commercial Code result in reduced capital support for the loan? Should standby letters of credit or personal guarantees affect the amount of capital required to support a loan? The relative credit risks of other bank assets is not clear: Is a mortgage loan to IBM fully secured by real property collateral more risky than the purchase of Italian government bonds?

The credit risks of still other assets may be difficult to appraise: Is the credit risk of a mortgage-backed security (or, for that matter, any asset-backed security) to be determined by the creditworthiness of the issuer of the security, by the nature of the underlying mortgages that back the collateral, or by some other means? With respect to all bank assets, to what extent should reliance be placed on the bank examination process rather than on capital adequacy requirements? These and many other issues are important in determining the credit risk of individual assets and the resultant capital support required.

The point is that the emphasis in the Basle Agreement is on credit risk, *not* interest rate or currency risk. But it must be recognized that interest rate and currency risk *do* "creep into" the Basle Agreement and the Board's final regulations. As is stated in the latter document:

> The focus of these guidelines is principally on broad categories of *credit* risk, although the risk-based framework does take some transfer risk considerations, as well as limited instances of *interest rate and market risk,* into account in assigning certain assets to risk categories. The measure does not take explicit account of other factors that can affect an organization's financial condition, such as overall interest rate exposure....[4]

---

[4] 54 Fed. Reg. 4186, 4187 (January 27, 1989).

The creeping in of country risk is quite obvious with respect to claims on central governments. Lower risk weights are assigned to obligations of central governments that are members of the Organization for Economic Cooperation and Development (OECD) than to those of non-OECD central governments.[5] Both interest rate and currency risk creep in with respect to the treatment of swaps. As discussed later in the text, interest and exchange rate volatilities are used to measure replacement cost, which in turn is the proxy for the credit risk on swap contracts.

The stress on credit risk in the Basle Agreement can be contrasted with the emphasis in the risk-based capital regulations recently proposed by the Federal Home Loan Bank Board for savings and loan associations (S&Ls).[6] The proposal would require S&Ls to maintain an 8 percent capital/risk-weighted assets ratio, but interest rate risk would be explicitly considered along with credit risk.[7] Like the Basle Agreement, the Bank Board proposes to slot assets held by S&Ls into categories based on credit risk. The greater the risk of default by the obligor, the more capital support would be required.[8] But unlike the Basle Agreement, the Bank Board's proposal would require capital support based on an S&L's exposure to interest rate risk.[8]

---

[5] *See* Basle Agreement, 11-13.

[6] 53 Fed. Reg. 51800 (proposed December 23, 1988). *See also* "Stiffer Thrift Capital Rules Proposed by Bank Board," *Wall Street Journal*, December 20, 1988, at A16; "Stricter Thrift Capital Rules Are Proposed," *Wall Street Journal*, November 29, 1988, at A4; "Loss Prevention Rules Considered for Federally Insured Thrifts," Federal Home Loan Bank Board Press Release, November 28, 1988.

[7] The risk associated with collateralized borrowings by S&Ls would also be explicitly recognized. Borrowings secured by specific assets would require capital support in an amount equal to 3 percent of such borrowings. 53 Fed. Reg. 51800, 51801, 51811 (proposed December 23, 1988).

[8] 53 Fed. Reg. 51800, 51801, 51804-51808 (proposed December 23, 1988).

The Bank Board's proposal would explicitly account for interest rate risk by using a discounted cash-flow analysis "to estimate the effect on an institution's value (market value of portfolio equity) of an immediate and permanent 200-basis-point movement in interest rates, either up or down."[9] That is, the effect of a 2 percent change in interest rates on the market value of an S&L's equity would be calculated. An S&L "will be required to maintain capital in an amount equal to 50 percent of the larger of the possible decreases in the market value of [its] net equity consequent to the 200 basis point increase or decrease, as a protection against interest-rate risk."[10]

B. The Five Risk Categories for On-Balance-Sheet Assets

Five risk categories are established in the Basle Agreement: zero percent, 10 percent, 20 percent, 50 percent, and 100 percent. The 100 percent category is also known as the "standard" risk category. The classification scheme is presented in Table 1. The scheme that appears in the final Board regulations is somewhat different. Some of the differences are discussed in this section.

Table 1
Risk-Weight Categories for On-Balance Sheet Assets[11]

Zero Percent
1. Cash.
    This includes, at the discretion of national authorities, gold bullion held in vaults.
2. Claims on central governments and central banks which are denominated in national currency and funded in that currency.

---

[9] *Id.* at 51810.
[10] *Id.*
[11] This table is adapted from Annex 2 of the Basle Agreement (with some modifications). Reference was made to B. Orr, "The Fed Drops the Other Shoe," 70 ABA *Banking Journal* 124 (October 1988). The scheme in the Board's final regulations is somewhat different.

Table 1
(Continued)

3. Other claims on central governments and central banks of the OECD.

    At present, 24 countries are full members of the OECD: Australia, Austria, Belgium, Canada, Denmark, Federal Republic of Germany, Finland, France, Greece, Iceland, Ireland, Italy, Japan, Luxembourg, the Netherlands, New Zealand, Norway, Portugal, Spain, Sweden, Switzerland, Turkey, the United Kingdom, and the United States. In addition, countries that have special lending arrangements with the International Monetary Fund are counted as OECD countries. At present, only Saudi Arabia has such an arrangement.

4. Claims that are
    a. Collateralized by cash,
    b. Collateralized by OECD central government securities, or
    c. Guaranteed by OECD central governments.

    If a commercial loan is partly covered by such collateral or partly guaranteed, then only that part of the loan that is covered will attract the zero percent risk weight.

Zero, 10, 20, or 50 Percent (at national discretion)
1. Claims on domestic public-sector entities, excluding the central government.
2. Loans guaranteed by domestic public-sector entities, excluding the central government.

20 Percent
1. Claims on multilateral development banks (the World Bank, the Inter-American Development Bank, the Asian Development Bank, the African Development Bank, and the Export-Import Bank).
2. Claims guaranteed by, or collateralized by securities issued by, multilateral development banks.

    If a commercial loan is partly covered by such collateral or partly guaranteed, then only that part of the loan that is covered will attract the zero percent risk weight.

3. Claims on banks incorporated in the OECD.
4. Loans guaranteed by banks incorporated in the OECD.
5. Claims on banks incorporated in countries outside the OECD with a remaining (residual) maturity of up to one year.
6. Loans with a residual maturity of up to one year that are guaranteed by banks incorporated outside the OECD.

Table 1
(Continued)

7. Claims on nondomestic OECD public-sector entities, excluding central governments.
8. Loans guaranteed by nondomestic OECD public-sector entities, excluding central governments.
9. Cash items in the process of collection.

50 Percent
1. Loans fully secured by a mortgage on residential property that is or will be occupied by the borrower or that is rented.

100 Percent (Standard)
1. Claims on the private sector.
2. Claims on banks incorporated outside the OECD with a remaining maturity of over one year.
3. Claims on central governments outside the OECD, unless such claims are denominated and funded in national currency.
4. Claims on commercial companies owned by the public sector.
5. Premises, plant and equipment, and other fixed assets.
6. Real estate and other investments, including nonconsolidated investment participations in other companies.
7. Capital instruments issued by other banks, unless deducted from capital.
8. All other assets.

The capital/risk-weighted assets ratio is represented in a simple form in equation 4.

Equation 4.

$$\frac{[\text{Tier One (as adjusted)} + \text{Tier Two capital}] - \text{investments in certain unconsolidated subsidiaries}}{\text{Risk-weighted assets}}$$

Equation 3 from Chapter 3 can be substituted into the numerator of equation 4 to highlight the elements of capital. The risk-weighting scheme is used to calculate the denominator. For each on-balance-sheet asset type, the value of the assets of that type (as stated on the balance sheet of the bank or BHC) is multiplied by the risk weight applicable to that asset type. The product is the risk-weighted asset. This multiplication process is repeated for each asset type on the balance sheet. The sum of the risk asset values for on-balance-sheet assets plus the risk asset values for off-balance-sheet items is the denominator of the ratio.

C. Some Weighty Matters: Risk Weights for Treasuries, Mortgage-Backeds, CMOs, and Strips

Three controversies concerning the items categorized in Table 1 result in differences between the Basle Agreement and the Board's final regulations. The first concerns the weighting for Treasury securities held by banks and bank holding companies. The second concerns holdings of mortgage-backed securities, including collateralized mortgage obligations (CMOs). The third involves securities known as "stripped mortgage-backed securities," or "strips."

(1) Treasury Securities: Should Interest Rate Risk Be Considered?

Under the Basle Agreement, the Federal Reserve is free to establish different risk weights for Treasuries with different maturities.[12] For example, the Board is free to assign Treasuries with a maturity of less than one year to the zero-risk category and those with a maturity greater than one year to the 10 percent category. However, it is reported that the Board will weight all Treasuries at zero in its final regulations.[13] The Board's final regulations place all direct obligations of OECD governments in the zero risk category,

---

[12] Basle Agreement, 10-11. The U.S. Treasury issues three principal types of securities: Treasury bonds, which are the longest maturity instrument, Treasury notes, which are medium-term, and Treasury bills, which have the shortest maturity. *See* G. Bollenbacher, *U.S. Government Securities Markets* 31-68 (1988).

[13] "Impact of Risk-Based Capital Rules to Be Eased," *American Banker*, October 28, 1988, at 3.

whether the obligations are short- or long-term.[14] This eliminates the 10 percent risk category listed in the Basle Agreement.[15]

While the emphasis in the Basle Agreement is on credit risk, the only plausible rationale for a nonzero weighting for securities like Treasuries would be to capture interest rate risk. This is because of the negligible possibility that the U.S. Government will default on its obligations. The issue is thus whether risk-based capital regulations should focus exclusively on credit risk or attempt to capture interest rate risk.

It is more or less generally accepted that the credit risk on Treasuries is zero. Indeed, many bankers have argued—and Robert Clarke, the Comptroller of the Currency, has agreed—that "regardless of their maturities, claims on the U.S. Government carry no [credit] risks to banks and other holders and thus should carry no capital requirements."[16] But it is also acknowledged that these securities bear some interest rate risk. Federal Reserve Board Chairman Alan Greenspan agrees that Treasuries carry no credit risk but points out that the interest rate risk varies with maturity.[17] This is because long-term securities are more volatile than short-term securities.

"Volatility" in this context refers to the sensitivity of the security's price to changes in interest rates. The price of a fixed-income security like a Treasury is calculated as the present discounted value of the expected stream of cash flows. The cash flows are a stream of periodic interest payments followed by repayment of principal. The present

---

[14] 54 Fed. Reg. 4186, 4190, 4202 (for banks), 4214 (for BHCs); (January 27, 1989).

[15] December 14, 1988, Board Staff Memorandum, 5.

[16] "Impact of Risk-Based Capital Rules to Be Eased," *American Banker,* October 28, 1988, at 3.

[17] *Id.*

discounted value formula for a long-term security has more terms than one for a short-term security. There is a term for each cash flow, as each cash flow is discounted back to the present. So the longer the maturity, the greater the number of expected cash flows. The interest rate appears in each term of the formula. Thus, a change in the interest rate affects the price of a long-term security more than that of a short-term security, because it impacts on more terms.

(2) Mortgage-Backed Securities: Look at the Obligor

Mortgage-backed securities are not treated by the Basle Agreement.[18] They are treated in the Board's final regulations.[19] The treatment is consistent with the general focus of the Basle Agreement and the regulations on credit risk. The crucial inquiry is the nature of the obligor: Who is the issuer or guarantor of the mortgage-backeds? Since credit risk is the risk of counterparty default (or, more broadly, the risk that the obligor will fail to make good on its obligations), to focus on credit risk is to focus on the identity of the obligor.

The obligor on a mortgage-backed security is the issuer or guarantor. There are three possible issuers or guarantors: a U.S. Government agency (namely, the Government National Mortgage Association, GNMA); a government-sponsored agency (the Federal National Mortgage Association, FNMA, or the Federal Home Loan Mortgage Corporation, FHLMC); and a private issuer or guarantor. The final regulations on mortgage-backeds are implicitly organized according to these three types of obligors.

---

[18] For a summary article on mortgage-backeds, *see* P. Murray and B. Hadaway, "Mortgage-Backed Securities: An Investigation of Legal and Financial Issues," 11 *The Journal of Corporate Law* 203 (Winter 1986).

[19] 54 Fed. Reg. 4186, 4191-4192, 4202-4203 (for banks), 4214-4216 (for BHCs); (January 27, 1989).

RISK-WEIGHTING SYSTEM

Private issuers, of course, are not affiliated with the government. The difference between a government agency and a government-sponsored agency is subtle but critical. Only securities of government agencies carry the *explicit* full faith and credit backing of the U.S. Government.[20] Securities of government-sponsored agencies carry no such explicit guarantee.[20]

Mortgage-backeds issued or guaranteed by the GNMA are commonly called Ginnie Maes. Mortgage-backeds issued or guaranteed by the FNMA are known as Fannie Maes, and those issued or guaranteed by the FHLMC are dubbed Freddie Macs. The Board's final regulations state that if the issuer or guarantor is a U.S. Government agency or a U.S. Government-sponsored agency, the mortgage-backeds "are assigned to the risk weight category appropriate to the issuer or guarantor."[21] This translates into two different weightings: Ginnie Maes are placed in the zero percent category, while Fannie Maes and Freddie Macs receive a 20 percent risk weighting.[22] The reason for the de facto two-tiered market is the explicit U.S. Government guarantee — Ginnie Maes have it but Fannie Maes and Freddie Macs do not, so there is less credit risk in holding Ginnie Maes.[23]

If mortgage-backeds are privately issued, then the regulations treat the securities:

---

[20] *Id.* at 4191-4192, note 27 at 4202 and note 32 at 4203 (for banks), note 30 at 4214 and note 35 at 4215 (for BHCs).

[21] *Id.* at note 10 at 4192, 4202 (for banks), 4214 (for BHCs).

[22] *Id.* at 4202-4203 (for banks), 4214-4215 (for BHCs).

[23] The fact that Ginnie Maes would be weighted differently from Fannie Maes or Freddie Macs was revealed before the final regulations were published. *See* "Risk-Based Capital Rules Will Not Require Capital for Ginnie Maes, Fed Official Says," *BNA Banking Report* (October 24, 1988).

as essentially indirect holdings of the underlying assets. Accordingly, such securities are generally assigned to the same risk weight appropriate to the highest risk-weighted asset in the underlying asset pool, except that in no case will these securities be assigned to the zero percent risk category, which is reserved for *direct* claims on central governments.[24]

That is, the regulations allow the same risk weighting for privately issued mortgage-backeds as for the mortgages that underlie them—but only if certain conditions are met. Generally, for a mortgage-backed to get the same risk-weighting as the underlying asset pool, "the risk of holding the mortgage-backed security [must] not, in fact, exceed the risk of holding the underlying assets that back that security."[25] More specifically, the regulations require that:

A privately issued mortgage-backed security may be treated as an indirect holding of the underlying assets provided that: (1) The underlying assets are held by an independent trustee and the trustee has a first priority, perfected security interest in the underlying assets on behalf of the holders of the security; (2) either the holder of the security has an undivided *pro rata* ownership interest in the underlying mortgage assets or the trust or single-purpose entity (or conduit) that issues the security has no liabilities unrelated to the issued securities; (3) the security is structured such that the cash flow from the underlying assets in all cases fully meets the cash flow requirements of the security without undue reliance on any reinvestment income; and (4) there is no material reinvestment risk associated with any funds awaiting distribution to the holders of the security. In addition, if the underlying assets of a mortgage-backed security are composed of more than one type of asset, for example, U.S. Government-sponsored agency securities and privately issued pass-through securities that qualify for the 50 percent risk category, the entire mortgage-backed security is

---

[24] 54 Fed. Reg. 4186, 4192 (January 27, 1989).
[25] December 14, 1988, Board Staff Memorandum, 8.

generally assigned to the category appropriate to the highest risk-weighted asset underlying the issue. Thus, in this example, the security would receive the 50 percent risk weight appropriate to the privately issued pass-through securities.[26]

Any privately issued mortgage-backeds that do not meet these conditions are automatically assigned to the 100 percent risk category.[27] As an example, consider a private issuance of mortgage-backeds whose underlying asset pool consists solely of mortgages eligible for placement in the 50 percent risk category. (They would be eligible for this weight as long as they are "loans fully secured by first liens on one- to four-family residential properties, either owner-occupied or rented;... [they] have been made in accordance with prudent underwriting standards, including a conservative loan-to-value ratio; [they] are performing in accordance with their original terms; and [they] are not 90 days or more past due or carried in nonaccrual status."[28] This issuance would be placed in the 50 percent risk category.

Two interesting questions are raised by the Board's treatment of mortgage-backeds in its final regulations. First, with respect to privately issued mortgage-backeds, why look to the risk-weighting on the underlying assets? Why not simply impose a flat rule (as with commercial loans) that because the obligor is a private party, the 100 percent risk weight is triggered? Second, will other countries follow the Board's lead?

There are three answers to the first question. The analogy to commercial loans is not quite correct because certain types of collateral pledged to secure a commercial loan are

---

[26] 54 Fed. Reg. 4186, note 23 at 4202 (for banks), note 26 at 4214 (for BHCs); (January 27, 1989).
[27] Id. at 4192, 4202 (for banks), 4214 (for BHCs).
[28] Id. at 4203 (for banks), 4215 (for BHCs).

recognized by the Basle Agreement and the Board's final regulations. In other words, the Basle Agreement and the final regulations do "look through" commercial loans to see whether any qualifying collateral has been pledged. As is clear from Table 1, commercial loans that are categorized by cash or OECD central government securities or guaranteed by OECD central governments receive a zero percent risk-weighting. Loans guaranteed by multilateral development banks or collateralized by their securities receive a 20 percent risk weight. And certain mortgage loans are eligible for a 50 percent weighting. Thus, it is not inconsistent for the final regulations to look through the private issuer of a mortgage-backed to the underlying assets. The treatment of secured loans serves as the precedent for this treatment.

The second answer is that it would be an unfair penalty to those who securitize assets with preferential risk weights to attach a higher risk weight to the security than to the underlying assets. If a pool of mortgages receives a 50 percent weighting, why should securities backed by the pool receive a 100 percent weighting? Isn't it a tautology that the securities are as good as the underlying assets? There is some truth to this argument, but it is deceptive in that it neglects the different types of mortgage-backeds and the bankruptcy risk (an extreme form of credit risk) associated with each type.[29]

Mortgage-backed securities may be structured in one of three ways: pass-through certificates, mortgage-backed bonds, or pay-through bonds. An investor in pass-throughs owns an undivided interest in the underlying asset pool (i.e., in the mortgages) and receives an income stream link-

---

[29] The following discussion is drawn from H. Scott, "Securitization of Assets by Banks," in *Current Developments in International Banking and Corporate Financial Operation*. National University of Singapore, ed., 1989 (forthcoming).

ed directly to the returns (i.e., the mortgage payments) on that pool. An investor who holds a mortgage-backed bond owns only the bond, not the underlying assets. He has a security interest in the assets. His return is based on a contractual rate set by the issuer and not necessarily directly linked to the returns on the underlying asset pool. Pay-throughs are a hybrid of pass-throughs and mortgage-backed bonds. Like the holder of a mortgage-backed bond, an investor in a pay-through does not have an ownership interest in the underlying asssets. He has a security interest in these assets. But like the investor in a pass-through, a pay-through investor receives returns that are tied directly to the income stream on the underlying assets. Generally, all three structures are issued or guaranteed by a special payment vehicle (SPV), which is a separate corporation or trust to which the pooled assets are initially transferred by the mortgage originators (the original lending bank or banks).

What happens if the SPV goes bankrupt? This could occur if several mortgagors default on their mortgage payments, so there is no investment income to be channeled to investors. The answer depends on bankruptcy law, but the critical point to remember is that only with pass-throughs do investors actually own the mortgages. If mortgage-backed bonds or pay-throughs are held, investors will be creditors of the SPV and there will undoubtedly be a delay in recovering from the bankrupt SPV. The bankruptcy trustee of the SPV will retain control over the mortgages and any forthcoming mortgage payments. Hence, holding a mortgage-backed bond or pay-through is *not* as good as holding the underlying assets. Indeed, these are not at all equivalent.

This leads to a general point that the final regulations can be said to treat mortgage-backeds generously because they do not differentiate among the three structures. If the regulations were tougher, they would not give as favorable a risk-weighting to mortgage-backed bonds or pay-throughs as to pass-throughs because of the higher bankruptcy risk of the former structures.

The third answer is that the regulations would be remarkably unsophisticated and "blunt-edged" if they did not take note of the assets underlying privately issued mortgage-backeds. These securities are different from other privately issued securities like equities or bonds. It is only sensible for the regulations to treat mortgage-backeds in some special way. The problem with the answer that a special case deserves special treatment is that almost anything can be made into a special case. Once mortgage-backeds are treated as a special case, there is the danger of sliding down a "slippery slope," because arguments will be made to give special treatment to other financial instruments.

The second issue raised by the treatment of mortgage-backeds in the final regulations concerns international policy coordination. Since the Basle Agreement is silent on mortgage-backeds, will banking regulators in other countries follow the treatment outlined by the Federal Reserve? The answer may be no. The Bank of England has apparently decided to require British banks to place all mortgage-backeds in the 50 percent category.[30] If so, then British banks will have to support holdings of Ginnie Maes, Fannie Maes, Freddie Macs, and their British counterparts, and possibly privately issued mortgage-backeds, with more capital than American banks.

(3) Collateralized Mortgage Obligations: How About a 20 Percent Risk Weight?

Collateralized mortgage obligations are a form of pay-

---

[30]"Banks Given Deadline for Meeting Capital Standards Agreement," *Financial Times,* November 3, 1988, at 12.

through bond.[31] Typically, they are privately issued or guaranteed and are backed not by mortgage loans but by mortgage-backed securities. Thus, it is not uncommon to find an issue of CMOs backed by Ginnie Maes, Fannie Maes, or Freddie Macs. The investment return on CMOs is divided into different classes, called "tranches." As Professor Scott explains:

> A CMO is divided into several maturity classes, called tranches, in order to meet the different time horizons of different investors and to allocate the risk of prepayment of the mortgage loans. Prepayments can result from refinancings undertaken by mortgagors as a result of interest rate changes. Payments to bondholders are prioritized, with interest receiving the highest priority and principal payments coming second. No payments of interest or principal are made to holders in one tranche until all prior tranches have been paid. Thus, interest is paid to the first tranche first, then to the second, third, etc. Lower-ranking tranches carry greater risk, and therefore offer higher returns.[32]

In principle, CMOs could be treated like any other mortgage-backeds: they could attract a zero percent risk weight if issued or guaranteed by a U.S. Government agency, a 20 percent risk weight if issued or guaranteed by a U.S. Government-sponsored agency, and a risk weight that depends on the underlying asset pool if privately issued.

In practice, CMOs are treated differently from other mortgage-backeds. Under the Board's final regulations, most CMOs are placed in the 20 percent category. "[C]laims

---

[31] For a survey article on CMOs, *see* G. Parseghian, "Collateralised Mortgage Obligations: A Primer," *The Journal of International Securities Markets* 87 (Winter 1987).

[32] H. Scott, "Securitization of Assets by Banks," in *Current Developments in International Banking and Corporate Financial Operation.* National University of Singapore, ed., 1989 (forthcoming).

that are collateralized by securities issued or guaranteed by ... U.S. Government agencies [or by] U.S. Government-sponsored agencies" receive a 20 percent weighting.[33] So also do "[c]ertain privately issued securities representing indirect ownership of mortgage-backed U.S. Government agency or U.S. Government-sponsored agency securities."[34]

This means that the obligor does not matter. As long as the CMO issue is collateralized by or represents an indirect ownership in a pool of mortgage-backeds sponsored by a U.S. Government agency or a U.S. Government-sponsored agency, a 20 percent risk weight applies. For example, "a collateralized mortgage obligation ... backed by Federal National Mortgage Association securities would be assigned to the 20 percent risk category," the same category to which Fannie Maes are assigned.[35] Yet so also would a CMO backed by Ginnie Maes, even though Ginnie Maes receive a zero percent weight.

(4) Stripped Mortgage-Backed Securities: These Are Really Risky!

The Basle Agreement does not treat strips, which include interest only (IO) and principal only (PO) securities. They are placed in the 100 percent risk category, regardless of issuer or guarantor.[36] The reason for this is not credit risk, but interest rate risk—another example of the creeping in of other types of risk. When interest rates change, the prices of IOs and POs also change, sometimes dramatically. As stated by the Board staff:

---

[33] 54 Fed. Reg. 4186, 4207 (for banks), 4220 (for BHCs); (January 27, 1989). *See also* 4203 (for banks) and 4215 (for BHCs).
[34] *Id. See also* 4192.
[35] December 14, 1988, Board Staff Memorandum.
[36] 54 Fed. Reg. 4186, 4192, 4202-4203 (for banks), 4214-4215 (for BHCs); (January 27, 1989).

> Due to extreme price volatility of these instruments, a conservative treatment for risk-based capital purposes would appear to be warranted. Indeed, a number of banks have experienced significant losses as a result of holding these types of instruments without fully understanding their market risk and sensitivity to *interest rate* changes.[37]

In other words, interest rate risk creeps in because the risk-weighting of strips is based on it. This contrasts with the treatment of mortgage-backeds, where the crucial fact is who issues or guarantees the securities.

Interest rate risk also creeps in—in another way. During the Board's discussion of the final regulations, Federal Reserve Governor Wayne Angell "balked at the 100 percent risk-weight assignment given interest only (IOs) and principal only (POs) securities, noting that some banks use such securities effectively to hedge against interest rate risk."[38] It was reported that "Angell agreed to approve the final guidelines after the Fed Staff agreed to apply the regulatory language it developed for its proposed treatment of interest rate swaps to IOs and POs."[39] Presumably, the "regulatory language" referred to is as follows:

> [T]he board recognizes that these instruments [IOs and POs] can be used to hedge risk and does not want to discourage their use for this purpose. Accordingly, examiners will take into account the manner in which an organization uses IOs and POs, as well as other instruments, in its hedging strategy before making an overall judgment on the organization's capital adequacy. ... The treatment of stripped mortgage-backed securities will also be considered in connection with efforts to develop a means for incorporating interest rate risk into the risk-based

---

[37] December 14, 1988, Board Staff Memorandum, 9 (emphasis supplied).
[38] "Fed Adopts Risk-Based Capital Guidelines; Will Also Propose Minimum Leverage Ratios," 52 *BNA Banking Report* 4, 5 (January 2, 1989).
[39] *Id.*

capital standard. These efforts will endeavor to recognize the risk-reducing (hedging) characteristics of these instruments when they are used properly. Finally, the treatment of IOs, POs, and similar instruments may also be considered in future discussions of the Basle Supervisors' Committee intended to refine the risk-based capital framework.[40]

Perhaps the phrase "other instruments" in the second sentence and "similar instruments" in the final sentence are references to swaps. However, why that passage or one like it is not repeated in the portions of the regulations pertaining to swaps remains something of a mystery. This point is developed in Chapters 5 and 6.

D. Calculating the Credit Equivalent Amount for Off-Balance-Sheet Items

Conceptually, off-balance-sheet items other than swaps are treated in the same manner as on-balance-sheet assets. A risk weight is applied to the item according to the nature of the counterparty obligor. What is different about off-balance-sheet items (including swaps, as explained later), is that the value to which the risk weight is applied is not necessarily the full face value of the item. This is because the actual credit risk to which a bank or bank holding company is exposed on an off-balance-sheet item is not necessarily the full face value of the item.

For instance, a bank may issue a credit line to a customer of up to $50 million but retain the right to cancel the credit line at any time for any reason. It is unlikely that the bank would be liable for the full $50 million, given that the line is cancelable even without a material adverse change. Similarly, a bank may issue to an importer a standby letter of credit for $25 million, which is to be drawn on only if a shipment of goods arrives 30 or more days early. Since the

---

[40] 54 Fed. Reg. 4186, 4192 (January 27, 1989).

importer typically receives goods on schedule or late, the letter of credit is an insurance policy to be drawn on only in the unlikely event that the goods arrive so early that the importer cannot pay for them.

To account for different probabilities that credit exposure will occur, the Basle Agreement establishes credit conversion factors for off-balance-sheet items other than swaps. There are four such factors: 100 percent, 50 percent, 20 percent, and zero percent. One factor is applied to the full face value of each off-balance-sheet exposure to get the credit equivalent amount of the exposure. The credit equivalent amount is deemed to be the actual credit exposure on the item. A high factor (100 percent or 50 percent) is applied to the full face value of the exposure if the chance is high that the bank or bank holding company will be exposed to the full face value. The credit conversion factors are presented in Table 2.

E. A Gearing Ratio: Does This Capture Interest Rate Risk?

Finally, it is at least theoretically possible for a bank to hold only assets with zero credit risk. In such a case, no capital support would be required to support the asset portfolio under the guidelines. The Board's final regulations indicate that an overall leverage or gearing ratio will be used to supplement the capital/risk-weighted asset ratio.[42] This will require a minimum amount of capital based on total unadjusted assets. Specifically, "the existing primary and total capital-to-*total* asset ratios (leverage ratios) will be retained, at least until" the end of 1990.[42]

The stated reason for employing an overall gearing ratio is that "the risk-based capital standard alone does not limit

---

[42] 54 Fed. Reg. 4186, 4193 (January 27, 1989). *See also* December 14, 1988, Board Staff Memorandum, 2-3, and "Risk-Based Capital Rules Will Not Require Capital for Ginnie Maes, Fed Official Says," *BNA Banking Report* 698 (October 24, 1988).

Table 2
Credit Conversion Factors for Off-Balance-Sheet Items Other Than Swaps[41]

100 Percent
1. Direct credit substitutes.
   For example:
   - General guarantees of indebtedness, such as standby letters of credit serving as financial guarantees for loans and securities.
   - Acceptances, including endorsements with the character of acceptances.
2. Sale and repurchase agreements with recourse.
   Some credit risk remains with the bank because of the possibility of recourse.
3. Asset sales with recourse.
   Again, some credit risk remains with the bank.
4. Forward asset purchases, forward deposits, and partly paid shares and securities that represent commitments with certain drawdown.

50 Percent
1. Transaction-related contingent items.
   For example:
   - Standby letters of credit related to particular transactions.
   - Performance bonds.
   - Bid bonds.
   - Warranties.
2. Note issuance facilities (NIFs) and revolving underwriting facilities (RUFs).
3. Other commitments with a maturity over one year.
   For example:
   - Formal standby credit facilities with an original maturity over one year.
   - Credit lines with an original maturity over one year.

20 Percent
1. Short-term trade-related contingencies that are self-liquidating.
   For example:
   - Documentary credits collateralized by the underlying shipments.

Zero Percent
1. Commitments with an original maturity of up to one year that can be unconditionally canceled at any time.

---

[41] This table is adapted from the Basle Agreement, Annex 3 at 1-2.

total leverage with respect to those assets assigned to the zero percent risk category."[43] Capital should be available to avoid losses arising for reasons other than credit risk—for example, interest rate risk. Indeed, the Board staff says:

> ...retention of an overall leverage constraint is important since, in the absence of such a constraint and without a comprehensive measure for *interest rate* risk, the assignment of a significant volume of assets to the zero percent risk category... could allow a banking organization an unwarranted degree of leveraging and risk-taking.[44]

F. Chapter Summary

The focus of the risk-weighting system in the Basle Agreement is credit risk, not interest rate or currency risk. Credit risk is the risk that the obligor (counterparty) will not make good on its obligations (i.e., will default). There is at least a theoretical credit risk associated with every on-balance-sheet asset and off-balance-sheet activity.

Five credit risk categories are established in the Basle Agreement: Zero, 10, 20, 50, and 100 percent. The 100 percent category is also known as the standard risk category. Every on-balance-sheet asset of a bank and every off-balance-sheet activity in which the bank engages must be slotted into one of these five categories.

For on-balance-sheet assets, the appropriate risk weight is simply applied to the amount of that type of asset held. For example, Treasury securities are given a zero credit risk-weighting, because there is deemed to be almost no chance that the U.S. Government will default on its obligations. Treasury securities are not differentiated by maturity, so the increased interest rate risk associated with longer-term Treasuries (for instance, T-bonds as opposed to T-bills) is not considered in the risk-weighting. By contrast,

---

[43] December 14, 1988, Board Staff Memorandum, 3.
[44] 54 Fed. Reg. 4186, 4193 (January 27, 1989); (emphasis supplied).

all commercial loans, regardless of the borrower, are slotted into the standard risk category.

The treatment of mortgage-backed securities, collateralized mortgage obligations, and stripped mortgage-backed securities is not discussed in the Basle Agreement. However, these instruments are mentioned in the Federal Reserve Board's final regulations. The weight attached to a mortgage-backed depends on the nature of the obligor (the issuer or guarantor). Mortgage-backeds issued or guaranteed by a U.S. Government agency like the GNMA receive a zero risk weight. Fannie Maes and Freddie Macs, which are mortgage-backeds issued or guaranteed by government-sponsored agencies (the FNMA and the FHLMC, respectively) are slotted at 20 percent. The weight applied to privately issued mortgage-backeds depends on the weight that would attach to the underlying pool of mortgages. CMOs are generally weighted at 20 percent, regardless of the issuer or guarantor. All strips are placed in the standard risk category.

For off-balance-sheet activities other than swaps, a credit conversion factor is applied to the full face value of the item. There are four credit conversion factors: 100, 50, 20, and zero percent. The product of the credit conversion factor and the face value is called the credit equivalent amount. The appropriate risk weight is applied to this amount. Thus, only if the 100 percent credit conversion factor is used is the risk weight applied to the full face value of the off-balance-sheet item.

The risk-weighting scheme yields the denominator of the capital/risk-weighted assets ratio. The denominator is the sum of all on-balance-sheet assets and all credit equivalent amounts of off-balance-sheet items, where each asset and amount is weighted by the appropriate risk weight.

While the focus of the risk-weighting system is credit risk, other forms of risk do creep in. For instance, strips are placed in the standard risk category because of their interest rate risk. Similarly, the retention of an overall gearing ratio may be an attempt to capture interest rate risk.

5
The ABCs of Swaps

Key Concepts	
Exchange of obligations	Basis swap
Hedging	Currency swap
Cost reduction	Cross-currency interest
Plain vanilla swap	rate swap

A. An Exchange of Obligations

A swap is an exchange of obligations.[1] Specifically, it is "an exchange of one kind of interest obligation for another, which may occur in the same currency or in different currencies."[1] As Henderson explains:

> Regardless of form, the underlying principle of a swap is the agreement of each of two parties to provide the other with a series of cash flows, based on fixed or floating interest rates and in the same or different currencies. At the outset, the parties view the respective values of the two streams as equal. In other words, when the agreement is formed, the present values of the respective cash flows at the current prevailing interest rates and, if applicable, exchange rates are equal.[2]

The classic types of swap transactions are the plain vanilla (or fixed/floating) swap, the basis swap, the currency swap, and the cross-currency interest rate swap.[3] In a *plain vanilla*

---

[1] B. Gendreau, "Interest Rate and Currency Swaps," 1 *Commercial Lending Review* 47 (Fall 1986). *See also* D. Lereah, "The Growth of Interest Rate Swaps," 169 *The Bankers Magazine* 36 (May/June 1986).

[2] S. Henderson, "Swap Credit Risk: A Multi-Perspective Analysis" 2 (1988); (paper submitted to Singapore Conference on Current Developments in International Banking and Corporate Financial Operations).

[3] *See, e.g.,* "International Capital Markets: Just a Simple Idea," *Financial Times,* June 29, 1988, Survey Section at 5.

103

swap, one party has issued fixed interest rate debt and the counterparty has issued a floating-rate instrument. The first party agrees to make the floating interest payments on the counterparty's instrument. The counterparty agrees to make the fixed interest payments on the first party's debt.[4] The first party is thus the *floating-rate payor,* while the counterparty is the *fixed-rate payor.*[5] As Morris and Merfeld explain:

> An interest rate swap is a contract in which one party—the fixed rate payer—agrees to make a sequence of level payments to another party—the floating rate payer—in exchange for a sequence of payments that vary with prevailing interest rates. This contract can be thought of as the exchange—that is, the "swapping"—of interest payments on some underlying fixed-rate and floating-rate loans without an exchange of the principal.[6]

If the payment dates specified in the swap contract are the same—if the first party is to make the floating-rate

---

[4] Henderson describes an interest rate swap as an agreement that obligates the first party to pay an amount equal to interest which would accrue on an agreed amount during a given period at one type of interest rate and obligates the second party to pay an amount equal to interest which would accrue on that agreed amount during that period at another type of interest rate. To the extent that payment dates are simultaneous, the parties typically would net the payments, with the party owing the larger amount paying the difference to the other party.

[5] The terms "fixed-rate payor" and "floating-rate payor" are defined in Article 2, §§ 2.1 and 2.2, respectively, of the ISDA's 1986 Rate Swap Code. A fixed-rate payor is "a party obligated to make payments from time to time during the Term of the Rate Swap Transaction of amounts calculated by reference to a fixed per annum rate." A floating-rate payor is "a party obligated to make payments from time to time during the Term of the Rate Swap Transaction of amounts calculated by reference to a floating per annum rate."

[6] C. Morris and T. Merfeld, "New Methods for Savings and Loans to Hedge Interest Rate Risk," 73 Federal Reserve Bank of Kansas City *Economic Review* 3, 11 (March 1988).

payment on the same date that the counterparty is to make the fixed-rate payment—then the payments may be netted. That is, a net payment will be made by one party. Who makes the payment (the direction of the net cash flow) will depend on changes in interest rates. If the index to which the floating rate is tied has risen, then the floating-rate payor may be obligated to make an interest payment that exceeds the fixed-rate payment it receives. Alternatively, if the index has fallen, the floating-rate payor may be a net recipient. When the fixed-rate debt and the floating-rate instrument mature, no principal is exchanged. The swap agreement does not alter the underlying debtor-creditor relationship. The first party remains legally obligated to repay principal to the holder of the fixed-rate debt, and the counterparty must repay principal to the holder of the floating-rate instrument.

Basis swaps are a type of interest rate swap in which obligations to make floating-rate payments are exchanged. Basis swaps are also called floating/floating swaps. The floating rates are tied to different indexes, or bases. Thus, the parties to the swap contract exchange obligations; each obligation is to make floating interest rate payments, but the index to which the floating rate on one obligation is tied is different from the index to which the other floating rate is tied.[7]

For instance, one party may be obligated to make interest payments at one percent over the prime rate (prime + 1), while the counterparty has debt with an interest rate at 1.25 percent above the rate on 90-day Treasury bills (T-bill + 1.25). A basis swap between these two parties would result in

---

[7] *See* S. Henderson and L. Klein, "Glossary of Terms Used in Connection with Rate Swap, Currency Swap, Cap and Collar Agreements," *Butterworths Journal of International Banking and Financial Law* 2 (June 1987 Supplement).

the first party assuming the duty of paying interest at T-bill plus 1.25 and the counterparty paying interest at prime + 1. As with a plain vanilla swap, no principal would be exchanged upon maturity. In another example, one obligation might be tied to the London Inter-Bank Offered Rate (LIBOR), while the other obligation might be tied to the Federal Funds rate. These would be swapped so that each party traded its initial payment obligations in exchange for the payment obligations of the other party.

A *currency swap* involves the exchange of both interest and principal in one currency for interest and principal in a second currency.[8] One party may have issued a fixed-interest obligation denominated in dollars and a counterparty may have issued a similar obligation but denominated in sterling. Under the swap contract, the first party agrees to make sterling payments on the obligation issued by the counterparty, and the counterparty agrees to make dollar payments on the obligation issued by the first party.

Finally, a *cross-currency interest rate swap* is a hybrid of the plain vanilla and the currency swap. One party exchanges its fixed-interest obligation denominated in one currency for the counterparty's fixed-interest obligation denominated in a different currency.

Swaps are not placed in a category of their own by the

---

[8]T. Arnold, "How to Do Interest Rate Swaps," 62 *Harvard Business Review* 96 (Sept./Oct. 1984).
Henderson describes currency swaps as follows:
> A typical currency swap involves an agreement under which the first party agrees to pay an amount in one currency, usually at periodic intervals, and the second party agrees to pay an amount in a different currency at the same or different intervals. These amounts may be expressed as either stated amounts due at stated times (in which case the interest rate and principal components are implicit in the specified amounts) or in terms of interest accruing on principal amounts in different currencies plus payment of those principal amounts at maturity.

Basle Agreement. Rather, they come under the more general rubric of "interest rate contracts" or "exchange rate contracts." The former are defined to include "single-currency interest rate swaps, basis swaps, forward rate agreements, interest rate futures, interest rate options purchased and similar instruments."[9] A "single-currency interest rate swap" is simply a different term for a plain vanilla swap. "Exchange rate contracts" are defined to include "cross-currency interest rate swaps, forward foreign exchange contracts, currency futures, currency options purchased and similar instruments."[9] (Exchange rate contracts with an original maturity of 14 days or less are excluded from this definition.[9])

B. The Swap Market and the ISDA

Data on swap transactions suggest their growing importance in international finance. As of mid-1988, the volume of interest rate and currency swap contracts, as measured by the outstanding notional principal, was over $1 trillion.[10] The "outstanding notional principal" is the debt principal upon which the exchange of obligations is based.[11] In mid-1987, the outstanding notional principal amount was $500 billion.[12] In contrast with the 1988 and

---

[9] Basle Agreement, Annex 3 at 3.

[10] "Survey Shows Losses Are Low in Swap Market," *American Banker*, July 20, 1988, at 2.

[11] E. Comiskey, C. Mulford, and D. Turner, "Bank Accounting and Reporting Practices for Interest Rate Swaps," 1 *Bank Accounting and Finance* 3 (Winter 1987-88).

[12] S. Henderson, *supra* note 253. Alternative sources provide a lower estimate. For example, one source suggests that in the first half of 1987, the outstanding notional principal amount on interest rate and currency swaps was $225 billion. *See* "International Capital Markets: Just a Simple Idea," *Financial Times*, June 29, 1988, Survey Section at 5. *See also* E. Comiskey, C. Mulford, and D. Turner, *supra* note 264.

1987 figures, the total outstanding principal at the end of 1986 was only $175 billion.[13]

The International Swap Dealers Association (ISDA) is a group of major "commercial, merchant and investment banks that act as dealers in swap transactions."[14] As of May 1, 1987, there were 77 members.[15] All of the parties used in the illustrations of swap transactions in this chapter are ISDA members. The ISDA is not a regulatory authority, although it issues comments on regulations that affect the swap market. For instance, a comment letter on the U.S.-U.K. Joint Proposal was sent to the Federal Reserve and the Bank of England.[16]

The ISDA was formed in part to facilitate development of the swap market. Its strategy has been to standardize and simplify swap documentation.[17] In 1985, the ISDA developed a *Code of Standard Wording, Assumptions and Provisions for Swaps* (also known as the *1986 Swaps Code*). Initially, the *1986 Swaps Code* served as a dictionary of standard terms for swap parties to use in contracts that they drafted.[18] In 1987, a standard interest rate swap agreement was developed (the Master Rate Agreement). It incorporates terms from the *1986 Swaps Code*.[19] This Master Agreement may be used only for U.S. dollar-denominated interest rate swaps.

---

[13] E. Comiskey, C. Mulford, and D. Turner, *supra* note 264.

[14] Letter from Patrick de Saint-Aignan, chairman, ISDA, to Brian Quinn, head of banking supervision, Bank of England, and William Wiles, secretary, Board of Governors of the Federal Reserve System (May 28, 1987); (discussing calculation of credit equivalent amounts for interest rate and currency swaps).

[15] *Id.* at Annex A.

[16] May 28, 1987, ISDA Comment Letter.

[17] *See* ISDA, *User's Guide to the Standard Form Agreements* 1 (1987).

[18] S. Henderson and L. Klein, "A User's Guide to ISDA Master Swap Agreements," 1 *The Journal of International Securities Markets* 41 (Autumn 1987).

[19] *Id.* at 42.

Also in 1987, a standard interest rate and currency exchange agreement (the Master Rate and Currency Agreement) was developed for use in any interest rate or currency swap transaction. Terms from the *1986 Swaps Code* were not incorporated, but a companion guidebook, *Interest Rate and Currency Exchange Definitions,* may be used.[20]

C. Substantive Functions of Swaps

There is no one substantive purpose for entering into a swap transaction, just as there is no one substantive function of capital. Hedging, cost reduction, brokerage, and speculation are conceivable motives for "doing a swap."

(1) Hedging Interest Rate and Currency Risk

A common purpose for doing a swap is to hedge interest rate and currency risk.[21] Banks are often motivated to enter into swap transactions as principals in order to reduce interest rate or currency risk that arises from mismatches between assets and liabilities. Using plain vanilla swaps to hedge interest rate risk has been recommended for savings and loan associations. Many S&Ls are vulnerable to interest rate changes because their asset portfolios consist of long-term, fixed-interest mortgage loans funded by short-term, floating-interest liabilities. Increases in interest rates may

---

[20] *Id.*

[21] With respect to hedging against interest rate risk, *see* J. Bicksler and A. Chen, "An Economic Analysis of Interest Rate Swaps," 41 *Journal of Finance* 645 (July 1986) and D. Lereah, "The Growth of Interest Rate Swaps," 169 *The Bankers Magazine* 36 (May/June 1986). With respect to hedging currency as well as interest rate risk, *see* B. Gendreau, "Interest Rate and Currency Swaps," 1 *Commercial Lending Review* 47 (Fall 1986), and T. Arnold, "How to Do Interest Rate Swaps," 62 *Harvard Business Review* 96 (Sept./Oct. 1984). For a discussion of other functions of swaps, such as the exploitation of market imperfections, *see* G. Hammond, "Recent Developments in the Swap Market," 27 *Bank of England Quarterly Bulletin* 66 (February 1987).

narrow the spread between the fixed and floating interests. Morris and Merfeld explain how plain vanilla swaps reduce this risk:

> Interest rate swaps are useful for hedging the interest rate risk of S&L's because swaps essentially allow S&L's to trade a variable-rate cost of funds for a fixed-rate cost of funds. S&L's lose when interest rates rise and gain when interest rates fall because their costs of funds rise and fall with interest rates but the receipts from fixed-rate mortgages do not change. An S&L can insulate itself from changes in interest rates by becoming the fixed-rate payer and floating-rate receiver in a swap. The S&L can use the receipts from its portfolio of fixed-rate mortgages to make the fixed-rate swap payments. Since the floating-rate swap receipts vary with interest rates, the swap receipts can be used to pay the S&L's variable-rate cost of funds. Thus, if interest rates change, the S&L's cost of funds is, in effect, fixed because its swap payment is fixed while changes in its variable-rate swap receipts would match changes in the costs of its liabilities.[22]

(2) Cost Reduction

A second purpose a bank may have in entering a swap contract as a principal is to lower its cost of funds.[23] The law of comparative advantage makes cost reduction through swaps possible. Again, this purpose is irrelevant—addition-

---

[22] C. Morris and T. Merfeld, "New Methods for Savings and Loans to Hedge Interest Rate Risk," 73 Federal Reserve Bank of Kansas City *Economic Review* 3, 11 (March 1988).

[23] B. Gendreau, "Interest Rate and Currency Swaps," 1 *Commercial Lending Review* 47 (Fall 1986). Hedging risk and lowering cost of funds may be accomplished simultaneously, though in Figures 2-6 they are treated separately. The use of swaps to hedge and lower cost simultaneously is discussed in J. Whittaker, "Interest Rate Swaps: Risk and Regulation," 72 Federal Reserve Bank of Kansas City *Economic Review* 3, 4-7 (March 1987) and in S. Felgram, "Interest Rate Swaps: Use, Risk, and Prices," Federal Reserve Bank of Boston *New England Economic Review* 22, 23-25 (Nov./Dec. 1987).

al capital support is required for swaps even if the cost of funds is reduced.

(3) Brokerage

A bank may enter into swap contracts on an agency basis as an intermediary, acting as a pure broker. The bank matches parties and earns a fee for its services.[24] As a pure broker, the bank does not assume any credit risk in the swap transaction because it does not enter into a swap contract with either party.

Alternatively, an intermediary bank may do more than act as a pure broker: It may also enter into a swap contract with each party. There are then two swap contracts involved in the single swap transaction. The bank collects a fee for matching and for taking on the risk that either party will default on the swap transaction. If one counterparty defaults, the bank's swap contract with the defaulting counterparty will terminate automatically. However, the bank's swap contract with the other counterparty will not terminate. Thus, the intermediary bank will remain obligated to perform on the swap contract with the nondefaulting counterparty.

(4) Speculation

Still another purpose for entering into a swap contract is to speculate on interest rate or foreign exchange rate movements. A bank may believe that interest rates are likely to fall and so may enter into a plain vanilla swap transaction as a principal in order to become a floating-rate payor and shed a fixed-rate obligation. A bank may enter a currency swap as a principal to take on a yen obligation because it believes yen will depreciate relative to the dollar. When

---

[24] D. Lereah, "The Growth of Interest Rate Swaps," 169 *The Bankers Magazine* 36 (May/June 1986).

speculation is the motive, the transacting bank stands to lose if it guesses wrong.

D. Illustrations of Hedging and Cost Reduction Functions

In Figures 2 through 6, a bank enters into a swap contract with a corporate counterparty. In each case, the bank acts as a principal and is able to *hedge interest rate and/or currency risk* or *lower its cost of funding*. In each case, the bank is an "end user" of the swap—it does not stand between two parties as a third-party intermediary.

The hedging function is illustrated because the requirements that capital support be provided for swaps performing this function is curious, even ironic. There may be little doubt that a speculative swap should be supported with additional capital, but what about a swap used to hedge interest rate or currency risk? The cost reduction function is illustrated because it, like the hedging function, is a common reason for entering into a swap contract.[25]

In reality, many of these contracts would be arranged through a third-party intermediary (a swap broker), which would likely be a commercial or investment bank. The intermediary might act as a pure broker, or it might sign a swap contract with each counterparty. In the latter event, two swap contracts would be involved, and the intermediary would be exposed to the credit risks of both counterparties. Since the two swap contracts are automatically matched with one another, the intermediary does not stand to hedge interest rate or currency risk, or to lower its cost of funding, by virtue of its middle position in the transaction. The intermediary will earn a fee for its brokerage services and for assuming the credit risk of each party.

---

[25] *See generally* T. Andersen, *Currency and Interest Rate Hedging* 238-239 (1987).

Figure 3 shows an example of the role of a swap broker. In principle, the role would be similar in all of the other illustrations. The critical point regarding a swap arranged through an intermediary is that the presence of the intermediary does not frustrate the hedging or cost reduction purpose of the swap from the perspective of an end user.

(1) Anatomy of a Plain Vanilla Swap

(*a*) Eliminating a Mismatch.—Suppose that Manufacturers Hanover Trust (MHT) recently made a floating-interest-rate loan to a corporate borrower and funds this loan by selling a fixed-rate certificate of deposit. The loan and the CD are of the same maturity.[26] Since the interest rate on the loan floats, there is a mismatch on MHT's books: a floating-rate asset is associated with a fixed-rate liability. The mismatch exposes MHT to interest rate risk. At the time MHT made the loan, there was a positive spread between the floating interest receivable and the fixed interest payable. But if interest rates fall, the spread could become zero or negative, thereby eliminating any interest income from the loan and possibly resulting in losses to MHT. Thus, MHT would like to eliminate the risk of loss from a fall in interest rates.

Suppose that the General Motors Acceptance Corporation (GMAC) recently made numerous fixed-interest-rate loans to purchasers of GM automobiles. It provided the funds to finance these automobile loans by issuing floating-rate debt of approximately the same maturity as the loans. There is a mismatch on GMAC's books: it has a fixed-rate asset (the portfolio of automobile loans) associated with a floating-rate liability (the debt issuance). Interest rate risk arises because a rise in interest rates could eliminate any

---

[26] The problem of maturity mismatches is not considered in any of these illustrations.

positive spread between interest receivable from borrowers who purchased their GM cars with GMAC loans and interest payable to holders of GMAC debt. GMAC seeks to hedge against the risk of a rise in interest rates.

Officials from MHT and GMAC might meet directly and agree to a fixed/floating-interest-rate swap contract. Under this contract, each agrees to pay the interest obligations of the other. That is, MHT takes on the obligation to pay the floating rate due to holders of the GMAC bonds, and GMAC agrees to pay the fixed rate due the purchasers of MHT's CD. The principal sum on which the interest is calculated would be the same. For instance, MHT would agree to make floating payments on $100 million of GMAC bonds and GMAC would agree to make fixed payments on $100 million of MHT CDs.

When the swap contract is entered into, the present value of the cash flow each party expects to receive equals the present value of the cash flow payment each party expects to make. In other words, the present value of the expected net cash flow to MHT is the same as that to GMAC. This equality will be lost as time passes because interest rates will change.

For example, if interest rates rise, then MHT's obligation increases relative to what it receives. In practice, MHT passes on the floating-rate payments directly to GMAC, and GMAC then remits the interest payment to the GMAC bondholders. Similarly, GMAC pays the fixed rate to MHT, which then pays the CD holders. The interest payments may be made semiannually, pursuant to the underlying obligations of MHT and GMAC, and may be made on the same date.

If the payments are made on the same date, then one net payment may be made. That is, if the payment owed MHT exceeds that owed GMAC because interest rates have fallen (that is, the floating rate has fallen below the fixed rate), then one net payment will be made by GMAC to MHT. The reverse net cash flow will occur if interest rates have risen. When the swap contract expires, no principal is exchanged. MHT is responsible for repaying principal to holders of its CD, and GMAC is responsible for returning the investment made by its bondholders.

MHT has thus eliminated the risk of a decline in interest rates because it is the floating-rate payor. GMAC has hedged against a rise in interest rates because it is the fixed-rate payor. This swap transaction is depicted in Figure 2.

Alternatively, officials from MHT and GMAC might contact a swap broker—possibly an investment bank like Salomon Brothers—and request it to find a suitable counterparty. MHT and GMAC would then be brought together through this intermediary. It is likely that two separate swap contracts would be made: MHT would sign a swap agreement with the broker, and GMAC also would sign a swap contract with the broker. It is also likely that MHT's payments to holders of the GMAC bonds would be made through the swap broker, who would remit the payments to GMAC, and GMAC's payments to MHT's CD holders likewise would be made through the intermediary. Again, the payments would be made semiannually, possibly one net payment would be made on each payment date, and no principal would be exchanged upon expiration of the contract. This swap transaction is depicted in Figure 3.

(b) **Lowering the Cost of Funds.** — Suppose that Marine Midland Bank seeks to raise funds at a fixed interest rate—but because of its large portfolio of poorly performing loans to Latin American countries and to energy and real estate businesses in Texas, Moody's has downgraded its rating of Marine's bonds. If Marine issues medium-term, fixed-interest-rate debt, it will have to offer prospective investors a slightly higher rate in order to induce them to hold the

PERSPECTIVES ON RISK-BASED CAPITAL

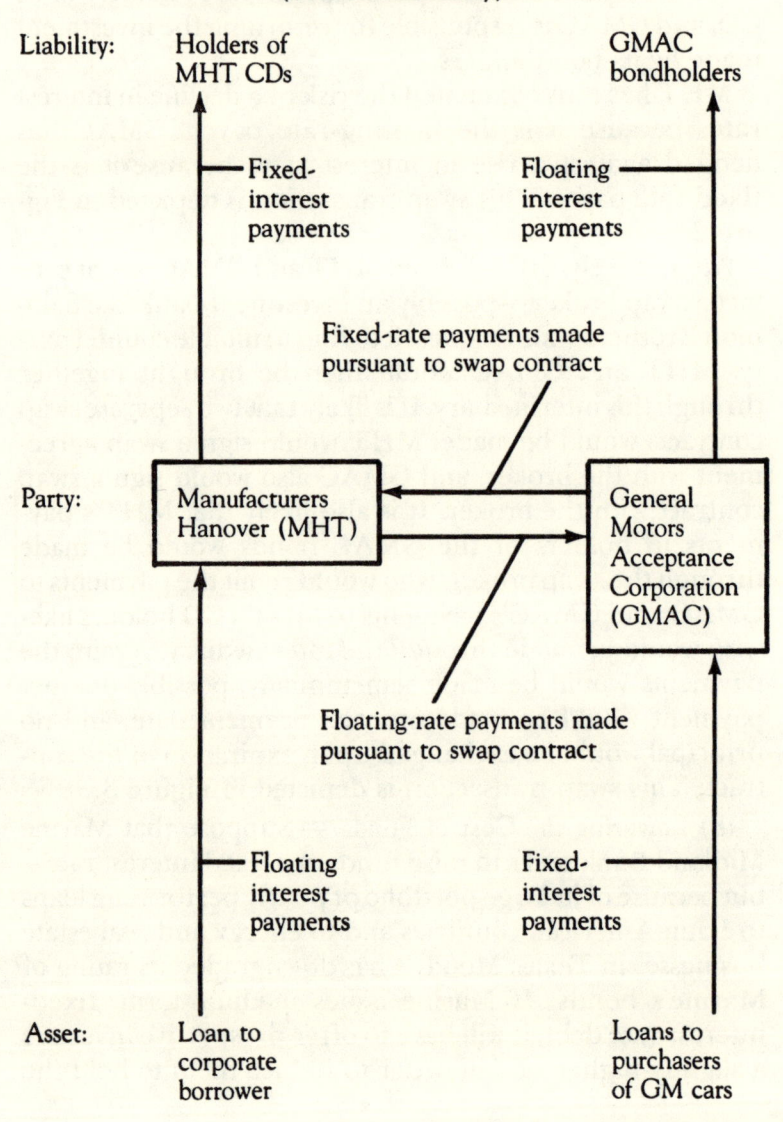

Figure 2
Flowchart of Hypothetical Interest Rate Swap Between Manufacturers Hanover and GMAC
(No Intermediary)

Liability:	Holders of MHT CDs	GMAC bondholders
	↑ Fixed-interest payments	↑ Floating interest payments
	Fixed-rate payments made pursuant to swap contract	
Party:	Manufacturers Hanover (MHT) ⇄	General Motors Acceptance Corporation (GMAC)
	Floating-rate payments made pursuant to swap contract	
	↑ Floating interest payments	↑ Fixed-interest payments
Asset:	Loan to corporate borrower	Loans to purchasers of GM cars

116

ABCs OF SWAPS

Figure 3
Flowchart of Hypothetical Interest Rate Swap Between Manufacturers Hanover and GMAC (with Intermediary)

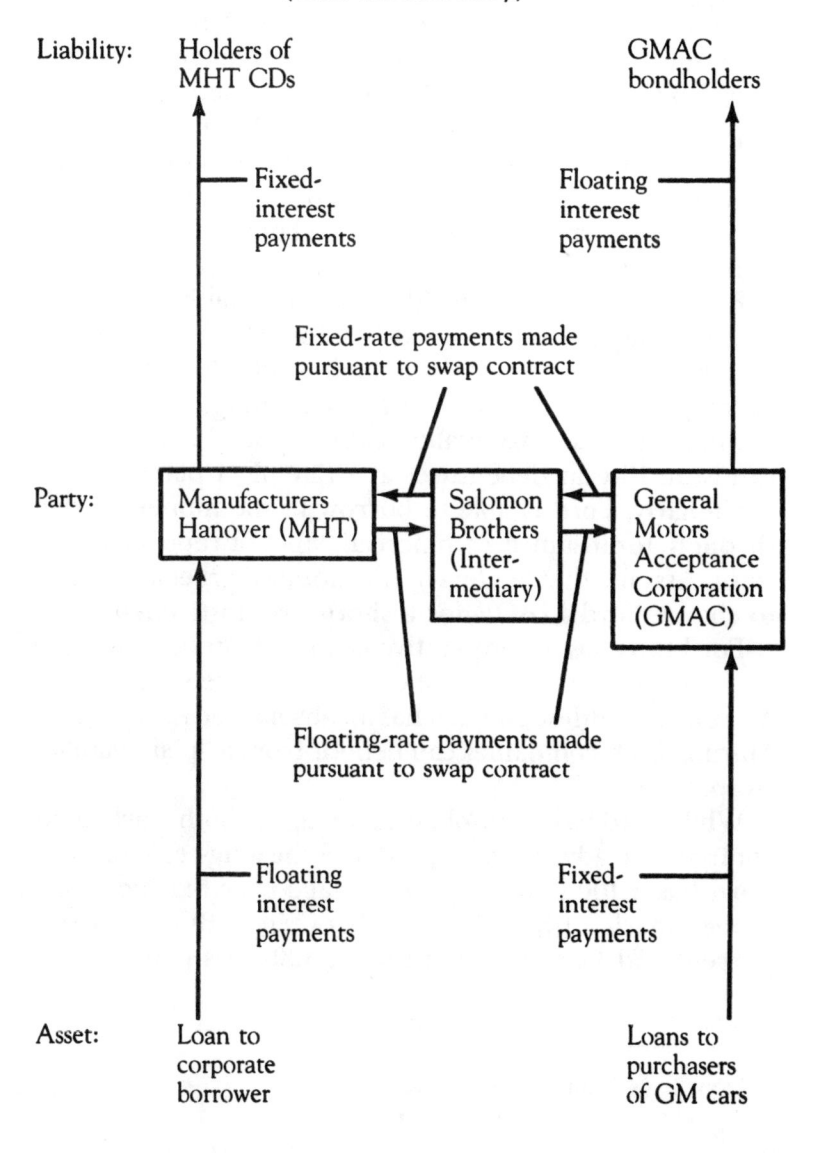

Liability:	Holders of MHT CDs		GMAC bondholders
	↑ Fixed-interest payments		↑ Floating interest payments
		Fixed-rate payments made pursuant to swap contract	
Party:	Manufacturers Hanover (MHT) ←	Salomon Brothers (Intermediary) ← →	General Motors Acceptance Corporation (GMAC)
		Floating-rate payments made pursuant to swap contract	
	↑ Floating interest payments		↑ Fixed-interest payments
Asset:	Loan to corporate borrower		Loans to purchasers of GM cars

117

bonds, in light of the higher default risk associated with the bank. Assume that Marine must pay 14 percent on a five-year debenture.

Suppose that Marine's ability to borrow in the money market (the market for short-term funds) has also been adversely affected because of its exposure in Latin America and Texas. For example, Marine must issue commercial paper (which, in practice, Marine calls "loan notes") at a larger discount, or must pay a higher rate on repurchase agreements (repos) than its competitors. Assume that Marine can borrow funds for a period of less than a year at LIBOR + 1 percent.

By contrast, suppose that the financial health of the Ford Motor Company is appraised by Moody's as excellent, so that Ford's long-term debt is high-grade. Ford's current earnings and its earnings forecasts are strong, as the word is out in the market that quality really is "Job 1" at Ford. Ford can issue 10-year debentures at a rate of 11 percent.

Similarly, Ford is able to borrow in the money market through, for instance, commercial paper or repos, at cheap rates. Assume that lenders in the money market are willing to charge Ford LIBOR for a short-term instrument.

Ford thus has a comparative advantage in borrowing in both the long-term and short-term markets relative to Marine. But although Ford has an absolute advantage over Marine, both companies can benefit from a "plain vanilla" swap.

While Ford has an absolute advantage in both markets, its comparative advantage is greater in the long-term market. Ford has a 100-basis-point advantage over Marine in the money market (the difference between LIBOR plus one percent and LIBOR).[27] Ford has a 300-basis-point advan-

---

[27] One basis point = .01 percent.

ABCs OF SWAPS

tage over Marine in the long-term debt market (the difference between 14 percent and 11 percent). Assume that Ford issues an 11 percent debenture and Marine places commercial paper paying LIBOR + 1 with a private investor.

The difference between the 300-basis-point comparative advantage and the 100-basis-point comparative advantage (200 basis points) is the source of potential gain for Ford and Marine from a plain vanilla swap. Marine could agree to pay Ford's debenture holder 11 percent and Ford could agree to make floating-rate payments to the investor in Marine's commercial paper.

It is obvious that Marine benefits, because it can obtain long-term, fixed-rate funding at a lower rate than with its own debenture. Marine would have had to pay 14 percent if it had issued a debenture, but instead it pays only 11 percent to the holder of the Ford debenture.

Ford also reduces its cost of funds. Since Ford has an absolute borrowing advantage, Marine must induce it to enter into the swap agreement. The incentive offered by Marine can take two forms. Ford can pay Marine a rate less than LIBOR + 1 — that is, less than what is due to the holder of Marine's commercial paper. Specifically, Ford can pay less than LIBOR, which is what Ford would have paid if it had issued the commercial paper. Or Ford can demand that Marine pay it more than the 11 percent due to the Ford debenture holder. Then Ford can retain the excess. Assume that Ford chooses the first option and pays Marine less than LIBOR.

The analysis of the cash flows in Table 3 summarizes the amount the swap saves both Marine and Ford. The sum of the cost savings to the two banks equals 200 basis points. It is assumed that Ford pays Marine LIBOR − 1 percent. The two split the 200-basis-point potential gain evenly, as each saves 100 basis points.

(2) Anatomy of a Basis Swap

(*a*) **Eliminating a Mismatch.** — The most obvious purpose of a basis swap is to eliminate a mismatch. This is because insofar as different interest rate indexes track each other closely, basis swaps may not provide significant cost advantages. One can construct a sample basis swap by simply modifying the Manufacturers Hanover-GMAC example (see Figure 4).

Table 3
Cash Flow Analysis of Hypothetical Interest Rate Swap Between Marine Midland and Ford

Cash Flow Analysis: Marine

Receives from Ford: (swap inflow)	LIBOR − 1%
Payments made:	
(1) To Ford (swap outflow)	11%
(2) To investors in commercial paper (pass-through)	LIBOR + 1%
Net cash outflow:	13%[28]
Best alternative to raise long-term, fixed-interest debt:	14%
Net savings: (comparison of net cash outflow with best alternative)	1%, or 100 basis points

Cash Flow Analysis: Ford

Receives from Marine:	11%
Payments made:	
(1) To Marine	LIBOR − 1%
(2) To investors in debenture	11%

ABCs OF SWAPS

Table 3 (Continued)

Net cash outflow:	LIBOR − 1%[29]
Best alternative to raise short-term, floating-interest debt:	LIBOR
Net savings: (comparison of net cash outflow with best alternative)	1%, or 100 basis points
Total savings to Marine and Ford:	200 basis points (100 basis points each)

Suppose that the loan made by MHT bears an interest rate that is tied to LIBOR. Suppose also that the interest rate on the GMAC bonds varies and the index to which it is tied is LIBOR. The interest rate payable is also tied to LIBOR.

Under these assumptions, neither party suffers from a mismatch on its books in the sense of having a fixed-rate asset and a floating-rate liability, or vice versa. Yet each is exposed to interest rate risk because of the mismatch in the index (the basis) to which its asset and liability are tied. MHT's asset (the loan) is tied to LIBOR, but its liability (the MHT CD) is tied to the discount rate on T-bills. GMAC's asset (the loans) is tied to the T-bill rate, but its liability (the Chase CD) is tied to LIBOR.

If the T-bill rate and LIBOR are perfectly correlated,

---

[28] [LIBOR − 1] − [(11) + (LIBOR + 1)]
   = LIBOR − 1 − 11 − (LIBOR + 1)
   = LIBOR − 1 − 11 − (LIBOR − 1
   = − 1 − 11 − 1
   = − 13, or a net payment of 13 percent.

[29] 11 − [(LIBOR − 1) + 11]
   = 11 − (LIBOR − 1) − 11
   = −(LIBOR − 1), or a net payment of LIBOR − 1 percent.

121

then in practice no risk exists. Yet the correlation may not be perfect, and the movement of one rate may lag in response to a change in the other rate. MHT prefers that LIBOR exceed the T-bill rate, for only then is there a positive spread on the interest rates associated with uses and sources of funds. By contrast, GMAC prefers that the T-bill rate remain above LIBOR so it obtains a positive spread. Each may seek to eliminate the interest rate exposure by entering into a swap agreement with the other, or with a broker. MHT would substitute for its liability tied to the T-bill rate one tied to LIBOR, and GMAC would receive a liability tied to the T-bill rate in exchange for one tied to LIBOR.

MHT thereby eliminates its mismatch because its LIBOR asset is matched with LIBOR-indexed payments. Conversely, GMAC matches its T-bill-linked loans with T-bill-linked payments. This swap transaction is depicted in Figure 4.

(b) Lowering the Cost of Funds. — Although short-term interest rates to which floating-rate payments on a swap might be indexed move in tandem, a basis swap can still be used to lower the cost of funds. Differentials between short-term rates should not persist because of interest rate arbitrage activity. Nevertheless, at least a theoretical example of cost saving from a basis swap can be constructed. The source of the saving is hypothesized to be comparative borrowing advantages.

Suppose that the Union Bank of Switzerland (UBS), being well known in the European financial markets, can issue short-term, interest-bearing Eurodollar notes at 25 basis points over LIBOR (LIBOR + 25). To borrow dollars in the U.S., where it is less well known, UBS would have to pay one percent over the prime rate (Prime + 1).

Irving Trust seeks to borrow dollars in the European markets and pay a rate tied to LIBOR. However, because of uncertainty surrounding Irving's merger into the Bank of

ABCs OF SWAPS

Figure 4
Flowchart of Hypothetical Basis Swap Between Manufacturers Hanover and GMAC

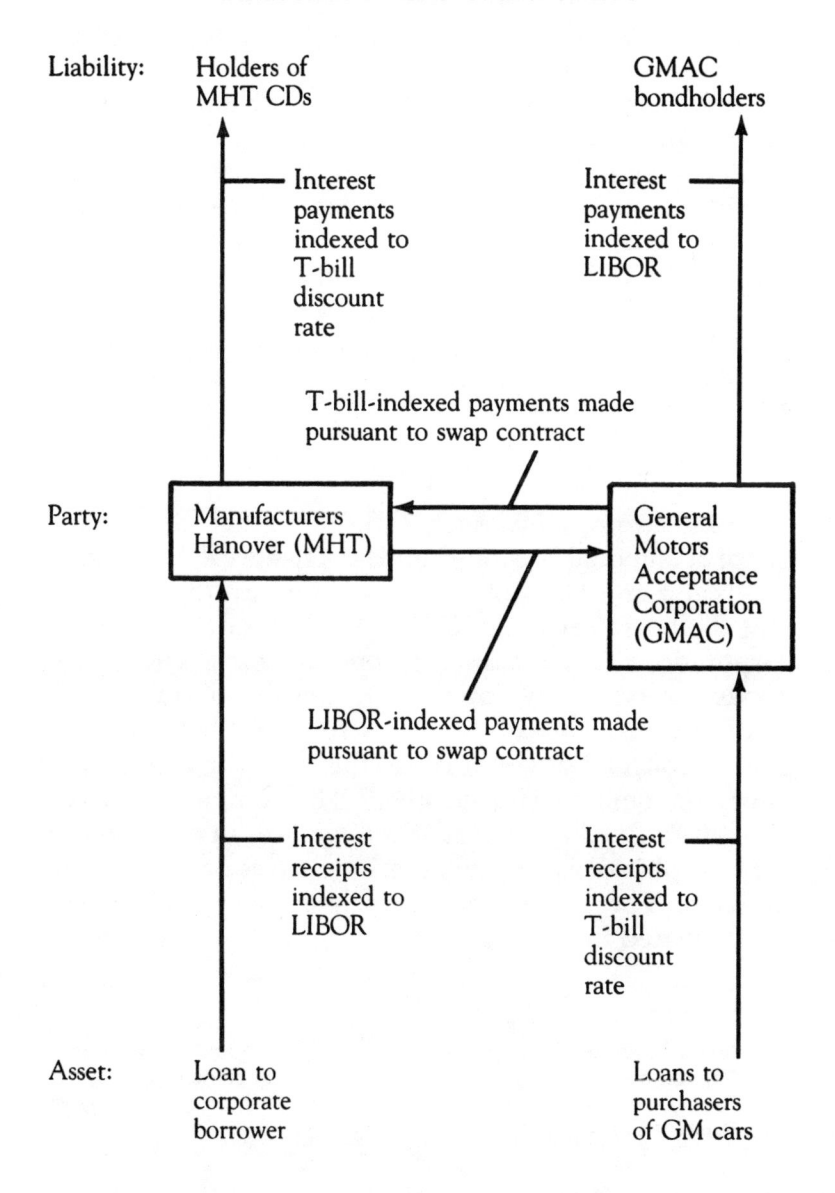

Liability:	Holders of MHT CDs	GMAC bondholders
	↑ Interest payments indexed to T-bill discount rate	↑ Interest payments indexed to LIBOR
	T-bill-indexed payments made pursuant to swap contract	
Party:	Manufacturers Hanover (MHT) ⇄	General Motors Acceptance Corporation (GMAC)
	LIBOR-indexed payments made pursuant to swap contract	
	↑ Interest receipts indexed to LIBOR	↑ Interest receipts indexed to T-bill discount rate
Asset:	Loan to corporate borrower	Loans to purchasers of GM cars

New York (BNY), European lenders will purchase Irving's obligations only if they receive 1.25 percent over LIBOR (LIBOR + 125). By contrast, American lenders are willing to charge Irving the prime rate on the strength of a guarantee from its new parent, BNY.

Under a basis swap arrangement, UBS would borrow Eurodollars at LIBOR plus 25 and Irving would borrow dollars at the prime rate. UBS would then assume Irving's obligations, paying the prime rate. Since this is one percent less than what UBS would have paid had it borrowed directly in the U.S. market, UBS would effectively reduce its cost of funds. Conversely, Irving would assume UBS's LIBOR plus 25 obligation, thereby saving itself one percent (the difference between LIBOR plus 125 and LIBOR plus 25).

(3) Anatomy of a Currency Swap

(*a*) **Eliminating a Mismatch.** — Suppose that the London office of National Westminister Bank (Natwest) has made a two-year Eurodollar loan at a fixed interest rate. Assume that the borrower is the U.K. subsidiary of an American corporation. This borrower may require dollars to pay for goods or services it has obtained from suppliers in the U.S. Interest and principal payments from the borrower are paid in dollars. Natwest finances this loan with commercial paper denominated in sterling.[30] The commercial paper also pays a fixed interest rate and matures in two years. It may be placed with a large private investor or bank in England. The interest and principal payments must be denominated in sterling.

---

[30] Sterling commercial paper is a relatively new financial instrument. Legal impediments to its usage were removed by the Bank of England in 1986. *See* G. Penn, "Sterling Commercial Paper," 1 *Banking and Finance Law Review* 195 (1987-88).

There is a currency mismatch on Natwest's books. Natwest has a dollar-denominated asset associated with a sterling-denominated liability. If the dollar-sterling exchange rate moves unfavorably (if the dollar depreciates relative to the pound), the interest Natwest earns from its borrower will be worth relatively less, and interest paid to the investor in its commercial paper will be relatively more costly. That is, the value of Natwest's asset will depreciate relative to the value of its liability. This is currency risk.

Suppose that Procter and Gamble (P&G) earns sterling-denominated income from the sale of its products in the U.K. Suppose also that P&G has taken out fixed-interest-rate, dollar-denominated loans from various U.S. banks. P&G thus earns sales revenue in sterling but has dollar-denominated loan liabilities. There is a currency mismatch on P&G's books, which results in exposure to foreign exchange risk. If sterling depreciates relative to the dollar, the value of P&G's sales revenues will decline relative to the value of its liability.

A currency swap would allow Natwest and P&G to hedge against the currency risk each faces because of the mismatch on its books. Natwest would agree to make the fixed rate, dollar-denominated interest payments on the loans incurred by P&G. Natwest would then have a fixed-rate dollar liability matched to its fixed-rate dollar asset. Conversely, the sterling-denominated, fixed-interest payments on the commercial paper issued by Natwest would be made by P&G. P&G West would then have a fixed-interest obligation matched to a fixed-interest rate asset, both denominated in sterling.

Unlike the situation in interest rate swaps, in a currency swap principal is exchanged upon maturity of the contract. This swap agreement is depicted in Figure 5. Like any swap, this transaction may be arranged through an intermediary.

(b) **Lowering the Cost of Funds.**— Suppose that Citibank recently purchased a long-term, fixed-interest bond issued

Figure 5
Flowchart of Hypothetical Currency Swap Between Natwest and Procter & Gamble

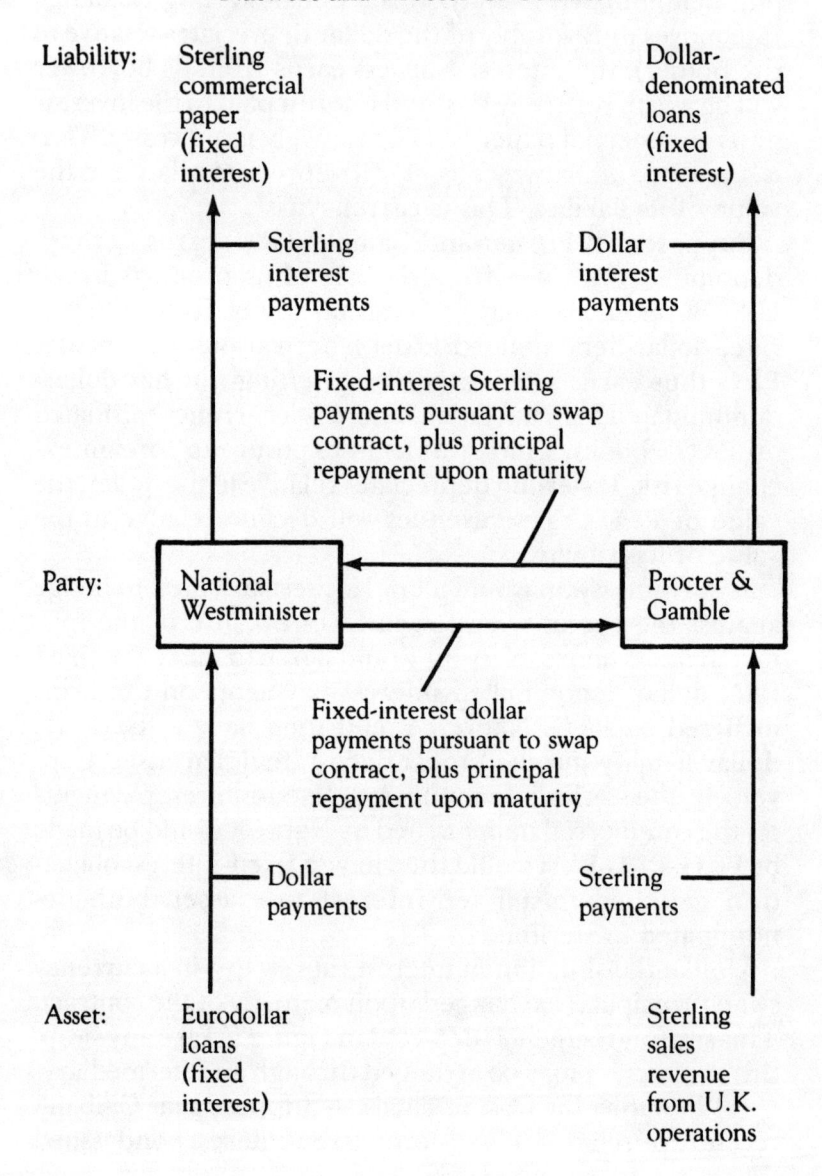

Liability:	Sterling commercial paper (fixed interest)	Dollar-denominated loans (fixed interest)
	↑ Sterling interest payments	↑ Dollar interest payments
	Fixed-interest Sterling payments pursuant to swap contract, plus principal repayment upon maturity	
Party:	National Westminister ← →	Procter & Gamble
	Fixed-interest dollar payments pursuant to swap contract, plus principal repayment upon maturity	
	↑ Dollar payments	↑ Sterling payments
Asset:	Eurodollar loans (fixed interest)	Sterling sales revenue from U.K. operations

by the French government. The bond is denominated in French francs. This purchase was financed through long-term, dollar-denominated subordinated debentures recently issued in the U.S. Citibank would like to match its franc-denominated asset with a franc-denominated liability. One possibility would be for Citibank to issue a long-term debt instrument in France. But borrowing in the French market is costly to Citibank because it is not as well known in France as the major French banks, such as Banque Nationale de Paris and Credit Lyonnais. Because it is a less well-known credit risk, Citibank will be forced to offer slightly higher rates to induce French investors to purchase its debt.

Suppose that the Chanel Company (which manufactures Chanel No. 5 perfume) recently purchased a long-term Eurodollar bond that bears a fixed interest rate. It funded this purchase by issuing a long-term, fixed-rate bond denominated in French francs. Chanel would like to match its dollar-denominated asset with a dollar-denominated liability. Chanel is well known in the United States for its perfume, but it cannot issue long-term, dollar-denominated debt instruments at a interest rate as low as that offered by Citibank on its debt.

In this situation, Citibank enjoys a comparative advantage in the market for long-term, dollar-denominated debt, and Chanel possesses a comparative advantage in the market for long-term, franc-denominated debt. A currency swap would be mutually beneficial. Citibank would be obligated to make interest payments and principal repayment to those holding franc-denominated bonds issued by Chanel. The interest rate on those payments would be less than what Citibank would have paid had it issued its own franc-denominated obligations. Citibank thereby lowers its cost of funds by entering into the swap contract. Chanel would make dollar-denominated payments (interest plus principal) to holders of Citibank's debentures. Such payments are at a lower interest rate than Chanel would have paid if it had sold its own dollar-denominated bonds. Chanel thus reduces its cost of funds as well.

(4) Anatomy of a Cross-Currency Interest Rate Swap

(a) Eliminating Two Mismatches.—Suppose that the London branch of Bankers Trust has made a one-year Eurodollar loan that bears a fixed interest rate. The borrower is the U.K. subsidiary of an American company. This subsidiary may require dollars to pay for goods or services from the United States. Interest and principal payments received from the borrower are denominated in dollars. Bankers Trust finances this loan with a short-term, floating-rate CD denominated in sterling. The CD may be purchased by a large private investor or bank in England. The interest and principal payments must be denominated in sterling.

Bankers Trust faces two sorts of mismatches. First, it has a dollar-denominated asset associated with a sterling-denominated liability. If the dollar-sterling exchange rate moves unfavorably (if the dollar depreciates relative to the pound), the dollars received from the borrower will be worth relatively less, and the sterling paid to the investor in its commercial paper will be relatively more costly. That is, the value of Bankers Trust's asset will depreciate relative to the value of its liability. This is currency risk. Second, Bankers Trust has a fixed-interest asset but a floating-rate liability. This is interest rate risk. If short- and medium-term interest rates rise, the spread between the interest rate Bankers Trust receives on its loan and the rate paid on its commercial paper will narrow and perhaps even turn negative.

Suppose that British Petroleum (BP) holds a two-year floating-rate note (FRN) denominated in sterling. This was purchased with funds from an issuance of fixed-rate commercial paper denominated in Eurodollars. The issuer of the FRN that BP holds may be the American subsidiary of a British company that needs to pay sterling for goods or services from England. The investor in BP's commercial paper could be a large private investor or bank in the

BP also faces two mismatches resulting in exposure to two forms of risk. It is exposed to currency risk because if sterling depreciates relative to the dollar, the value of its asset depreciates relative to the value of its liability. It is exposed to interest rate risk because if short- and medium-term interest rates fall, the spread between the interest rate received and the rate paid narrows.

A cross-currency interest rate swap would eliminate the risks to which each bank is exposed. Bankers Trust would agree to make the fixed-rate interest payments, in Eurodollars, on the commercial paper issued by BP. Bankers Trust would then have a fixed-rate Eurodollar liability matched to its fixed-rate Eurodollar asset. Conversely, BP would make the sterling-denominated floating interest payments on the CD sold by Bankers Trust. BP would then have a floating-rate obligation matched with a floating-rate asset, both denominated in sterling. This swap is depicted in Figure 6.

(b) *Lowering the Cost of Funds.* — Suppose that Continental Illinois National Bank wishes to raise funds denominated in Swiss francs that bear a floating rate. Continental may wish to do this in order to match a floating-rate sterling asset it has acquired. Because of Continental's troubles in the early 1980s, Swiss investors are unwilling to invest in any of its obligations without charging a default risk premium.[31] Thus, Continental must pay LIBOR plus 3

---

[31] A discussion of Continental Illinois' troubles is found in I. Sprague, *Bailout* 149-212 (1986).

PERSPECTIVES ON RISK-BASED CAPITAL

Figure 6
Flowchart of Hypothetical Cross-Currency Interest Rate Swap Between Bankers Trust and British Petroleum

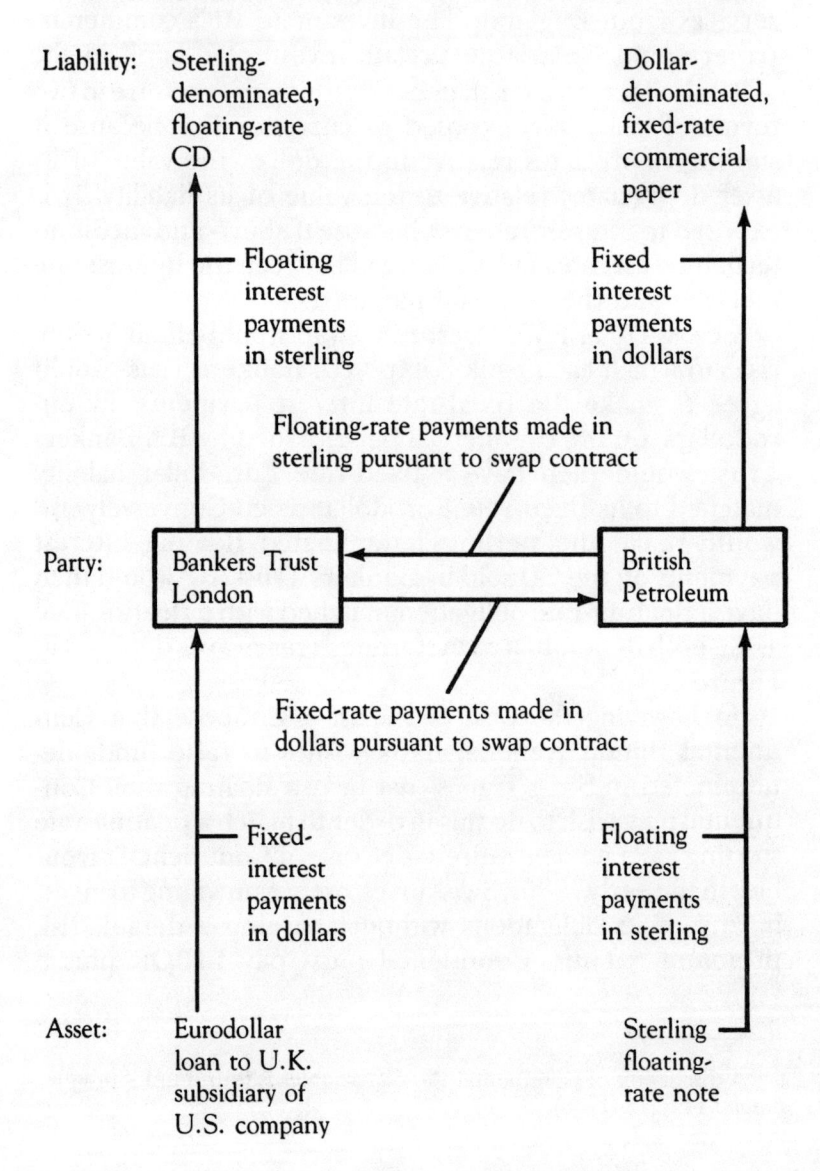

Liability:	Sterling-denominated, floating-rate CD	Dollar-denominated, fixed-rate commercial paper

Floating interest payments in sterling ↑   Fixed interest payments in dollars ↑

Floating-rate payments made in sterling pursuant to swap contract

Party:	Bankers Trust London ← →	British Petroleum

Fixed-rate payments made in dollars pursuant to swap contract

Fixed-interest payments in dollars ↑   Floating interest payments in sterling ↑

Asset:	Eurodollar loan to U.K. subsidiary of U.S. company	Sterling floating-rate note

130

percent (LIBOR + 3) on debt issued in Swiss francs. Assume that Continental can raise dollar-denominated, fixed-rate funds in the United States at a rate of 9.75 percent. While American investors know of Continental's history, they are confident about its new banking strategies and optimistic about its future.

Jardine Matheson Holdings (JMH) is a diversified holding company incorporated in Bermuda. Suppose that JMH seeks to raise dollar-denominated funds bearing a fixed interest rate. It can do so at a rate of 10 percent. JMH is perceived by American investors as quite creditworthy and enjoys a strong reputation among Swiss investors. JMH can issue debt in Switzerland at just 1 percent above LIBOR (LIBOR + 1). These funds are denominated in Swiss francs.

JMH has a comparative advantage in the Swiss franc-denominated debt market. If Continental were to borrow directly in this market, it would have to pay 2 percent more than JMH (the difference between LIBOR + 3 and LIBOR + 1). JMH does not enjoy the same comparative advantage in the American market. JMH can issue dollar-denominated debt paying a fixed interest of 10 percent, whereas Continental need pay only 9.75 percent. This gives Continental a 25-basis-point advantage in the American market.

A cross-currency fixed/floating swap contract may save costs for each party. Because of JMH's comparative advantage in the floating-rate Swiss franc market, it should raise funds in this market. Continental, with a comparative advantage in the fixed-rate dollar market, should raise funds there. Then the two should swap obligations. Continental would agree to make the floating-rate interest payments, denominated in Swiss francs, on the debt issued by JMH. Conversely, JMH would make the dollar-denominated fixed-rate interest payments on the debt issued by Continental.

Continental saves 2 percent by borrowing in the floating-rate Swiss market indirectly through the swap, and JMH saves one-quarter percent (25 basis points) by borrowing in the fixed-rate dollar market indirectly through Continental. It is, of course, possible that the parties will negotiate a somewhat different sharing of the benefits from the transaction. For instance, JMH may insist on receiving slightly more than LIBOR + 1 from Continental or may pay Continental slightly less than 9.75 percent.

E. Chapter Summary

The building blocks of the Basle Agreement on risk-based capital are capital and risk. One way to approach risk is to study the treatment of swaps.

A swap is nothing more than an exchange of obligations between two parties. In an interest rate swap (a plain vanilla swap), one party exchanges its obligation to make fixed interest payments for the counterparty's obligation to make floating interest payments. In a basis swap, obligations that are tied to different interest rate indexes are exchanged.

A currency swap entails the exchange of obligations to make payments in different currencies: One party trades its obligation to make payments in, say, dollars for the counterparty's obligation to make payments in, say, yen. Unlike plain vanilla or basis swaps, currency swaps also involve the exchange of underlying principal, not just the exchange of payments.

Finally, a cross-currency interest rate swap is the exchange of an obligation to make fixed interest payments in one currency for an obligation to make floating interest payments in another currency.

Swaps may be used for a variety of purposes, including the hedging of interest rate or currency risk. A bank can correct a mismatch on its books by entering into a swap contract. It can also use a swap contract to lower its cost of funds.

6
Substance, Form, and the Treatment Of Swaps

Key Concepts	
Swap credit risk	Delay costs
Status quo ante	ISDA Master Agreements
Bankruptcy	Netting
Executory contract	Credit enhancements
Assumption/rejection	Replacement cost
Cherry picking	Current credit exposure
Adequate protection	Potential future exposure

A. Swaps, Irony, and Overinclusion

Perhaps the most complicated part of the Basle Agreement pertains to swaps. The underlying swap transactions for which capital support is required are themselves somewhat involved. This is why the mechanics of swaps are discussed in some detail in Chapter 5.

The key point to be made about the treatment of swaps is that the Basle Agreement is overinclusive. This is ironic in light of the risk-hedging function that some swap transactions fulfill. Banks often enter into swap contracts to reduce interest rate or currency risk. But because the Basle Agreement focuses on credit risk, the hedging function is ignored. *The capital support required to cover credit risk acts as a disincentive to use swaps to reduce interest rate and currency risk.*

In substance-form terms, the irony is that the Basle Agreement neglects the underlying substantive purposes for entering into swap transactions. A formal rule based on credit risk is applied: If a swap contract is signed, credit exposure is deemed to exist, so capital support is required. That the Basle Agreement is overinclusive in treating swaps is not surprising. It is well known that formal rules tend to

133

be over- or underinclusive (and sometimes both).

This irony is heightened when two points are considered. First, the *effect* of counterparty default on the nondefaulting party, even in the worst-case scenario—default because of counterparty bankruptcy—is not necessarily that great. Typically, counterparty default results in restoration of the status quo ante to the nondefaulting party. That is, default puts the nondefaulting bank back in its initial unhedged position. The interest rate or currency risk it was exposed to before the swap contract was signed once again appears after counterparty default. In this sense, the nondefaulting bank is not any worse off than before it signed the swap contract.

This definition of the status quo ante is implied by Brealey and Myers and by Gendreau. Brealey and Myers write, "The recurring nightmare for swap managers is that one party will default, leaving the bank with a large *unmatched* position."[1] Similarly, Gendreau points out that:

> swaps are not riskless. In swaps, as in any financial instrument involving promises of future payments, there is a chance of default. In the event of default on a liability swap, a participant might be forced to make debt payments at a higher cost than would have been incurred under the swap. But perhaps just as important, a participant would likely find that it is no longer hedged. Because swaps "*undo*" a mismatch in the structure of interest payments or currency payments in a participant's balance sheet, a default on a swap would restore the *original,* risky mismatch. In this sense, swaps represent contingent liabilities: there is some chance beforehand that a participant may wind up with an unfavorable interest rate risk or foreign-exchange risk exposure.[2]

---

[1] R. Brealey and S. Myers. *Principles of Corporate Finance* 620 (1988); (emphasis supplied).

[2] B. Gendreau, "Interest-Rate and Currency Swaps," 1 *Commercial Lending Review,* 47, 54 (Fall 1986); (emphasis supplied).

Admittedly, the status quo ante can be defined differently, as the position the nondefaulting party was in just prior to counterparty default. Indeed, this is the definition implied in the Basle Agreement. The problem with this definition is that it can be loaded; under it, default by a counterparty automatically renders the nondefaulting party worse off, regardless of the function the swap played, so long as the swap yielded net payments to the nondefaulting party. But if the position of the nondefaulting party after default is compared with its position not just before default but just before the swap contract was signed, then the effect of default is not automatically adverse.

Under either definition, it could be said that the nondefaulting bank is worse off in one sense. Because of the Basle Agreement, the bank has to provide capital support for a swap on which the counterparty later defaults. If no swap contract had been signed, no capital support would be required.

The second irony involves the Basle Agreement's emphasis on credit risk. This emphasis helps explain why the Board's final regulations do not provide for different risk weights for Treasuries of different maturities. With respect to calculating the required capital support for swaps, the regulations *do* look to interest rate and currency risk. As discussed later in this chapter, credit risk on a swap is measured by the replacement cost of the swap. Replacement cost is measured in relation to interest and foreign exchange rate movements.

(1) Complexity

Even though the purposes for swaps are simple—hedging, cost reduction, brokerage, and speculation — swap transactions, specifically the cash flows involved, can be complicated. Yet simple regulations can be applied to complicated transactions, and simplicity is a desirable feature for any regulation because it can minimize the costs of interpretation, compliance, and enforcement. A regulation may be complex because of a desire to strike some sort of balance between different regulatory goals—in the broadest sense, between an efficient outcome and an equitable one.

No such balancing act appears to explain the complexity of the Basle Agreement in this area. Swaps are different from other off-balance-sheet items in two respects. The credit risk associated with a swap is not the face value (also called the notional principal) of the swap contract. Thus, it is not easy to calculate exactly what amount is at risk. Moreover, the potential loss arising from counterparty default may change over time. This change must be accounted for somehow.

Like other off-balance-sheet items, swaps are treated in two stages by the Basle Agreement. In the first stage, a credit equivalent amount of the swap is found. In the second stage, this amount is slotted into a particular risk-weight category. But unlike other off-balance-sheet items, swaps require several steps for calculation of the credit equivalent amount.

Herein lies the source of the complexity. The Basle Agreement purports to take account of both current and future risk associated with the swap. This is because the value of these contracts may change over time, and thus the potential loss resulting from counterparty default may change. By contrast, the value of such off-balance-sheet items as letters of credit is not viewed as subject to future changes. This view may be questionable, since account party risk associated with (risk) the party on whose behalf the bank extending credit looks to for repayment may vary.

(2) Irony and Overinclusion

While the attempt to grapple with underlying substantive realities of swaps may lead to complexity in the Basle Agreement, there is an irony in this complexity. The Basle Agreement requires a bank that enters into a swap contract to provide capital support for the swap because of credit risk, even though the swap may lower the bank's interest rate or currency risk. The irony results from a failure to differentiate among the various functions swaps fulfill. Under the Basle Agreement, whether a bank enters into a swap as a principal to hedge, lower costs, or speculate is immaterial. Whether a bank enters into a swap on an agency basis and contracts with both end users is immaterial. All that matters is the formality of the swap contract. If a bank enters into such a contract, it must provide capital support.

It is because the focus of the Basle Agreement is on credit risk that the substantive reason for doing a swap is ignored. As Henderson points out, "certain swap-driven transactions may in fact result in a decrease in one type of risk at the cost of an increase in credit risk."[3] There is no "intent requirement" in the Basle Agreement. The rule requiring capital support for swaps is a per se rule! Herein lies the irony. Even if a bank enters into a swap contract for the purpose of reducing interest rate or currency mismatches on its balance sheet, it must provide capital support for the swap.

Is the risk of counterparty default on swaps great? The answer depends in part on the source consulted. The ISDA contends that few losses from swap transactions have occurred. It reports that as of mid-1988, of the $1 trillion outstanding notional principle on swap contracts, only $33 million in losses had been reported.[4] Alternatively, the

---

[3] S. Henderson, "Swap Credit Risk: A Multi-Party Perspective" 46 (1988); (paper submitted to Singapore Conference on Current Developments in International Banking and Corporate Financial Operations).

[4] "Survey Shows Losses Are Low in Swap Market," *American Banker,* July 20, 1988 at 2.

thesis of Henderson's paper is that credit risks are real.[5] Henderson examines these risks from five perspectives: each of the two contracting parties, a lender to one of the contracting parties, a government regulator, and the financial markets.

B. But Can You Differentiate Among the Substantive Functions?

Adverse effects of counterparty default on a swap contract exist at least as a theoretical possibility, which should be enough to cause concern to the legal mind. Yet the risk-reducing purpose of swaps cannot be ignored, nor can the contractual mechanisms to reduce credit risk.

Bank examiners may argue that it is difficult to discern such purposes in a routine bank examination. The ISDA's May 28, 1987, Comment Letter did not make the argument forcefully that purpose is discernible. Two perspectives can be offered on this issue. First, an admittedly limited, informal, and unscientific survey of bankers at money-center banks who are involved in or know about swap transactions reveals that at least some banks' swap records state the purpose for each swap transaction. One banker reports that his bank's swap book has a column in which the purpose is recorded alongside such essential information as name of the counterparty, dates, and terms.

Second, other legal rules turn on the motive for entering into a swap contract: recently proposed regulations on the recognition of income from and changes in the market value of swaps, and tax provisions on swaps.

(1) Proposed Regulations of the Federal Financial Institutions Examination Council

The Federal Financial Institutions Examination Council (FFIEC) is an interagency body formed by Congress in 1978

---

[5]S. Henderson, *supra* note 287.

to deal with specific regulatory matters.[6] It consists of a governor of the Federal Reserve Board, the FDIC chairman, the comptroller, the Bank Board chairman, and the chairman of the National Credit Union Administration Board.[7] One regulatory matter with which the FFIEC is concerned is the development of uniform report forms and reporting standards for financial institutions.[7]

The FFIEC recently proposed regulations applicable to all FDIC-insured commercial banks concerning the reporting standards for interest rate and cross-currency interest rate swaps.[8] Currency swaps would not be covered by this regulation.[9] There are currently no generally accepted accounting principles concerning the reporting of swap income and the recording of changes in the market value of swaps. The FFIEC is concerned about misleading disclosures in the Reports of Condition and Income (call reports) periodically filed by banks with federal banking regulators. Under the proposal, the regulations were to take effect on March 31, 1989, and were to apply to all interest rate and cross-currency interest rate swaps entered into after December 31, 1988.[10]

The proposed regulations address two questions. First, should a bank be allowed to recognize all income from a swap when the swap transaction is entered into, or should the bank have to recognize the income over the life of the

---

[6] C. Golembe and D. Holland, *Federal Regulation of Banking 1986-87* 29 (1986). The FFIEC was created pursuant to the Financial Institutions Regulatory and Interest Rate Control Act of 1978. *Id.*

[7] *Id.* at 35-36.

[8] 53 Fed. Reg. 45,386 (proposed November 9, 1988). *See also* "FFIEC May Require Banks to Recognize Interest Rate Swap Income Gradually," *BNA Banking Report,* November 14, 1988.

[9] This is clear from the definition of interest rate swaps in the proposed regulations at 53 Fed. Reg. 45,386, 45,387.

[10] "FFIEC May Require Banks to Recognize Interest Rate Swap Income Gradually," *BNA Banking Report,* November 14, 1988.

swap? There are two sources of income from swaps. The first, called "spread income," is any excess of payments received from the counterparty over payments made to the counterparty. The second is any fee the bank earns—say, from acting as a broker. The FFIEC proposes that swap income be amortized over the life of the swap:

> In no case shall income be recognized at the inception of a swap. Arrangement fees must be recognized as income over the life of the swap contract. Spread income, i.e., the difference between future cash receipts and payments for a portfolio of swaps, must be recognized only as accrued for the current period, i.e., not beyond the [call] report date.[11]

To recognize all swap income immediately might overstate income. Indeed, the general accounting principle is that "income earned as a result of a contractual obligation should be recognized over the life of the contract."[12] Furthermore, whenever a bank acts as a principal in a swap transaction, the costs and risks of the swap are distributed across the life of the swap. It would be inconsistent to recognize all income immediately when credit risk, interest rate risk, and administrative costs are incurred throughout the life of the swap.

The second question is whether a bank should be required to record changes in the market value of a swap it has entered into. A comparison of the FFIEC's answer with the Basle Agreement's is revealing. The FFIEC proposal "would require that changes in the market value of swaps *(except most swaps accounted for as hedges)* be recorded in the period in which they occur."[13] That is, the general rule would be to record a change in the market value of a swap

---

[11] 53 Fed. Reg. 45,386, 45,387 (proposed November 9, 1988).
[12] *Id.* at 45,386.
[13] *Id.* (emphasis supplied).

when the change occurs. No deferral would be permitted. The idea behind the rule is that "any losses in value in a bank's swap portfolio would be reflected in current period income rather than being deferred, thus providing more discipline to banks engaging in the swap market."[14]

However, an exception to this general rule would be made for swaps used to reduce interest rate or currency risk. Such swaps could be reported as hedges, and changes in their market value would be accounted for in the same manner as changes in the market value of the underlying hedged item. For instance, suppose an interest rate swap is used to hedge an item whose changes in market value are not recorded immediately under the accounting principles applicable to that item. The swap used to hedge the item will be accounted for in the same way: Changes in the market value of the swap will be reported whenever changes in the market value of the hedged item are reported. The accounting principles of the item govern the swap used to hedge it. In a different example, suppose the underlying hedged item is carried at market value (marked to market). Changes in the market value of the swap that hedges the interest rate risk associated with that item cannot be deferred.[15]

How would federal regulators examining a bank's call report know whether a swap is used as a hedge? The FFIEC proposal states that "banks must fully document their swap hedging policies and transactions."[16] For single-currency interest rate swaps, the proposal would require banks to

---

[14] *Id.* at 45,386–45,387.

[15] *Id.* at 45,388. There is an exception to the exception. A swap used to hedge another swap may not be reported as a hedge. "For example, offsetting swaps for which a bank is acting as an intermediary are not swaps that reduce its interest rate risk exposure." *Id.*

[16] *Id.* at 45,387.

satisfy the accounting rules for futures contracts. For crosscurrency interest rate swaps, banks would have to meet the rules for foreign currency translation:

> Swaps that are used to reduce a bank's interest rate risk exposure may be reported as hedges of such risk if... all of the hedging criteria set forth in FASB Statement No. 80 have been fulfilled. Therefore, for example, the specific item to be hedged must expose the enterprise to price (or interest rate) risk, and the swap must reduce that exposure and be designated as a hedge of that item. Swaps denominated in more than one currency that are used to reduce a bank's interest rate or foreign exchange risk may be reported as hedges of such risks if... all of the hedging criteria set forth in FASB Statement No. 52 have been met.[17]

The bottom line is that the proposed FFIEC regulations would recognize the hedging function of swaps and give banks a break for such swaps, but the Basle Agreement ignores the hedging function. It simply *cannot* be that federal banking regulators would be unable to discern which swaps are used to hedge interest rate or currency risk if this information were disclosed on banks' call reports. Thus, *the inability to differentiate among the functions of swaps is no justification for requiring capital support for all swaps.*

(2) Section 988 of the Internal Revenue Code

While the Basle Agreement may ignore the substantive functions a swap agreement fulfills, the Internal Revenue Code (IRC) does not. Swaps are covered under section 988 of the IRC.[18] This section was part of the Tax Reform Act of 1986.[19] Exactly how gains and losses arising from swap

---

[17] *Id.* at 45,387–45,388.

[18] 26 U.S.C. § 988. S. McGarry, "The Taxation of Exchange Gains and Losses: A Road Map," 14 *The International Tax Journal* 25, 38, 42 (Winter 1988). McGarry does not identify the different types of swaps.

[19] S. McGarry, "The Taxation of Exchange Gains and Losses: A Road Map," 14 *The International Tax Journal* 25, 41, (Winter 1988).

transactions are to be taxed is not clear, since the Treasury Department has yet to issue final regulations on this matter.[20] Nevertheless, it is intriguing that the hedging function of interest rate and currency swaps is acknowledged in section 988. It implies that taxpayer intent matters.

Section 988 is what is known in tax jargon as a "characterization" section.[21] "It defines when income is realized, its source, whether it is capital gain or ordinary income, and the basis." Transactions (such as swaps, forwards, futures, and some options) that are covered by section 988 are creatively labeled "section 988 transactions." The general rule is given in section 988(a)(1)(A): "Except as otherwise provided in this section, any foreign currency gain or loss attributable to a section 988 transaction shall be computed separately and treated as ordinary income or loss (as the case may be)." If nothing were "otherwise provided," it would mean that gain or loss would have to be computed on each swap contract, transaction by transaction.[22]

The "otherwise provided" comes in section 988(d)(2). A "988 hedging transaction" is defined as one:

(A) entered into by the taxpayer primarily—
  (i) to reduce risk of currency fluctuations with respect to property which is held or to be held by the taxpayer, or
  (ii) to reduce risk of currency fluctuations with respect to borrowings made or to be made, or obligations incurred or to be incurred, by the taxpayer, and
(B) identified by the Secretary *or the taxpayer* as being a 988 hedging transaction.[23]

The language concerning reduction of currency risk in

---

[20] *Id.* at note 143 at 50.
[21] *Id.* at 41.
[22] A description of the calculation is found in *Merten's Law of Federal Income Taxation* § 45-3.27 (1987).
[23] Emphasis supplied.

sections 988(d)(2)(A)(i) and (ii) certainly covers currency swaps and probably also cross-currency interest rate swaps. It does not cover interest rate swaps.

Since section 988(d)(2)(B) allows the taxpayer to identify a swap transaction as a 988 hedge, a bank need only identify swaps that fulfills the section 988(d)(2)(A) requirement of risk reduction as being "988 hedging transactions." McGarry writes that for a swap to qualify, the taxpayer must make an election before the close of business on the day the transaction occurs.[24]

What difference does it make whether a swap qualifies as a "988 hedging transaction"? Qualification means that the taxpayer need not calculate gain or loss on each individual swap. Rather, section 988(d)(1) provides that "all transactions which are part of such 988 hedging transaction shall be integrated and treated as a single transaction...."

The purpose of this digression into the bowels of the IRC is not to inquire whether a bank can obtain tax benefits from bundling swap transactions into one section 988 hedge. Rather, the issue is whether an election by a taxpayer that is sufficient for IRS agents would be sufficient for federal bank examiners too.

C. Interest Rate and Currency Risk Arising from Swaps

While a swap can be used to hedge against exposure to interest rate and currency fluctuations arising from mismatches, the swap itself generates some interest rate and currency risk. When a swap is entered into, the present value of the expected stream of payments to be made equals the present value of the expected stream of payments to be

---

[24] S. McGarry, "The Taxation of Exchange Gains and Losses: A Road Map," 14 *The International Tax Journal* 25, 43 (Winter 1988).

received. That is, equivalent values (in discounted terms) are swapped. However, interest and foreign exchange rates will change during the term of the swap contract, and the longer the term, the greater the exposure to such change. Thus, the actual amount paid and received may turn out not to be equivalent. As Henderson explains:

> The rate risk (including currency risk if applicable as well as interest rate risk) is that, based on movement of rates in the future, the counterparty will be the net payor under the swap. Worded another way, after all payments have been made, the swap payments made by the counterparty will turn out to have been more valuable than those received by it. This is the risk that the swap becomes unfavorable to it.[25]

For example, in the plain vanilla swap illustrated in Figure 2, GMAC is the fixed-rate payor, making fixed-rate payments to MHT at a contractually agreed rate. GMAC receives floating-rate payments. The swap contract would specify the index to which the floating rate is tied. If the index declines relative to the fixed rate, then payments received will not equal payments made. Specifically, the net present discounted value of the expected payments, which equals the present value of payments to be received minus the present value of payments to be made, will become negative. GMAC will thus become a net payor, and the swap contract will have become unfavorable. Alternatively, a rise in the interest rate index will cause GMAC to become a net recipient.

Similarly, in the currency swap depicted in Figure 5, each party is vulnerable to exchange rate movements. As the sterling payor and dollar recipient, P&G stands to lose if sterling appreciates relative to the dollar. Natwest stands to lose from a depreciation in sterling. Finally, there is expo-

---

[25] S. Henderson, *supra* note 287.

145

sure to both interest and foreign exchange rates in a cross-currency interest rate swap (see Figure 6).

Swap participants are aware of the market risks generated by swaps and attempt to hedge these risks through various financial techniques.[26] One method is to make use of futures and options.[27] For example, if a party is vulnerable to a decline in interest rates (as GMAC is in the plain vanilla swap in Figure 2), it can purchase an interest rate futures contract—for example, a 180-day contract for T-bills—and can continue to roll over that contract during the life of the swap. If interest rates do fall, then the price of T-bills (and correspondingly of T-bill futures) will rise. The futures contract can be closed out (sold) at a price higher than the purchase price, generating a gain.

An alternative way to hedge market risks from swaps is to maintain a swap portfolio consisting of matched pairs. This is also known as "running a matched book" of swaps. Swaps can be matched just as the payment streams from any on-balance-sheet assets and liabilities can be matched. If a bank acts as an intermediary between two parties and enters into a swap contract with each party, the two swap agreements are automatically matched.

For instance, suppose two parties enter into a plain vanilla swap through Salomon Brothers. Two swap agreements are involved: one between the first party and Salomon and one between Salomon and the second party. If the first party is the fixed-rate payor, it will make fixed-interest-rate payments to Salomon and will receive floating-rate payments from Salomon. The second party, the floating-rate payor, will make floating-rate payments to Salomon and

---

[26] *Id.*
[27] For a comparative study of foreign exchange hedging tools, *see* S. Khoury and K. Chan, "Hedging Foreign Exchange Risk: Selecting the Optimal Tool," 5 *Midland Corporate Finance Journal* 40 (Winter 1988).

receive fixed-rate payments. Salomon makes floating-rate payments to the first party and fixed-rate payments to the second party. If interest rates rise, Salomon will have to pay more to the first party, but it will receive more from the second party. The swaps are thus matched.

Even if a bank participates in swaps as an end user, it can engage in matched pairs of swap contracts. Thus, as the fixed-rate payor in Figure 2, GMAC would seek to enter into a swap contract in which it is a floating-rate payor. Similarly, in Figure 5 P&G would seek to pay dollars to a swap counterparty in order to match its sterling payments to the counterparty in the first swap. That is, on the first swap P&G would pay sterling and receive dollars, and on the second swap P&G would pay dollars and receive sterling. Any change in the dollar-sterling exchange rate would affect the two contracts equally but in opposite directions.

The counterparty in the second swap, which matches the first, may or may not be the same counterparty as in the first swap. If it is the same, and if one of the ISDA's Master Agreements is used, then both swap transactions will be covered by this single agreement. This raises the topic of netting, which is discussed later in this chapter.

D. Swap Credit Risk, Take No. 1: The Effect of Counterparty Default Where the Counterparty Does Not Go Bankrupt

(1) Reasons for Counterparty Default

Credit risk is the risk of default of the counterparty, which can arise for several reasons. Careful attention should be given to the *effect* on the nondefaulting party of counterparty default. The distinction to be drawn is *whether counterparty default merely reinstates the status quo ante, so that the nondefaulting party is in the same position as before it entered into the swap contract,* or whether counterparty default actually leaves the nondefaulting party worse off than before it entered into the swap contract. The argument is that so long as the counterparty does not go bankrupt—so long as the Bankruptcy Code rules are not triggered — the nondefaulting party is *no worse off* than before it entered into the swap contract. Where the counterparty defaults because of insolvency, triggering Bankruptcy Code rules, the solvent nondefaulting party could be worse off.

In a formal sense, reasons for default may be provided in the swap contract. Clauses covering events of default or termination events are fairly common. The ISDA's *1986 Swaps Code* requires the parties to the contract to specify events of default and termination events.[28] It also contains definitions of typical events of default and termination events, in Article 11, section 11.7. Typical events include breach of covenant, credit support default, failure to give notice of default or termination events, illegality, and misrepresentation.[29]

If such an event occurs and if bankruptcy law does not operate, the nondefaulting party may terminate the swap contract early and thereby be excused from further performance. This follows from section 11.1 of the *1986 Swaps Code* and sections 5, 6(a), and 6(b) of the Master Rate Agreement. Section 11.1 states, "a party to a Rate Swap Agreement may designate an Early Termination Date: (a) if an Event of Default in respect of the other party has occurred...or (b) if a Termination Event in respect of either party has occurred ...."

A swap contract may also be terminated because it is economically efficient for a swap counterparty to breach its contract. "Economically efficient breach" is not a concept in

---

[28] C. Nicolaides, "Overview of the 1986 ISDA Rate Swap Code," 1 *Butterworths Journal of International Banking and Financial Law* 44, 47 (September 1986).
[29] *Id.*

the ISDA materials, nor is it discussed much in the literature on swaps. Nevertheless, it is at least a theoretical possibility. A party may elect early termination because the swap has become unfavorable due to interest or exchange rate fluctuations. Even though the defaulting party is required to pay a damage fee to the counterparty, termination may still offer a net cost advantage.

(2) Counterparty Default and Restoration of the Status Quo Ante

If a counterparty fails to meet its payment obligations on the swap, the nondefaulting party is deprived of the cash-flow streams it had expected pursuant to the swap agreement. This is an adverse effect if the status quo ante is defined as the situation just before default *and if* the swap had a positive net present value to the nondefaulting party (that is, the nondefaulting party was a net recipient of payments).

An alternative is to compare the nondefaulting party's position just after default with that just before it entered into the swap contract. This leads to a more benign view of the effect of counterparty default. Here the status quo ante that is restored is the nondefaulting party's position at "time zero."[30]

If the status quo ante is defined as the position of the nondefaulting party just before default, any adverse effect of the default arises because of interest or exchange rate fluctuations. This is an instance where other types of risk creep into the analysis.

Specifically, the nondefaulting party may wish to replace the lost cash flow. But this might be costly because of

---

[30] Under either definition, the status quo ante is not reinstated for an intermediary that entered into a swap contract with each party. The intermediary must continue to perform with the nondefaulting party.

changes in interest and exchange rates between the time the contract was entered into and the moment of default. *Thus, the effect of counterparty default is ultimately a function of interest and exchange rate changes.* It is *not* pure credit risk that matters. Credit risk is intimately linked with interest rate and currency risk. The actual loss suffered by the nondefaulting party in the event of counterparty default depends on market risks. Henderson explains the link as follows:

> Swap agreements invariably contain provisions providing for one party to terminate the agreement if the other party is in breach or if significant adverse credit events (such as bankruptcy) occur with respect to the other party. Since each party generally has assets and liabilities, or another matching swap agreement, being hedged by the now terminated swap agreement, failure to replace the terminated swap agreement will result in exposure going forward. If each party were to attempt to replace the swap agreement at the point of termination either with another swap agreement or by a combination of investment and borrowing, the (almost certain) change in rates since the effective date of the original agreement would result in one party being able to do so at a profit and the other party being required to do so at a loss. If, at closeout, rates have moved in favour of a party such that it can only replace the swap agreement by paying a substantial fee to a new counterparty or by requiring more funds for an investment to recreate income than are obtained from a borrowing to recreate a liability, that party has suffered a loss on early termination. Worded another way, that party has an interest (or equity) in the continuance of the agreement.[31]

This point can be tied in with the themes of irony and overinclusion. It is not really credit risk that is important here. If there is a loss from counterparty default, it is

---

[31] S. Henderson, "Termination of Swaps Under U.S. Insolvency Laws," 3 *International Financial Law Review* 17 (December 1984).

SWAPS

because of interest or exchange rate movements, not because of the default per se. *Capital support for swaps cannot be justified in terms of credit risk where bankruptcy law is not applicable to the defaulting counterparty.* Assuming bankruptcy law is inapplicable, it can be justified only if the status quo ante is defined as the situation that prevailed just prior to default and if interest rate and currency fluctuations have occurred.

An example will clarify the point. Suppose a bank enters into a swap contract for hedging purposes — that is, to match cash flows tied to a particular type of interest rate or denominated in a particular currency and thereby hedge interest rate or currency risk. Suppose further that the counterparty defaults. Define the status quo ante as the situation just before the bank entered into the swap contract. Default will cause the original mismatch to be reinstated, because the cash flow stream from the swap is lost.[32] If the worst that happens is restoration of the status quo ante, why should capital be required to support a swap used for hedging purposes? *Is the bank any worse off after counterparty default than it would have been had it never entered into the swap contract?* It appears that in either instance—entering into a swap to hedge a mismatch resulting in counterparty default, or not entering into any swap—the bank's economic position is the same. It is stuck with an interest rate or currency mismatch.

In sum, it is ironic that risk-based capital support must be maintained for a risk-reducing tool that is itself safe. The capital support requirement could well act as a disincentive to use the tool to reduce risk.

---

[32] However, suppose the function of the swap was to reduce the cost of funding by taking advantage of relative borrowing advantages in different markets. This advantage will be lost upon counterparty default.

E. Swap Credit Risk, Take No. 2: The Effect of Counterparty Default Where the Counterparty Does Go Bankrupt

Swaps are used to hedge interest rate or currency risk, and default by a nonbankrupt counterparty merely restores the nondefaulting party to its initial unhedged position. There is an irony in requiring capital support: banks are discouraged from doing a "good" thing—namely, reducing other forms of risk while not exposing themselves to serious credit risk. The Basle Agreement and the Board's final regulations result in overinclusion.

Perhaps the most serious cause of counterparty default, from the perspective of a participant bank, is bankruptcy of the counterparty. This situation deserves special attention because it triggers an entire body of law, the Bankruptcy Code. How is the irony affected if default occurs because of counterparty bankruptcy? Can the guidelines be said to be overinclusive in this case too?

Default and damage clauses, and credit enhancements, may not be helpful if the defaulting counterparty becomes bankrupt. This is true if the defaulting party is a nonfinancial institution subject to the Bankruptcy Code.[33] It is also true if the defaulting counterparty is a financial institution subject to receivership regulations of the FDIC or the Federal Savings and Loan Insurance Corporation (FSLIC). Counterparty default may impose certain costs on the solvent nondefaulting party to a swap contract *if* the counterparty declares itself or is adjudicated bankrupt. In particular, there may be costs of delay, because bankruptcy proceedings take time. Consequently, the capital support requirement for swaps can be justified in terms of credit risk *if* counterparty default because of bankruptcy is en-

---

[33] 11 U.S.C. § 101 *et seq.*

visioned. That is, *counterparty bankruptcy is an argument in favor of requiring some sort of risk-based capital support for swap contracts.*

(1) Banks as Creditors Under the Bankruptcy Code

Section 109(b)(2) of the Bankruptcy Code specifies that domestic financial institutions, such as banks and savings and loans, cannot be debtors under Chapter 7 (the liquidation chapter) of the Bankruptcy Code. The same specification is made in section 109(b)(3) for foreign financial institutions. Section 109(d) indicates that a "person" cannot be a debtor under Chapter 11 of the Bankruptcy Code (the reorganization chapter) unless the "person" can be a debtor under Chapter 7.[34] A "person" is defined in section 101(35) to include an individual, partnership, or corporation. Thus, domestic and foreign banks are excluded from the Bankruptcy Code as debtors in both liquidation and reorganization contexts. The reason for this exclusion, as stated in the legislative history, is that alternative regulatory provisions apply to the liquidation or reorganization of financial institutions.[35]

However, domestic and foreign banks may be creditors under the Bankruptcy Code. A creditor is defined in section 101(9)(A) as an "entity that has a claim against the debtor that arose at the time of or before the order for relief concerning the debtor." Under section 101(14), an "entity" includes a person, and therefore it includes a corporation. A claim is defined in section 101(4)(A) as a "right to payment, whether or not such right is reduced to judgment, liquidated, unliquidated, fixed, contingent, matured, un-

---

[34] An exception is made for stockbrokers, commodities brokers, and railroads.
[35] H.R. Rep. No. 595, 95th Cong. 1st Sess. 318-319 (1977). *See also* S. Henderson, "Termination of Swaps Under U.S. Insolvency Laws," 3 *International Financial Law Review* fn 5 at 17 (December 1984).

matured, disputed, undisputed, legal, equitable, secured, or unsecured." Thus, a bank that participated in a swap contract with a counterparty subject to the Bankruptcy Code would become a creditor if the counterparty became legally bankrupt. The bank's claim would be to the expected future cash flow from the counterparty on the swap contract, plus any unpaid prior obligations on the contract.

Nonfinancial institutions (such as P&G in Figure 5 and Chanel in another Chapter 5 example) are subject to the Bankruptcy Code under section 109(a). Bankruptcy proceedings commence when the debtor files a voluntary petition under section 301 or three or more creditors file an involuntary provision under section 303(b)(1).[36] Absent voidable preference or fraudulent conveyance problems, if a swap contract has been effectively terminated before a bankruptcy petition is filed, the filing will have no effect on the contract. However, if the contract has not been effectively terminated prior to filing, the contract will be affected. This is because of the power of the bankruptcy trustee to assume or reject executory contracts and the delay costs associated with bankruptcy proceedings.

(2) No Grabbing!

Suppose that a nonfinancial institution files a voluntary petition or creditors file an involuntary petition. Suppose further that none of the swap contracts to which the debtor is a party has been effectively terminated. Immediately upon filing, the automatic stay provision found in section 362(a) suspends all claims of creditors. Parties with whom the debtor has swap contracts will become creditors.

They cannot unilaterally terminate the swap contract and

---

[36] An involuntary petition can be filed by fewer than three creditors in the situations described in §§ 303 (b) (2) and (3).

make use of any credit enhancements, for the purpose of section 362(a) is to prevent individual creditor remedies (what Professor Jackson calls in the classroom a "grab race" among creditors) and instead promote a collective solution. All swap contracts are assembled by the bankruptcy trustee (or receiver or debtor-in-possession) as part of the debtor's estate, and creditors are obligated to continue to perform on the swap contracts—that is, to make payments to the debtor's estate. Yet no payments will be made to the creditors from the debtor's estate until the trustee decides whether to assume or reject the swap contracts.

(3) Executory Contracts and Financial Accommodations

Assumption or rejection of each swap contract follows from the treatment of a swap contract as executory. While the Bankruptcy Code does not define the term "executory contract," the definition generally used in bankruptcy law is the classic one offered by Professor Countryman. He wrote that a contract is executory if it is one "under which the obligation of both the bankrupt and the other party to the contract are so far unperformed that the failure of either to complete performance would constitute a material breach excusing the performance of the other."[37]

Jackson points out that executory contracts "are nothing more than mixed assets and liabilities arising out of the

---

[37] V. Countryman, "Executory Contracts in Bankruptcy (pt. 1)," 57 *Minnesota Law Review* 439, 460 (1973). Jackson's wording of the definition is somewhat simpler:

An executory contract ... is generally considered for purposes of bankruptcy to be a contract on which performance remains due, to some material extent, on the part of *both* contracting parties, so that failure of either side to fulfill its remaining performance obligations would constitute a breach, justifying the failure of the other party to complete *its* unperformed obligations under the contract.

T. Jackson, *The Logic and Limits of Bankruptcy Law* 105 (1986).

same transaction."[38] A conventional loan is not considered executory, since performance is due only from one side.[39] The lender has already disbursed the loaned funds, and no further performance is due. Performance is due only from the borrower, who must pay interest and repay principal. To the lender, the loan is an asset. From the borrower's perspective, it is an unperformed liability.

By contrast, a swap contract is executory because performance is due from both sides.[40] Dissection of a swap transaction reveals both asset and liability features. The expected cash inflow from the counterparty is similar to an account receivable: the expected cash outflow resembles an account payable.

The trustee in bankruptcy has the power to assume or reject all executory contracts.[41] This power exists whether the debtor is liquidating under Chapter 7 or reorganizing under Chapter 11.[42] An exception to this power is provided in section 365(c)(2) of the Bankruptcy Code. No executory contract can be assigned if "such contract is a contract to make a loan, or extend other debt financing or *financial accommodations,* to or for the benefit of the debtor, or to issue a security of the debtor."[43] A swap contract is not a loan or an extension of debt financing. The parties are mutual debtors and creditors. Nor is there a plausible argument that a swap contract is a contract to issue a security.

---

[38] T. Jackson, *The Logic and Limits of Bankruptcy Law* 106 (1986).
[39] H.R. Rep. No. 595, 95th Cong., 1st Sess. 347 (1977); S. Rep. No. 989, 95th Cong., 2d Sess. 58 (1978).
[40] Henderson writes that a swap contract "almost certainly constitutes an 'executory' contract, that is, one under which both parties have obligations remaining to be performed." S. Henderson, "Termination of Swaps Under U.S. Insolvency Laws," 3 *International Financial Law Review* 17, 19 (December 1984).
[41] 11 U.S.C. § 365(a).
[42] 11 U.S.C. § 103(a).
[43] Emphasis supplied.

Could a swap contract be a "financial accommodation"? The Bankruptcy Code does not define this term, and no case law exists on the issue.[44] Presumably, swap parties could insert a provision into their contract declaring the transaction to be a financial accommodation. In the event of counterparty bankruptcy, the nondefaulting party could then suspend its performance, be released from the automatic stay, and terminate the swap contract, without fear of assumption by the trustee.[45] Termination would follow from an *ipso facto* clause. Such a clause is respected by the Bankruptcy Code in an executory contract that is a financial accommodation. Yet, as Henderson points out, courts may be reluctant to accept a creditor's characterization of the contract when the creditor's intent is to circumvent a Bankruptcy Code provision.[46]

It can be argued on policy grounds that swaps are not financial accommodations, regardless of how parties characterize them in a contract. Section 365(c)(2) seems to provide for opt-out behavior so that creditors do not have to throw good money after bad, or be compelled to make unilateral extensions of credit to debtors in bankruptcy. Swaps are not unilateral extensions of credit, so there is no danger of this occurring.

(4) The Trustee's Power of Assumption or Rejection and the Risk of "Cherry Picking"

If a swap contract is executory and is not a financial accommodation, then the bankruptcy trustee does have the power to assume or reject the contract. In order to assume,

---

[44] S. Henderson, "Termination Provisions of Swaps Under U.S. Insolvency Laws," 3 *International Financial Law Review* 17, 19 (December 1984).
[45] *Id.*
[46] *Id.*

the trustee must cure any default and provide adequate assurance of future performance.[47] The assumption and rejection power allows the trustee to maximize the value of the debtor's estate for the benefit of unsecured creditors, whom the trustee represents.

The trustee will attempt to "cherry pick"—that is, assume all swap contracts that are favorable to the estate and reject all those that are unfavorable. Whether a contract is favorable or unfavorable will depend on the movements in interest and foreign exchange rates between the time the contract was entered into and the time of assumption or rejection. Favorable swap contracts are those that result in net receipts, and unfavorable contracts result in net payments.

If the defaulting counterparty had not entered into bankruptcy, its default would likely have excused any further performance by the nondefaulting party. As noted earlier, this would follow section 11.1 of the *1986 Swaps Code* and sections 5, 6(a), and 6(b) of the Master Rate Agreement. But where the Bankruptcy Code is involved, the nondefaulting party is *not* excused, since the trustee can assume swap contracts favorable to the estate.

Clauses that specify bankruptcy as a condition of default are known as *ipso facto*, or bankruptcy, clauses. Clauses that trigger default upon failure to maintain certain financial ratios are called financial ratio clauses. Insertion of either type of clause into the swap contract will not protect that party from the trustee's power of assumption or rejection. Parties sometimes specify that commencement of bankruptcy proceedings by either party will result in automatic termination of the swap contract. But *ipso facto* and financial ratio clauses in executory contracts are expressly rendered

---

[47] 11 U.S.C. § 365(b)(1).

ineffective by section 365(e)(1) of the Bankruptcy Code.[48] Thus, the nondefaulting party could not unilaterally terminate the swap contract pursuant to such a clause.

What effect would the trustee's rejection or assumption of a swap contract have on the nondefaulting counterparty? First, consider rejection. Would rejection of a swap contract unfavorable to the debtor's estate make the nondefaulting party worse off than before it had entered into the contract? As in the case where bankruptcy law does not apply, all that results from rejection is restoration of the status quo ante. If a nondefaulting party used the swap to hedge interest rate or currency risk, then rejection will cause the initial unhedged position to be restored (if the status quo ante is taken to be the situation before the contract was signed). Rejection simply means that the trustee will not perform on the contract in order to avoid any net loss to the estate. Any net benefit to the nondefaulting party (the creditor of the estate) is also avoided; this party is back to where it was before the swap. There is a distinction between merely losing a net benefit and being made worse off than before the net benefit arose. If this distinction is plausible, then it is difficult to justify capital support in terms of credit risk

---

[48] Section 365(e)(1) states that:
Notwithstanding a provision in an executory contract ... an executory contract ... of the debtor may not be terminated or modified, and any right or obligation under such contract ... may not be terminated or modified, at any time after the commencement of the case solely because of a provision in such contract ... that is conditioned on
(A) the *insolvency* or *financial condition* of the debtor at any time before the closing of the case;
(B) the *commencement of a case* under this title; or
(C) the *appointment of or taking possession by a trustee* in a case under this title or a custodian before such commencement. (emphasis supplied).
See also T. Jackson, *The Logic and Limits of Bankruptcy Law* 40 (1986).

when the worst-case scenario does not involve being worse off than before the net benefit arose.

Can the trustee's assumption of a swap contract favorable to the estate result in the nondefaulting party being worse off? No, because the well-being of the nondefaulting party does not turn on whether net payments are made to the trustee or to the counterparty. The situation is no worse than if there had been no default.

(5) Adequate Protection and the Risk of Delay Costs

Another issue that counterparty bankruptcy raises is the cost of delay. *Bankruptcy proceedings take time.* If a swap contract is executory and not a financial accommodation, the trustee may take weeks or months to decide whether to assume or reject. During this interim period, the nondefaulting party is exposed to two types of cost if it is obligated to continue performance on the contract. Henderson argues that such an obligation may exist:

> The status of the swap agreement in the interim between the commencement of the bankruptcy case and the assumption or rejection of the contract is unclear. Since the swap agreement is not terminated until it is rejected, if there are no other defaults under the swap agreement, the solvent party is arguably under a duty to perform. The debtor may be able to compel the solvent party to perform in such interim period if it is able to establish its own ability to perform under such agreement during such period. The solvent party may, however, be able to seek some type of adequate assurance as a precondition to its own performance in the interim between the commencement of the bankruptcy case and the assumption or rejection of the swap agreement.[49]

The first delay cost is *forgone interest.* Presumably a party to a swap contract could place any net cash flows received in

---

[49] S. Henderson, "Termination of Swaps Under U.S. Insolvency Laws," 3 *International Financial Law Review* 17, 20 (December 1984).

160

an interest-bearing account. While section 361 assures that creditors must be "adequately protected," this term is not defined in the Bankruptcy Code. The Supreme Court has held that adequate protection does not entitle an undersecured creditor to interest on the value of its collateral that accrues after the bankruptcy case begins.[50] A nondefaulting party that had required the counterparty to post collateral would fall within this ruling if the value of the collateral fell below the amount of the nondefaulting party's claim in a bankruptcy proceeding.

Some types of collateral that are recognized under the Basle Agreement as worthy of favorable treatment (that allow the asset they back to receive a lower risk-weighting) are also susceptible to fluctuations in value. These include U.S. Government or agency securities.[51] A nondefaulting party, though fully secured at the onset of a swap transaction, could become undersecured owing to subsequent fluctuations in the value of U.S. Government or agency securities taken as collateral.

A second cost associated with delay results from *changes in interest and foreign exchange rates between the time the petition is filed and the time the trustee decides whether to assume or reject the contract.* An unmatched (or unhedged) swap position creates an exposure to such rate changes. The nondefaulting party may decide to enter into another matching swap if it believes the trustee is likely to assume the swap contract of the debtor. If the nondefaulting party is wrong and the trustee does not assume, then it is left with an extra unmatched swap.

---

[50] *United Savings Association of Texas v. Timbers of Inwood Forest Associates, Ltd.*, 108 St. Ct. 626, 631 (1988) *See also* A. Schimberg, J. Clark, and D. Williams, "Legislative and Judicial Developments in 1987: Part 1," 44 *The Secured Lender* 20, 23-24 (Jan./Feb. 1988).

[51] *See* Table 1 and the discussions of credit enhancements and the treatment of swaps under the Basle Agreement.

Or the nondefaulting party may choose not to enter into a hedge because it expects the trustee to reject the contract. If the trustee does not reject, the nondefaulting party will be left with the unmatched hedge. Cunningham provides an example of potential costs resulting from rate changes:

> Solvent Party and Bankrupt Party (which at this time has not yet filed a bankruptcy petition) enter into a rate swap agreement with a term of seven years, pursuant to which Solvent Party pays at a fixed rate of 10 percent and receives LIBOR flat from Bankrupt Party.
>
> For two years, both parties perform. Bankrupt Party's financial condition deteriorates during these two years with the result that it files a bankruptcy petition two years into the term of the swap. Rates have moved so that if Solvent Party were to hedge its exposure and obtain a replacement swap at the time of the filing, Solvent Party would be required to pay a 12 per cent fixed rate in order to receive LIBOR flat. Solvent Party, however, does not know whether to hedge at the time of the filing because the trustee has not yet decided whether to assume or reject the rate swap agreement. Solvent Party must remember that, if the swap agreement is subsequently rejected, the breach will be deemed to have occurred immediately before the filing of the bankruptcy petition.
>
> One year after the filing in bankruptcy (and three years into the term of the rate swap), the trustee decides to reject the swap agreement. Rates have continued to move so that Solvent Party now will be required to pay a 14 per cent fixed rate to obtain a replacement swap that provides the necessary payments at a rate of LIBOR flat. If Solvent Party has waited to hedge, it must now pay 14 per cent but its claim will probably be based upon the 12 per cent rate prevailing at the time of the filing. If Solvent Party hedged at the time of filing, it ran the risk that the rate swap agreement would be assumed and it would be left with a hedge for which it has no need.[52]

---

[52] D. Cunningham, "Swaps: Codes, Problems and Regulation," 5 *International Financial Law Review* 26, 32 (August 1986).

(6) The Case of a Swap Counterparty Not Subject to the Bankruptcy Code

Even if a counterparty is not subject to the Bankruptcy Code, the nondefaulting party's efforts to minimize the risk of loss due to counterparty bankruptcy may be ineffectual. Banking institutions are subject to receivership regulations of the FDIC and savings and loan associations are subject to receivership regulations of the FSLIC. Both sets of regulations contain an automatic stay provision, and both the FDIC and the FSLIC have the de facto (if not de jure) power of assumption or rejection, just like a trustee operating under the Bankruptcy Code.

F. Contractual Mechanisms to Minimize Swap Credit Risk

Parties to swap agreements are aware of the risks of loss upon default, including the risks arising from counterparty bankruptcy. While financial techniques are used to hedge against the interest rate and currency risks generated by swaps, contractual mechanisms may be used to minimize losses from credit risk.[53]

(1) The ISDA's Master Agreements

Using one of the ISDA Master Agreements can help reduce credit risk in two ways. First, in the event of counterparty bankruptcy, the trustee may be prevented from "cherry picking" because all swap transactions with the same counterparty are covered by a single contract — the Master Rate Agreement or the Master Rate and Currency

---

[53] One contractual mechanism for reducing risk that is not discussed here is syndication, the sharing of risk among buyers of risk participations after initiation of the swap by a lead bank. Because of legal and financial difficulties, syndication of swap risk is rare. *See* B. Taylor, "Swap Risk," 4 *The Review of Financial Services Regulation* 17, 26 (February 3, 1988).

Agreement. A trustee must assume or reject the entire agreement and cannot unbundle the constituent swap transactions.

Indeed, the *1986 Swaps Code* explicitly differentiates between a swap contract and the underlying swap transactions. In Article 1, section 1.1, a "rate swap agreement" is defined as "an agreement... governing one *or more* Rate Swap Transactions" (emphasis supplied). A "rate swap transaction" is defined in section 1.2 as a "rate exchange or swap transaction." Cunningham explains the preclusive effect of a Master Agreement:

> The bankruptcy trustee's power to assume or reject any given swap agreement raises the concern that the trustee would be entitled to 'cherry pick' among all of the swaps between a bankrupt and a given counterparty (assuming those that current market conditions had made advantageous to the bankrupt counterparty while rejecting those that had become unfavorable). In response to this concern, many market participants have revised their forms of master agreement to provide that *all* swaps under a given master agreement constitute part of a *single* agreement *(which a trustee in bankruptcy would have to either assume or reject as a whole).*[54]

But as Cunningham also points out, this mechanism may be defeated by the trustee if the underlying swap transactions bear no relationship to one another:

> Unless it can be shown that several swaps under the same master agreement have some interrelationship, the provisions which attempt to integrate all swaps with one counterparty into a single agreement could be viewed simply as an ineffective attempt to defeat the trustee's ability to cherry pick. A bankruptcy trustee may be in a good position to resist these pro-

---

[54] D. Cunningham, "Swaps: Codes, Problems and Regulation," 5 *International Financial Law Review* 26, 32 (August 1986) (emphasis supplied).

visions and treat each swap separately unless some connection can be found between the various swaps.[55]

That is, the form of the Master Agreement will probably be attacked by the trustee in bankruptcy court if the underlying substantive transactions are unrelated.

The liquidated damage clause in the Master Agreements may help minimize the risk of loss from counterparty default. The rubric of section 6(e) of the Master Rate Agreement (and the same section in the Master Rate and Currency Agreement) is "payments on early termination." Upon default by the counterparty, the nondefaulting party may terminate the contract early (as provided for in section 6(e) of each Master Agreement) and is entitled to compensation from the defaulting counterparty.

In sections 6(e)(i)(1) and (2) of the Master Rate Agreement, damages are measured by the "agreement value — limited two-way payments." This term is defined in section 12.1(b) of the *1986 Swaps Code:*

> "Agreement Value—Limited Two Way Payments" means that on the Early Termination Date [i.e., the date of termination by the nondefaulting party on account of the counterparty's default] ... if there is a Defaulting Party, that party will be obligated to make a payment to the other party in the amount, if any, by which the Market Quotation determined by the other party exceeds zero.

The agreement value is calculated from market quotations provided by swap dealers.[56] As Cunningham explains:

> Under the Code, Agreement Value means that the termination value of the swap will be determined based on the cost to a party of obtaining a replacement swap providing the same economic

---

[55] *Id.*

[56] C. Nicolaides, "Overview of the 1986 ISDA Rate Swap Code," 1 *Butterworths Journal of International Banking and Financial Law* 44, 48 (September 1986).

terms as the terminated swap.... [T]he Agreement Value... is straightforward and easy to understand and... [market participants] believe it reflects the method that would actually be used to replace a terminated swap. The growing use of Agreement Value reflects in part the growth and maturity of the overall swap market and development of a secondary market for swaps.[57]

The phrase "limited two-way payments" refers to a situation in which the nondefaulting party gained from the counterparty's default. If the nondefaulting party benefited from the default because of changes in interest or exchange rates between the origination of the swap and the time of default, no payment is to be made to the defaulting party. The legal principle here is that a nondefaulting party should not have to pay damages to a defaulting counterparty.[58]

Agreement value is not the only way to measure damages from counterparty default in an interest rate swap transaction under the Master Rate Agreement. Section 6(e)(i)(3) of the Master Rate Agreement states that if a market quotation is unavailable and therefore the agreement value is not calculable, "indemnification—limited two-way payments" is to be used as the basis for calculating damages. This is defined in section 12.1(e) of the *1986 Swaps Code:*

> "Indemnification—Limited Two Way Payments" means that on the Early Termination Date... if there is a Defaulting Party, that party will be obligated to make a payment to the other in an amount equal to the positive amount, if any, of the other party's loss.

The approach to damages in the Master Rate and Cur-

---

[57] D. Cunningham, "Swaps: Codes, Problems and Regulation," 5 *International Financial Law Review* 26 (August 1986).

[58] *See* A. Gooch and L. Klein, "Damage Provisions in Swap Agreements," 3 *International Financial Law Review* 36, 37 (October 1984).

rency Agreement is similar to that just described although different terms are used. The "settlement amount" is the basis for the measure of damages under sections 6(e)(i)(1) and (2). This is defined in section 14 as the market quotation for the value of the terminated swap (again a proxy for replacement cost) or, if no quote is available, the amount of loss sustained by a party. The latter resembles the identification measure in the Master Rate Agreement. The settlement amount is measured in the "termination currency equivalent," which is the currency in which the parties agreed to measure damages when the contract was signed. It is listed in part 1 of the schedule attached to the Master Rate and Currency Agreement.

New York law governs both Master Agreements. This is indicated in Article 13, section 13.1, of the *1986 Swaps Code* for the Master Rate Agreement and in section 13(a) and part 4 of the schedule for the Master Rate and Currency Agreement. Cunningham points out that, under New York law, the agreement value approach to calculating damages may not be a reasonable *a priori* estimate of actual damages and may therefore be voidable as a penalty.[59]

Whether this is true depends on perceptions of the depth of the secondary market for swaps.[60] If the secondary market is seen as thin, the legitimacy of the agreement value as a proxy for actual replacement cost is questionable. By definition, a thin market would not yield objective, competitively determined prices. The concern Cunningham raises may be partly mollified in section 6(e)(iii) of the Master Rate Agreement: "The parties agree that the amounts recover-

---

[59] D. Cunningham, "Swaps: Codes, Problems and Regulation," 5 *International Financial Law Review* 26, 29 (August 1988).

[60] For a recent note on the secondary market for swaps, *see* "Legal Doctrines Restricting the Secondary Market in Interest Rate Swaps," 26 *Columbia Journal of Transnational Law* 313 (October 1988).

able ... are a reasonable pre-estimate of loss and not a penalty." The same disclaimer is found in section 6(e)(v) of the Master Rate and Currency Agreement.

(2) Netting

Netting refers to the treatment of swap contracts not on an individual basis but as a whole. In the words of the Basle Agreement, netting involves "weighting the net rather than the gross claims arising out of swaps ... with the same counterparties."[61] It is a form of contractual setoff triggered by a set of default events (including bankruptcy) specified in a swap contract.[62] As Houghton explains:

> Under the terms of [a] netting off agreement. ... the bank [i.e., the nondefaulting counterparty] is entitled to treat all unmatured deals as terminated. The bank will then be free to replace the contracts in the open market and will be able to prove for the net loss (if any) in the counterparty's liquidation. Alternatively, the bank will be able to set off the net position against a margin deposit or other security, if the netting off clause so provides.[62]

There are at least two types of netting provisions.[63] Under "payment netting," the parties keep track of the cumulative net balance owed on the swap but also keep each underlying obligation intact.[64] Under "netting by novation," swap contracts with the same counterparty that mature on the same day are matched. For each matched pair, the obligation to exchange two payments is extinguished and replaced by

---

[61] Basle Agreement, Annex 3 at 5.

[62] J. Houghton, "Regulatory Provisions on Off-Balance-Sheet Capital Requirements: Netting Off Agreements—The Legal Perspective," 2 *Journal of International Banking Law* 241, 242-243 (1987).

[63] For recent developments on the netting of cash payments, *see* "ManHan's Answer to Reduce Risk Capital," *International Financing Review* 1992 (June 18, 1988).

[64] *Id.* at 243.

one net payment.[65] One novated contract replaces, as a matter of fact and law, the two extinguished contracts. A novated contract is a substituted contract.[66]

Netting provisions may not raise legal problems when triggered by default events other than counterparty bankruptcy, but they are likely to when counterparty bankruptcy is the default event. This is why the December 1987 Basle Proposal did not recognize any form of netting in the treatment of swaps. Houghton discusses the problems under English insolvency law:

> Because it is a form of contractual setoff a netting off agreement is efficacious only if the counterparty defaults other than by reason of the commencement of its winding-up. Prior to the commencement of the counterparty's winding-up, contractual setoff provisions are enforceable as a matter of contract law... On the commencement of the counterparty's winding-up the *pari passu* principle applies, which means that all unsecured creditors receive equal treatment as regards the proportions of their claims which are admitted by the liquidator. The netting off clause does not create real rights over the counterparty's right to receive payment under the swap...contract, and so the bank is treated as unsecured for these purposes. Accordingly the netting off clause will be void as from the commencement of the counterparty's winding-up as it is then contrary to public policy. It is an attempt to contract out of the *pari passu* principle.[67]

---

[65] Basle Agreement, Annex 3 at 5, note 5. A similar definition is provided in the Board's final regulations at 54 Fed. Reg. 4186, note 51 at 4205 (for banks), note 55 at 4218 (for BHCs); (January 27, 1989).

[66] J. Calamari and J. Perillo, *Contracts* § 21-8 (3d ed. 1987). Calamari and Perillo point out that while courts use the terms "novated contract" and "substituted contract" synonymously, academic writers and the *Restatement (Second) of Contracts* use "novated contract" only if there is one obligor or obligee who was not a party to the original contract. *Id.*

[67] J. Houghton, *supra* note 350.

In terms of the U.S. Bankruptcy Code, the netting provision may become inoperative upon commencement of a bankruptcy case. Payment netting, as Houghton points out, plainly does not prevent a bankruptcy trustee from cherry picking, because the underlying obligations remain and are distinguishable. The trustee can pick the sweet cherries (the swaps that result in a positive net present value to the debtor's estate) and toss away the spoiled ones (those with negative net present values).

Netting by novation may keep the trustee away from the cherry trees if the novated contract replaces the two initial contracts as a matter of law prior to bankruptcy. Consequently, a bank negotiating swap contracts should try to keep the underlying transactions bundled into one contract and require cash flows to be replaced by single net payments. The ISDA has submitted draft legislation to Congress to resolve the uncertainties about netting provisions under the Bankruptcy Code.[68]

After the December 1987 Basle Proposal was circulated, numerous commentators asserted that netting reduces risk and should therefore be recognized in any risk-based capital guidelines. The Cooke Committee was persuaded by these comments that novated contracts do replace, in law as well as in fact, the initial two swap contracts.[69] Thus, netting by novation is recognized by the Basle Agreement for the purpose of calculating the credit equivalent amount of a swap.[70] However, no other form of netting is recognized. The same rule is set forth in the Board's final regulations.[71]

---

[68] S. 2279, 100th Cong. 1st Sess. (1988). *See* A. Pollard, "Treatment of Swaps in Bankruptcy," 3 *Butterworths Journal of International Banking and Financial Law* 515 (December 1988).

[69] August 1, 1988, Board Staff Memorandum, 31.

[70] *Id.*

[71] 54 Fed. Reg. 4186, 4205, and 4208 (for banks), 4218 and 4220 (for BHCs); (January 27, 1989).

As is stated in the agreement:

> Careful consideration has been given to the arguments put forward for recognising netting, i.e., for weighting the net rather than the gross claims arising out of swaps and similar contracts with the same counterparties. The criterion on which a decision has been based is the status of a netting contract under national bankruptcy regulations. If a liquidator of a failed counterparty has (or may have) the right to unbundle the netted contracts, demanding performance on those contracts favourable to his client and defaulting on unfavourable contracts, there is no reduction in counterparty risk.[72]

(3) Credit Enhancements

Credit enhancements, such as collateral, letters of credit, and guarantees, are yet another contractual mechanism used by swap participants to minimize the risk of loss from counterparty default. In a transaction between two end users, either or both may require the other to post collateral or obtain a letter of credit or a third-party guarantee. In a transaction through an intermediary, the intermediary may require a credit enhancement from one or both of the end users. If default occurs, collateral can be liquidated, or a letter of credit or guarantee can be drawn upon.

G. What Exactly Does the Basle Agreement Say About Swaps?

(1) The Concept of Replacement Cost

In principle, swap contracts are treated in the same manner as on-balance-sheet assets or such other off-balance-sheet items as letters of credit. A risk-weighting is assigned to each swap contract and figured into the denominator of the capital/assets ratio. In practice, the treatment of swap

---

[72] Basle Agreement, Annex 3, 5.

contracts under the Basle Agreement is not quite as straightforward as the treatment of on-balance-sheet assets or other off-balance-sheet items. What value should be attached to the risk weight?

Two methods are specified for valuing a swap contract: the current exposure method and the original exposure method. Under the Basle Agreement, banking regulators are free to specify which method should be used or alternatively to allow banking organizations to choose.[73] Most participants in the Basle negotiations, including the Federal Reserve, favored the current exposure method.[74] Indeed, this was the method recommended in the Joint U.S.-U.K. Proposal and in the Federal Reserve's March 1988 proposed regulations.[75] It was also favored by a majority of those who commented on the December 1987 Basle Proposal.[76] It is the method adopted in the Board's final regulations.[77]

The reason for the open tilt in favor of the current exposure method is that it more accurately captures actual credit risk exposure. It entails calculation of the current market value (the mark-to-market value) of a swap contract and estimation of future market value.

The original exposure method is simpler but less accurate. A credit conversion factor is applied to the notional principal amount of the swap contract.[78] No periodic marketing to market is involved.[79] Thus, the original expo-

---

[73] Basle Agreement, 16.
[74] Basle Agreement, Annex 3 at 3, 4, and note 4 at 4; August 1, 1988, Board Staff Memorandum, 45.
[75] *Id.*
[76] *Id.*
[77] 54 Fed. Reg. 4186, 4205, and 4208 (for banks), 4217-4218, and 4220 (for BHCs); (January 27, 1989).
[78] The credit conversion factors are listed in the Basle Agreement, Annex 3 at 4.
[79] August 1,1988, Board Staff Memorandum, 44.

sure method "could result in unrealistic assessments of credit risk because it is not based upon the calculation of actual credit exposure, or the known replacement cost."[80]

The key to grasping the current exposure method is understanding the concept of replacement cost. Intuitively, it means the cost to the nondefaulting party of replacing the cash flows that it was entitled to under the swap contract but that were lost because of counterparty default.[81] The implicit definition of the status quo ante is the position the nondefaulting party was in just before default. The replacement cost concept in the Basle Agreement is designed to return the nondefaulting party to this position—that is, to reinstate the cash flows that existed under the terminated swap contract.

That credit risk is operationalized as replacement cost can be seen from the definition of exposure in the Board's technical working paper on the treatment of swaps.[82] It is defined as "an estimate of the amount that might be lost on a contract that combines *both* present and *likely future replacement costs*."[83] The critical concept in this definition is "replacement costs." A problem arises because the measure of replacement cost *a priori* (before any default has actually occurred) is speculative. To estimate potential future exposure, the bank must make assumptions concerning future interest and exchange rates.

Nevertheless, the replacement cost concept works because a bank is not exposed to a loss in the amount of the full

---

[80] *Id.* at 45.
[81] *Id.* at 44-45.
[82] Federal Reserve Board, "Potential Credit Exposure on Interest Rate and Foreign Exchange Rate Related Instruments," 1987. This Technical Working Paper provides the methodological support for the U.S.-U.K. agreement on the treatment of swaps, published at 52 Fed. Reg. 9304 (proposed March 24, 1987). *See* note 2 at 9306.
[83] Technical Working Paper, 4 (emphasis supplied).

notional principal or face value of the swap contract. Exposure to credit risk is limited to the potential cost of replacing the cash flow from swap contracts that show a positive value (swap contracts that are beneficial to the nondefaulting party in that their net present value—the present value of payments to be received minus the present value of payments to be made—is positive).[84] If counterparty default occurs three years into a five-year swap contract whose notional value is $10 million, the bank will not lose $10 million and will not have to write off $10 million from one of its capital accounts. Rather, what the bank loses—and will seek to replace—is the cash flow from the counterparty in years four and five. To apply a risk weight to the notional value of the swap contract simply because risk weights are applied to the book values of on-balance-sheet assets and other types of off-balance-sheet items would be (to borrow a favorite classroom phrase of Dean Clark) "mere mindless analogizing."

Thus, the credit risk from a swap contract to which a participant bank is exposed (whether as a principal or an intermediary) can be thought of as the cost the bank would incur upon counterparty default to replace the old swap with a new swap that generated the *same* cash flow. This cost depends on when counterparty default occurs—it could occur today, or it could occur in the future. In either case, the current exposure method attempts to measure the cost to the bank of replacing the cash flow lost because of counterparty default with an identical cash flow from a different counterparty. Henderson explains this theory as follows:

> The sensible means of quantifying [swap credit] risk is through measuring the cost of replacing the cash flows under the swap if

---

[84] Basle Agreement, Annex 3 at 2; August 1, 1988, Board Staff Memorandum, 44. *See also* B. Taylor, "Swap Risk," 4 *The Review of Financial Services Regulation* 17, 19 (February 3, 1988).

Party X [i.e., the first party to the swap] defaults and the swap terminates. Since swaps involve reciprocal obligations and the possibility of bilateral cash flows, depending on rate movements there will almost certainly be a gain or loss to the counterparty if the swap terminates: a gain if, in recreating the future cash flows, the value of the termination of the counterparty's liability to pay under the swap exceeds its cost of replacing its income under the swap; and a loss, if termination of its liability is worth less than its cost of replacing its income under the swap.

This quantification cannot be precisely calculated in advance, that is to say prior to an actual default, since the counterparty does not know how rates will move and what their level will be at an indefinite time in the future. At best, a rough estimate can be made when entering into the swap of the range of exposures depending on theoretical rate movements.[85]

The current exposure method attempts to reflect present and possible future market values and requires a somewhat complicated calculation. Current replacement cost is known because current interest and foreign exchange rates are known. Future replacement costs are not known. Rather, they must be estimated based on forecasts of future interest and exchange rates.

What does an overall negative or an overall positive replacement cost (without regard to current and future components) mean? Overall replacement cost equals market value (if this value is positive). That is, it is the theoretical loss or profit that would result from counterparty default.[86] If default would result in a loss to the nondefaulting party, the replacement cost is positive. The loss arises because of a positive net present value of the expected cash flows. The interpretation of this positive value is that the nondefaulting party would have to *pay* another counterparty to enter

---

[85] S. Henderson, *supra note*, 287.
[86] Technical Working Paper, 4.

175

into a swap contract with the same terms, because interest or exchange rates have moved favorably (from the nondefaulting party's view) since the inception of the swap contract.

For instance, suppose in a five-year plain vanilla swap the nondefaulting party paid a fixed rate of 8 percent and received a floating rate indexed to the discount on Treasury bills (say, T-bill + 1/4 percent) on the same notional principal amount. The nondefaulting party is the fixed-rate payor and stands to benefit from any increase in medium-term (say, three- to five-year) fixed rates that occurs after the 8 percent rate is contractually established. This is because 8 percent will then represent a below-market rate.

Assume that the yield curve (the relationship between interest rates and maturities) slopes upward; medium- and long-term interest rates rise above short-term rates. This might occur because of inflation expectations or because of anticipated credit-tightening by the Federal Reserve. Assume that medium-term rates rise to 10 percent during the third year of the contract but short-term rates, as reflected by the discount on T-bills, stay relatively stable.

If the counterparty defaults during the third year, the nondefaulting party is worse off. Under the swap contract it has been paying 8 percent, but the three-year interest rate has risen to 10 percent. This is favorable to the nondefaulting party because it is now paying a below-market rate (8 percent instead of 10 percent). Presumably, no other counterparty would be willing to enter into a swap contract under which it received 8 percent and paid T-bill + 1/4 percent without some sort of additional compensation.

Absent such compensation, it would be preferable to engage in a borrow-investment strategy: borrow short-term funds at just above the T-bill rate and invest them in a three-year CD paying 10 percent. Thus, the nondefaulting party will incur a loss if it is forced to replace the cash flows from the swap.

If default would result in a theoretical gain to the nondefaulting party, the replacement cost is negative. The nondefaulting party would have to *be paid* by another counterparty to enter into a swap contract with the same terms, because interest or exchange rates had moved against the position of the nondefaulting party. In practice, a zero value is used for such a swap contract because the profits are assumed to be theoretical — not realizable.[87]

As an example, imagine a five-year fixed/fixed currency swap contract between a Japanese bank (say, Dai-Ichi Kangyo Bank), the nondefaulting party, and an American multinational company, which eventually defaults on the contract. Under the contract, the nondefaulting Japanese bank pays a fixed rate of 9.25 percent in yen and receives dollars at a fixed rate of 9.25 percent on the same notional principal amount.

Assume that during the second year, the dollar depreciates relative to the yen. This may occur through intervention in the foreign exchange markets by the Federal Reserve and other central banks to weaken the dollar relative to the currencies of major U.S. trading partners, to stimulate foreign demand for U.S. exports and reduce American demand for foreign imports. Such a movement would be adverse for the nondefaulting Japanese bank, because swap payments must now be made in a relatively more valuable currency (yen) and are received in a relatively less valuable currency (dollars). In other words, the Japanese bank is glad to be rid of its obligation under the swap agreement, and it would have to be paid to enter into another contract with the same terms.

(2) Calculating the Capital Support Required for Swaps

The theory underlying the current exposure method is

---

[87] *Id.*

that replacement cost is best measured by the market. But what does this mean? How is the amount of capital support required for a swap contract determined?

The Basle Agreement requires that under the current exposure method, a credit equivalent amount must be calculated for each swap contract.[88] A risk weight that depends on the counterparty obligor is applied to the credit equivalent amount. The same risk-weighting system that is used for on-balance-sheet assets is used for swaps. This includes favorable risk-weightings for swaps backed by acceptable collateral and guarantees.[89] Because swap counterparties are generally good credit risks, the risk weight is not to exceed 50 percent (though some countries that signed the Basle Agreement reserved the right to apply a 100 percent weight).[90] Thus, the amount of capital support required for a swap equals the product of the swap's credit equivalent amount and the appropriate risk weight.

Choosing the appropriate risk weight is not difficult. The trick is to calculate the credit equivalent amount. There are two parts to the credit equivalent amount: "current credit exposure" and "potential future exposure."[91] That is, the credit equivalent amount is the sum of current credit exposure and potential future exposure.[92]

Current credit exposure captures current replacement cost. How much, if anything, would the nondefaulting counterparty have to pay upon counterparty default to enter into the same swap contract? This is the mark-to-market value of the swap contract.[93]

---

[88]The method described here is set forth in the Board's final regulations. See 54 Fed. Reg. 4186, 4188, 4192-4193, 4205, and 4208 (for banks), 4217-4218, and 4220-4221 (for BHCs); (January 27, 1989).
[89]Basle Agreement, Annex 3 at 6.
[90]Id.
[91]August 1, 1988, Board Staff Memorandum, 17.
[92]Basle Agreement, Annex 3 at 3.
[93]Id. at 16.

SWAPS

Potential future exposure captures possible replacement costs if default occurs in the future. Since interest and foreign exchange rates are likely to change during the life of the swap contract, the replacement cost is likely to be different if counterparty default occurs in the future from what it would be today. As Taylor stated with respect to the December 1987 Basle Proposal, "In establishing conversion factors, the Basle Committee used a crystal ball resembling that which banks employ in assessing the underlying credit risk — a volatility analysis of interest rates and exchange rates."[94] The potential future exposure component of the credit equivalent amount is an add-on factor designed to reflect changes in replacement cost resulting from changes in these rates. No potential future exposure add-on is calculated for basis swaps.[95]

Potential future exposure is taken to be a percentage of the notional principal amount of a matched pair of swaps. The percentage depends on the type of swap and the residual (not original) maturity. The percentages are listed in Table 4.

Table 4
Percentage of Notional Principal Amount Used to Calculate Potential Future Exposure[97]

Residual Maturity	Plain Vanilla Swaps	Currency and Cross-Currency Interest Rate Swaps
Less than one year	0.0%	1.0%
One year of more	0.5%	5.0%

[96]This table is adapted from the Basle Agreement, Annex 3 at 3. No add-on factor is calculated for basis swaps.

---

[94]B. Taylor, "Swap Risk," 4 *The Review of Financial Services Regulation* 17, 19 (February 3, 1988).

[95]Basle Agreement, Annex 3 at 4. *See also* 54 Fed. Reg. 4186, 4205, and 4208 (for banks), 4217 and 4220 (for BHCs); (January 27, 1989).

PERSPECTIVES ON RISK-BASED CAPITAL

The methodology for deriving the percentages in Table 4 is set forth in the Technical Working Paper. In brief, the confidence intervals were constructed for the percentage of notional principal amount for matched pairs of swaps.[97] Construction of a confidence interval for any variable requires knowledge of the distribution (the probability density function) of that variable. Since potential future replacement cost depends on future movements of interest and exchange rates, the distribution of these rates was required. A log-normal distribution was assumed, tested, and found to fit well.[98] This distribution was used to generate a random series of interest and exchange rates over the lives of the matched pairs of swaps. Future market values of the matched pairs were then calculated for each future rate. Expected future replacement costs are these market values, and confidence intervals at various levels of confidence (e.g., 95, 98, and 99 percent) were constructed.[99] As explained in the Technical Working Paper:

> The results are expressed in terms of a percentage of notional principal for the *pair* of swaps. Thus a 95% confidence limit of 1.0% means that 95 times out of 100 the exposure on either one of the matched pair of swaps should be less than 2.0% of its own notional principal—because this is 1.0% of the notional principal of the pair and, of course, if one side is exposed the other cannot be.[100]

The point to note is the creeping in of interest rate and exchange risk. In order to measure the effect of counter-

---

[97] The summary of the methodology provided here applies only to plain vanilla swaps and floating/floating currency swaps. Adjustments are required to deal with fixed/fixed currency swaps and fixed/floating currency swaps. *See* Technical Working Paper, 22.
[98] Technical Working Paper, 14-15.
[99] The confidence intervals are presented in the tables attached to the Tehcnical Working Paper.
[100] Technical Working Paper, 21.

party default, (to capture credit risk), the concept of replacement cost is used. In order to measure replacement cost *a priori*, interest and exchange rate volatilities are studied.

H. The Turgid Miasma of Detail: The ISDA's Comment Letter

The ISDA's May 28, 1987, Comment Letter to the Federal Reserve Board and the Bank of England was directed at the Technical Working Paper. Judging from this letter, the debate between the ISDA and the banking regulators was in the trenches of detail, not on the high ground of theory. The bulk of the ISDA's effort is directed toward the methodology for calculating potential future exposure in the Technical Working Paper.

Considerably less space in the letter is devoted to broader issues. Surely the issue of what consideration, if any, should be given to the purpose for which a swap agreement was entered into counts as a broader issue. Yet the position that the purpose for which swaps are entered into should be considered is mentioned only once, on page 4 of the 11-page letter:

> The purpose for which a swap is entered into and the relationship to the counterparty should be considered in determining risk, but the [U.S.-U.K. Joint] Proposal ignores them. ISDA believes the regulation should not discourage financial institutions from entering into swaps in connection with their funding, investment and hedging activities. Swaps used to hedge assets or liabilities not held or incurred in a swap dealer capacity should be excluded from the Proposal. In addition, swaps between affiliates do not add to risk and should be excepted from the Proposal.

The lack of space devoted to this issue is startling. No argument is made that a bank examiner could discern whether a swap is entered into for hedging purposes based on a bank's swap records. No analogy is made to other areas of law, such as

Section 988 of the IRC. In short, the irony is missed entirely.

The only other broad issue raised in the ISDA letter concerns the risk weight to be applied to the credit equivalent amount of a swap contract. The discussion here includes the matter of recognizing certain types of collateral. Again, little space is devoted to this issue.[101] The letter notes that because of the high quality of swap counterparties and low default experience on swaps, a maximum 50 percent weight should be used. This recommendation was incorporated into the Basle Agreement. The ISDA's recommendation that collateral other than cash and U.S. Government and agency securities be recognized was rejected.

The balance of the May 28, 1987, ISDA Comment Letter is devoted to detailed criticisms of the methodology used to calculate potential future exposure in the Technical Working Paper. In particular, three criticisms are offered: (1) the use of confidence intervals is attacked; (2) the failure to account for the effects of changing interest and foreign exchange rates on potential future exposure is noted; and (3) the failure to discount potential future exposure (i.e. potential future replacement costs) back to the present is said to be a "serious flaw."[102]

The ISDA proposed a model for calculating the credit equivalent amount for matched pairs of swaps.[103] The credit equivalent amount would be the sum of the mark-to-market value of current replacement cost and a factor to measure the expected future replacement costs. The ideas of breaking down the calculation of the credit equivalent amount and using mark-to-market value for current replacement cost were consistent with the methods used in the Technical

---

[101]May 28, 1987 ISDA Comment Letter, 3, 8-10.
[102]*Id.* at Annex B, 1-2.
[103]*Id.* at 2 and Annex B.

Working Paper. There was, however, no resemblance in the methodology for calculating future replacement costs.

The ISDA characterized the calculation of the credit equivalent amount in the Technical Working Paper as follows: "[T]he total exposure on a swap is the sum of its mark-to-market value and the average replacement cost of a par swap for a given confidence interval."[104] The ISDA argues that confidence intervals should not be used to establish the percentage of notional principal amount on a matched pair of swaps that represents future replacement costs. Rather, the expected value—an exact estimate based on an integral, not a confidence range based on a distribution — should be used. This argument is based on the similarity between swaps and options. The ISDA distinguishes between par swaps (swaps that are at or near par) and premium, or discount, swaps (swaps that have moved substantially away from par).[105] The alleged similarity to options is explained in terms of risk profiles:

> The risk profile of a matched pair of swaps is similar to the return profile of an at-the-money put and call option combination. Option valuation and pricing is based on expected values, rather than values associated with specified confidence intervals. Requiring that specified confidence intervals be achieved grossly overstates the potential risk involved and would result in incorrect pricing of swaps relative to other assets.[106]

The problem with the argument is that it is unclear. Why are the risk profiles on swaps similar to the return profiles of options? Does a dissection of a swap transaction reveal option-like features? If so, why is this relevant? How does

---

[104] *Id.* at Annex B, 2.
[105] *Id.* at 2.
[106] *Id.* at Annex B, 1-2.

the analogy to options compare with the other approaches to credit risk?[107]

The ISDA also believes that confidence intervals overstated future replacement costs because of the volatility assumptions made in the construction of the intervals. The Comment Letter discusses changes in the measurement of interest and exchange rates that purport to result in more reliable volatility assumptions.[108]

Expected future replacement costs change as interest and exchange rates change. The ISDA contends that the changes in cost should be taken into account. For example, "as a swap moves further away from par its mark-to-market value becomes greater than its average expected replacement cost."[109] Presumably, when par is differentiated from premium or discount swaps, the cost changes can be considered. Par swaps have a mark-to-market value approximately equal to their average expected replacement cost. By contrast, mark-to-market value is a poor proxy for replacement cost for premium or discount swaps. The problem with this criticism is that it misses the whole point of what potential future exposure represents. The idea is to capture future changes in interest and exchange rates. The factor should not be adjusted every time rates change. It is a shortcut proxy for these changes, calculated *a priori*.

The ISDA's third technical criticism is that future replacement costs, however calculated, should be discounted to the present. As is stated in the Comment Letter,

---

[107] Ferron and Handjinicolaou review the options approach to measuring swap credit risk but reject it in favor of an approach they label the "Monte Carlo" simulation technique. *See* M. Ferron and G. Handjinicolaou, "Understanding Swap Credit Risk: The Simulation Approach," 1 *The Journal of International Securities Markets* 135, 137-139.

[108] May 28, 1987, ISDA Comment Letter, Annex B, 2-3.

[109] *Id.* at Annex B, 2.

"it is standard market practice to use discounting in determining the net replacement cost to be paid on the specified future date."[110] However, the choice of an appropriate discount rate may be problematical.

The ISDA presents an alternative model — in fact, a choice of two methods — for measuring potential future exposure. The simple method (Option B) is to take a flat percentage of the notional principal amount of a matched pair as the proxy for potential future exposure. Different percentages are assigned to different types of swaps.[111] Under the more complicated method (Option A), credit conversion factors are assigned to the notional principal amounts of matched pairs of swaps. This is more complicated, because swaps must be divided into par and premium or discount swaps and then further divided into certain categories.[112]

The criticisms of the methodology used in the Technical Working Paper to measure potential future exposure are, to borrow a classroom phrase of Professor Brudney's, "turgid miasma." (This discourse on the criticisms may not be safe from that phrase either.) What is clear is that the ISDA violated a basic rule of legal argumentation in its May 28, 1987, Comment Letter: put forth the best argument first.

The ISDA's best argument was the irony of requiring capital support for transactions that hedge against interest rate and currency risk by eliminating mismatches. The letter could have added that (1) hedging is a discernible purpose for doing swaps and (2) any credit risk, including any risk of counterparty bankruptcy, is at least partially hedged through the use of the ISDA's Master Agreements, netting by novation, and credit enhancements. In sum, the

---

[110] *Id.* at 2 and Annex B.
[111] *Id.* at 6-7 and Annex B, 5.
[112] *Id.* at 6.

case could have been made for an approach to swaps that resembles the approach to capital constituents: Look past the formality of the swap contract to the underlying substance of the transaction.

I. Chapter Summary

The second of the two building blocks of the Basle Agreement, risk, can be examined in detail through a study of the treatment of swaps. Here the central focus on credit risk is highlighted. Swaps entail very little credit risk, and indeed may hedge against interest rate and currency risk. Yet capital support must be provided for each swap contract because of a deemed credit risk. This is somewhat ironic and perhaps leads to the comment that the Basle Agreement is overinclusive with respect to swaps. Why not attempt to differentiate between swaps used to hedge interest rate or currency risk and swaps entered into for purely speculative purposes?

That swaps can be used to hedge against interest rate and currency risk was shown in Chapter 5. Swaps can be said to entail little credit risk for two reasons. First, the actual default experience is minimal. Second, as a theoretical matter, the effect of counterparty default on the nondefaulting party may not be that bad. Counterparty default will result in restoration of the status quo ante, which can be defined as the situation just before the swap contract was entered into. Thus, the nondefaulting party is no worse off than it was just before it signed the swap contract. Specifically, the initial unhedged position is restored.

The worst-case scenario is counterparty default because of bankruptcy (the counterparty defaults on its swap obligations because it goes bankrupt). If the ISDA's Master Agreements and netting by novation are used, the bankruptcy trustee will not be able to cherry pick among the various swap transactions. At most, the nondefaulting party will face some delay costs.

The amount of capital support required for a swap contract depends on how much it would cost to replace that swap if the counterparty defaulted on the contract. Computation of replacement cost involves two steps: calculation of current credit exposure and calculation of potential future credit exposure. Current credit exposure is the mark-to-market value of the swap (only positive values are used). Potential future exposure is found when a credit conversion factor is applied to the full face value of the swap. The conversion factor to be used depends on the type and maturity of the swap. The sum of the current and potential future exposures yields the replacement cost, or the credit equivalent amount, of the swap. A risk weight of not greater than 50 percent is then applied to this credit equivalent amount to determine the risk-weighted value of the swap.

Conclusion: The Building Blocks of Risk-Based Capital

Any risk-based capital regulation rests on a concept of capital and risk, the basic elements of the Basle Agreement. Propogation of risk-based capital guidelines by banking regulators presupposes that the regulators have made two strategic decisions: They have established criteria to evaluate possible capital constituents, and they have focused on a particular type or types of risk to which banks are exposed.

In the Basle Agreement, only one criterion, the ability to absorb losses, is used to evaluate possible capital constituents. The form the item takes—for instance, whether it is a financial instrument like preferred stock, or an intangible asset like goodwill—is not so important. What matters is its ability to perform the substantive function of absorbing losses. The more able the item can do this, the more likely it is to be placed in Tier One rather than Tier Two. One type of risk is emphasized in the Basle Agreement: credit risk. *The link between capital and risk is that capital must be available to absorb losses arising from counterparty default.*

The emphasis on credit risk is why Treasury securities are not differentiated by risk weights according to maturity. To place higher risk weights on longer-maturity Treasuries would be to recognize the higher interest rate risk associated with longer maturities. It is also why swaps are not differentiated according to the substantive function they play. Whether a bank uses a swap to lower interest rate or currency risk is irrelevant, for these forms of risk are not within the scope of the Basle Agreement. What matters is form—a swap contract is signed, it is deemed that there is credit risk associated with the swap transaction, so capital support is required.

Examination of what really happens to a nondefaulting party in the event of counterparty default reveals that the former may not be any worse off than before it signed the contract. True, the nondefaulting party will be deprived of any benefit (net cash flows) it enjoyed. But as long as the counterparty does not go bankrupt and the Bankruptcy Code does not apply, the original unhedged position of the nondefaulting party is restored. If bankruptcy law is triggered, then the nondefaulting party may face delay costs, since bankruptcy proceedings take time. But that may be the extent of the damage it suffers.

Whatever the actual loss to a nondefaulting party from counterparty default, it is curious that the Basle Agreement makes use of the replacement cost concept to measure the credit risk on swaps. There are two possible ways to define the status quo ante: 1) the situation that prevailed before the swap contract was entered into; or 2) the situation that prevailed just before the counterparty defaulted. The first definition is used to suggest that swaps may not really be that risky. The definition implicit in replacement cost is the second. The idea behind replacement cost is that the nondefaulting party should be put back in the position it was in just before default.

It is also curious that in measuring replacement cost, the Basle Agreement looks to a distribution of interest and foreign exchange rate movements. *Yet to look at such movements is to look at interest rate and currency risk.* It is as if the Basle Agreement stated, "The credit risk on swaps is measured by replacement cost, since a nondefaulting party will want to be put back in the position it was in just before default. How much it costs to replace the swap that was defaulted on depends on interest and foreign exchange rate movements. Thus, credit risk as proxied by replacement cost is a function of interest rate and currency risk." Is this a significant deviation from the Basle Agreement's

CONCLUSION

stated emphasis on credit risk? If so, shouldn't the hedging function of swaps be recognized explicitly?

Appendix
The Basle Agreement on Risk-Based Capital

Committee on Banking Regulations and Supervisory Practices

July 1988

International Convergence of Capital Measurement and Capital Standards

Introduction

1. This report presents the outcome of the Committee's[1] work over several years to secure international convergence of supervisory regulations governing the capital adequacy of international banks. Following the publication of the Committee's proposals in December 1987, a consultative process was set in train in all G-10 countries and the proposals were also circulated to supervisory authorities worldwide. As a result of those consultations some changes were made to the original proposals. The present paper is now a statement of the Committee agreed by all its members. It sets out the details of the agreed framework for measuring capital adequacy and the minimum standard to be achieved which the national supervisory authorities represented on the Committee intend to implement in their respective countries. The framework and this standard have been

---

[1]The Basle Committee on Banking Regulations and Supervisory Practices comprises representatives of the central banks and supervisory authorities of the Group of Ten countries (Belgium, Canada, France, Germany, Italy, Japan, Netherlands, Sweden, Switzerland, United Kingdom, United States) and Luxembourg. The Committee meets at the Bank for International Settlements, Basle, Switzerland.

endorsed by the Group of Ten central-bank Governors.

2. With a view to implementation as soon as possible, it is intended that national authorities should now prepare papers setting out their views on the timetable and the manner in which this accord will be implemented in their respective countries. This document is being circulated to supervisory authorities worldwide with a view to encouraging the adoption of this framework in countries outside the G-10 in respect of banks conducting significant international business.

3. Two fundamental objectives lie at the heart of the Committee's work on regulatory convergence. These are, firstly, that the new framework should serve to strengthen the soundness and stability of the international banking system; and secondly that the framework should be fair and have a high degree of consistency in its application to banks in different countries with a view to diminishing an existing source of competitive inequality among international banks. The Committee notes that, in responding to the invitation to comment on its original proposals, banks have welcomed the general shape and rationale of the framework and have expressed support for the view that it should be applied as uniformly as possible at the national level.

4. Throughout the recent consultations, close contact has been maintained between the Committee in Basle and the authorities of the European Community in Brussels who are pursuing a parallel initiative to develop a common solvency ratio to be applied to credit institutions in the Community. The aim has been to ensure the maximum degree of consistency between the framework agreed in Basle and the framework to be applied in the Community. It is the Committee's hope and expectation that this consistency can be achieved, although it should be noted that regulations in the European Community are designed to apply to credit institutions generally, whereas the Com-

APPENDIX

mittee's framework is directed more specifically with banks undertaking international business in mind.

5. In developing the framework described in this document the Committee has sought to arrive at a set of principles which are conceptually sound and at the same time pay due regard to particular features of the present supervisory and accounting systems in individual member countries. It believes that this objective has been achieved. The framework provides for a transitional period so that the existing circumstances in different countries can be reflected in flexible arrangements that allow time for adjustment.

6. In certain very limited respects (notably as regards some of the risk weightings) the framework allows for a degree of national discretion in the way in which it is applied. The impact of such discrepancies on the overall ratios is likely to be negligible and it is not considered that they will compromise the basic objectives. Nevertheless, the Committee intends to monitor and review the application of the framework in the period ahead with a view to achieving even greater consistency.

7. It should be stressed that the agreed framework is designed to establish *minimum* levels of capital for internationally active banks. National authorities will be free to adopt arrangements that set higher levels.

8. It should also be emphasised that capital adequacy as measured by the present framework, though important, is one of a number of factors to be taken into account when assessing the strength of banks. The framework in this document is mainly directed towards assessing capital in relation to credit risk (the risk of counterparty failure) but other risks, notably interest rate risk and the investment risk on securities, need to be taken into account by supervisors in assessing overall capital adequacy. The Committee is examining possible approaches in relation to these risks. Furthermore, and more generally, capital ratios, judged in

isolation, may provide a misleading guide to relative strength. Much also depends on the quality of a bank's assets and, importantly, the level of provisions a bank may be holding outside its capital against assets of doubtful value. Recognising the close relationship between capital and provisions, the Committee will continue to monitor provisioning policies by banks in member countries and will seek to promote convergence of policies in this field as in other regulatory matters. In assessing progress by banks in member countries towards meeting the agreed capital standards, the Committee will therefore take careful account of any differences in existing policies and procedures for setting the level of provisions among countries' banks and in the form in which such provisions are constituted.

9. The Committee is aware that differences between countries in the fiscal treatment and accounting presentation for tax purposes of certain classes of provisions for losses and of capital reserves derived from retained earnings may to some extent distort the comparability of the real or apparent capital positions of international banks. Convergence in tax régimes, though desirable, lies outside the competence of the Committee and tax considerations are not addressed in this paper. However, the Committee wishes to keep these tax and accounting matters under review to the extent that they affect the comparability of the capital adequacy of different countries' banking systems.

10. This agreement is intended to be applied to banks on a consolidated basis, including subsidiaries undertaking banking and financial business. At the same time, the Committee recognises that ownership structures and the position of banks within financial conglomerate groups are undergoing significant changes. The Committee will be concerned to ensure that ownership structures should not be such as to weaken the capital position of the bank or expose it to risks stemming from other parts of the group. The Committee will continue to keep these developments

APPENDIX

under review in the light of the particular regulations in member countries, in order to ensure that the integrity of the capital of banks is maintained. In the case of several of the subjects for further work mentioned above, notably investment risk and the consolidated supervision of financial groups, the European Community has undertaken or is undertaking work with similar objectives and close liaison will be maintained.

11. This document is divided into four sections. The first two describe the framework: Section I the constituents of capital and Section II the risk-weighting system. Section III deals with the target standard ratio; and Section IV with transitional and implementing arrangements.

I. The Constituents of Capital

(a) Core capital (basic equity)

12. The Committee considers that the key element of capital on which the main emphasis should be placed is equity capital[2] and disclosed reserves. This key element of capital is the only element common to all countries' banking systems; it is wholly visible in the published accounts and is the basis on which most market judgements of capital adequacy are made; and it has a crucial bearing on profit margins and a bank's ability to compete. This emphasis on equity capital and disclosed reserves reflects the importance the Committee attaches to securing a progressive enhancement in the quality, as well as the level, of the total capital resources maintained by major banks.[3]

---

[2] Issued and fully paid ordinary shares/common stock and non-cumulative perpetual preferred stock (but excluding cumulative preferred stock).

[3] One member country, however, maintains the view that an international definition of capital should be confined to core capital elements and indicated that it would continue to press for the definition to be reconsidered by the Committee in the years ahead.

13. Notwithstanding this emphasis, the member countries of the Committee also consider that there are a number of other important and legitimate constituents of a bank's capital base which may be included within the system of measurement (subject to certain conditions set out in sub-section (b) below).

14. The Committee has therefore concluded that capital, for supervisory purposes, should be defined in two tiers in a way which will have the effect of requiring at least 50 per cent of a bank's capital base to consist of a core element comprised of equity capital and published reserves from post-tax retained earnings (tier 1). The other elements of capital (supplementary capital) will be admitted into tier 2 up to an amount equal to that of the core capital. These supplementary capital elements and the particular conditions attaching to their inclusion in the capital base are set out below and in more detail in Annex 1. Each of these elements may be included or not included by national authorities at their discretion in the light of their national accounting and supervisory regulations.

(b) Supplementary capital
(i) Undisclosed reserves

15. Unpublished or hidden reserves may be constituted in various ways according to differing legal and accounting régimes in member countries. Under this heading are included only reserves which, though unpublished, have been passed through the profit and loss account and which are accepted by the bank's supervisory authorities. They may be inherently of the same intrinsic quality as published retained earnings, but, in the context of an internationally agreed minimum standard, their lack of transparency, together with the fact that many countries do not recognise undisclosed reserves, either as an accepted accounting concept or as a legitimate element of capital, argue for excluding them from the core equity capital element.

APPENDIX

(ii) Revaluation reserves

16. Some countries, under their national regulatory or accounting arrangements, allow certain assets to be revalued to reflect their current value, or something closer to their current value than historic cost, and the resultant revaluation reserves to be included in the capital base. Such revaluations can arise in two ways:
  (a) from a formal revaluation, carried through to the balance sheets of banks' own premises; or
  (b) from a notional addition to capital of hidden values which arise from the practice of holding securities in the balance sheet valued at historic cost.

Such reserves may be included within supplementary capital provided that the assets are considered by the supervisory authority to be prudently valued, fully reflecting the possibility of price fluctuations and forced sale.

17. Alternative (b) is relevant to those banks whose balance sheets traditionally include very substantial amounts of equities held in their portfolio at historic cost but which can be, and on occasions are, realised at current prices and used to offset losses. The Committee considers these "latent" revaluation reserves can be included among supplementary elements of capital since they can be used to absorb losses on a going-concern basis, provided they are subject to a substantial discount in order to reflect concerns both about market volatility and about the tax charge which would arise were such gains to be realised. A discount of 55 per cent on the difference between the historic cost book value and market value is agreed to be appropriate in the light of these considerations. The Committee considered, but rejected, the proposition that latent reserves arising in respect of the undervaluation of banks' premises should also be included within the definition of supplementary capital.

(iii) General provisions/general loan loss reserves

18. General provisions or general loan-loss reserves are created against the possibility of future losses. Where they are not ascribed to particular assets and do not reflect a reduction in the valuation of particular assets, these reserves qualify for inclusion in capital and it has been agreed that they should be counted within tier 2. Where, however, provisions have been created against identified losses or in respect of a demonstrable deterioration in the value of particular assets, they are not freely available to meet unidentified losses which may subsequently arise elsewhere in the portfolio and do not possess an essential characteristic of capital. Such specific or earmarked provisions should therefore not be included in the capital base.

19. The Committee accepts, however, that, in practice, it is not always possible to distinguish clearly between general provisions (or general loan loss reserves) which are genuinely freely available and those provisions which in reality are earmarked against assets already identified as impaired. This partly reflects the present diversity of accounting, supervisory, and, importantly, fiscal policies in respect of provisioning and in respect of national definitions of capital. This means, inevitably, that initially there will be a degree of inconsistency in the characteristics of general provisions or general loan-loss reserves included by different member countries within the framework.

20. In the light of these uncertainties, the Committee intends during the transitional period (see paragraphs 45 to 50 below) to clarify the distinction made in member countries between those elements which should conceptually be regarded as part of capital and those which should not qualify. The Committee will aim to develop before the end of 1990 firm proposals applicable to all member countries, so as to ensure consistency in the definition of general provisions and general loan-loss reserves eligible for inclusion in the capital base by the time the interim and final minimum target standards fall to be observed.

APPENDIX

21. As a further safeguard, in the event that agreement is not reached on the refined definition of unencumbered resources eligible for inclusion in supplementary capital, where general provisions and general loan-loss reserves may include amounts reflecting lower valuations for assets or latent but unidentified losses present in the balance sheet, the amount of such reserves or provisions that qualify as capital would be phased down so that, at the end of the transitional period, such items would constitute no more than 1.25 percentage points, or exceptionally and temporarily up to 2.0 percentage points, of risk assets within the secondary elements.

(iv) Hybrid debt capital instruments

22. In this category fall a number of capital instruments which combine certain characteristics of equity and certain characteristics of debt. Each of these has particular features which can be considered to affect its quality as capital. It has been agreed that, where these instruments have close similarities to equity, in particular when they are able to support losses on an on-going basis without triggering liquidation, they may be included in supplementary capital. In addition to perpetual preference shares carrying a cumulative fixed charge, the following instruments, for example, may qualify for inclusion: long-term preferred shares in Canada, titres participatifs and titres subordonnés à durée indéterminée in France, Genussscheine in Germany, perpetual debt instruments in the United Kingdom and mandatory convertible debt instruments in the United States. The qualifying criteria for such instruments are set out in Annex 1.

(v) Subordinated term debt

23. The Committee is agreed that subordinated term debt instruments have significant deficiencies as constituents of capital in view of their fixed maturity and inability to absorb losses except in a liquidation. These deficiencies justify an additional restriction on the amount of such

debt capital which is eligible for inclusion within the capital base. Consequently, it has been concluded that subordinated term debt instruments with a minimum original term to maturity of over five years may be included within the supplementary elements of capital but only to a maximum of 50 per cent of the core capital element, and subject to adequate amortisation arrangements.

(c) Deductions from capital

24. It has been concluded that the following deductions should be made from the capital base for the purpose of calculating the risk-weighted capital ratio. The deductions will consist of:

(i) goodwill, as a deduction from tier I capital elements:
(ii) investments in subsidiaries engaged in banking and financial activities which are not consolidated in national systems. The normal practice will be to consolidate subsidiaries for the purpose of assessing the capital adequacy of banking groups. Where this is not done, deduction is essential to prevent the multiple use of the same capital resources in different parts of the group. The deduction for such investments will be made against the total capital base. The assets representing the investments in subsidiary companies whose capital had been deducted from that of the parent would not be included in total assets for the purposes of computing the ratio.

25. The Committee carefully considered the possibility of requiring deduction of banks' holdings of capital issued by other banks or deposit-taking institutions, whether in the form of equity or of other capital instruments. Several G-10 supervisory authorities currently require such a deduction to be made in order to discourage the banking system as a whole from creating cross-holdings of capital, rather than drawing capital from outside investors. The Committee is very conscious that such double-gearing (or "double-

APPENDIX

leveraging") can have systemic dangers for the banking system by making it more vulnerable to the rapid transmission of problems from one institution to another and some members consider these dangers justify a policy of full deduction of such holdings.

26. Despite these concerns, however, the Committee as a whole is not presently in favour of a general policy of deducting all holdings of other banks' capital, on the grounds that to do so could impede certain significant and desirable changes taking place in the structure of domestic banking systems.

27. The Committee has nonetheless agreed that:

(a) individual supervisory authorities should be free at their discretion to apply a policy of deduction, either for all holdings of other banks' capital, or for holdings which exceed material limits in relation to the holding bank's capital or the issuing bank's capital, or on a case-by-case basis:

(b) where no deduction is applied, banks' holdings of other banks' capital instruments will bear a weight of 100 per cent;

(c) in applying these policies, member countries consider that reciprocal cross-holdings of bank capital designed artificially to inflate the capital position of the banks concerned should not be permitted;

(d) the Committee will closely monitor the degree of double-gearing in the international banking system and does not preclude the possibility of introducing constraints at a later date. For this purpose, supervisory authorities intend to ensure that adequate statistics are made available to enable them and the Committee to monitor the development of banks' holdings of other banks' equity and debt instruments which rank as capital under the present agreement.

II. The Risk Weights

28. The Committee considers that a weighted risk ratio in which capital is related to different categories of asset or off-balance-sheet exposure, weighted according to broad categories of relative riskiness, is the perferred method for assessing the capital adequacy of banks. This is not to say that other methods of capital measurement are not also useful, but they are considered by the Committee to be supplementary to the risk weight approach. The Committee believes that a risk ratio has the following advantages over the simpler gearing ratio approach:

(i) it provides a fairer basis for making international comparisons between banking systems whose structures may differ;
(ii) it allows off-balance-sheet exposures to be incorporated more easily into the measure;
(iii) it does not deter banks from holding liquid or other assets which carry low risk.

29. The framework of weights has been kept as simple as possible and only five weights are used—0, 10, 20, 50 and 100 per cent. There are inevitably some broad-brush judgements in deciding which weight should apply to different types of asset and the weightings should not be regarded as a substitute for commercial judgement for purposes of market pricing of the different instruments.

30. The weighting structure is set out in detail in Annexes 2 and 3. There are six aspects of the structure to which attention is particularly drawn.

(i) Categories of risk captured in the framework

31. There are many different kinds of risks against which banks' managements need to guard. For most banks the major risk is *credit risk*, that is to say the risk of counterparty failure, but there are many other kinds of risk—for example, investment risk, interest rate risk, exchange rate

risk, concentration risk. The central focus of this framework is credit risk and, as a further aspect of credit risk, country transfer risk. In addition, individual supervisory authorities have discretion to build in certain other types of risk. Some countries, for example, will wish to retain a weighting for open foreign exchange positions or for some aspects of investment risk. No standardisation has been attempted in the treatment of these other kinds of risk in the framework as the present stage.

32. The Committee considered the desirability of seeking to incorporate additional weightings to reflect the investment risk in holdings of fixed rate domestic government securities — one manifestation of interest rate risk which is of course present across the whole range of a bank's activities, on and off the balance sheet. For the present, it was concluded that individual supervisory authorities should be free to apply either a zero *or* a low weight to claims on the domestic government (e.g. 10 per cent for all securities or 10 per cent for those maturing in under one year and 20 per cent for one year and over). All members agreed, however, that interest rate risk generally required further study and that if, in due course, further work made it possible to develop a satisfactory method of measurement for this aspect of risk for the business as a whole, consideration should be given to applying some appropriate control alongside this credit risk framework. Work is already under way to explore the possibilities in this regard.

(ii) Country transfer risk

33. In addressing country transfer risk, the Committee has been very conscious of the difficulty of devising a satisfactory method for incorporating country transfer risk into the framework of measurement. In its earlier, consultative, paper two alternative approaches were put forward for consideration and comment. These were, firstly, a simple differentiation between claims on domestic institutions

(central government, official sector and banks) and claims on all foreign countries; and secondly, differentiation on the basis of an approach involving the selection of a defined grouping of countries considered to be of high credit standing.

34. The comments submitted to the Committee by banks and banking associations in G-10 countries during the consultative period were overwhelmingly in favour of the second alternative. In support of this view, three particular arguments were strongly represented to the Committee. Firstly, it was stressed that a simple domestic/foreign split effectively ignores the reality that transfer risk varies greatly between different countries and that this risk is of sufficient significance to make it necessary to ensure that broad distinctions in the credit standing of industrialised and non-industrialised countries should be made and captured in the system of measurement, particularly one designed for international banks. Secondly, it was argued that the domestic/foreign split does not reflect the global integration of financial markets and the absence of some further refinement would discourage international banks from holding securities issued by central governments of major foreign countries as liquid cover against their Euro-currency liabilities. To that extent a domestic/foreign approach would run counter to an important objective of the risk weighting framework, namely that it should encourage prudent liquidity management. Thirdly, and most importantly, the member states of the European Community are firmly committed to the principle that all claims on banks, central governments and the official sector within European Community countries should be treated in the same way. This means that, where such a principle is put into effect, there would be an undesirable asymmetry in the manner in which a domestic/foreign split was applied by the seven G-10 countries which are members of the Community

APPENDIX

compared with the manner in which it was applied by the non-Community countries.

35. In the light of these arguments, the Committee has concluded that a defined group of countries should be adopted as the basis for applying differential weighting coefficients, and that this group should be full members of the OECD or countries which have concluded special lending arrangements with the IMF associated with the Fund's General Arrangements to Borrow. This group of countries is referred to as the OECD in the rest of the report.

36. This decision has the following consequences for the weighting structure. Claims on central governments within the OECD will attract a zero weight (or a low weight if the national supervisory authority elects to incorporate interest rate risk); and claims on OECD non-central government public-sector entities will attract a low weight [see (iii) below]. Claims on central governments and central banks outside the OECD will also attract a zero weight (or a low weight if the national supervisory authority elects to incorporate investment risk), provided such claims are denominated in the national currency and funded by liabilities in the same currency. This reflects the absence of risks relating to the availability and transfer of foreign exchange on such claims.

37. As regards the treatment of interbank claims, in order to preserve the efficiency and liquidity of the international interbank market there will be no differentiation between short-term claims on banks incorporated within or outside the OECD. However, the Committee draws a distinction between, on the one hand, short-term placements with other banks which is an accepted method of managing liquidity in the interbank market and carries a perception of low risk and, on the other, longer-term cross-border loans to banks which are often associated with particular transactions and carry greater transfer and/or credit

risks. A 20 per cent weight will therefore be applied to claims on all banks, wherever incorporated, with a residual maturity of up to and including one year; longer-term claims on OECD incorporated banks will be weighted at 20 per cent; and longer-term claims on banks incorporated outside the OECD will be weighted at 100 per cent.

(iii) Claims on non-central-government, public-sector entities (PSEs)

38. The Committee concluded that it was not possible to settle on a single common weight that can be applied to all claims on domestic public-sector entities below the level of central government (e.g. states, local authorities, etc.), in view of the special character and varying creditworthiness of these entities in different member countries. The Committee therefore opted to allow discretion to each national supervisory authority to determine the appropriate weighting factors for the PSEs within that country. In order to preserve a degree of convergence in the application of such discretion, the Committee agreed that the weights ascribed in this way should be 0, 10, 20 or 50 per cent for domestic PSEs but that PSEs in foreign countries within the OECD should attract a standard 20 per cent weight. These arrangements will be subject to review by the Committee in pursuit of further convergence towards common weights and consistent definitions in member countries and in the light of decisions to be taken within the European Community on the specification of a common solvency ratio for credit institutions.

Commercial companies owned by the public sector will attract a uniform weight of 100 per cent inter alia in order to avoid competitive inequality vis-à-vis similar private-sector commercial enterprises.

(iv) Collateral and guarantees

39. The framework recognises the importance of collateral in reducing credit risk, but only to a limited extent.

APPENDIX

In view of the varying practices among banks in different countries for taking collateral and different experiences of the stability of physical or financial collateral values, it has not been found possible to develop a basis for recognising collateral generally in the weighting system. The more limited recognition of collateral will apply only to loans secured against cash or against securities issued by OECD central governments and specified multilateral development banks. These will attract the weight given to the collateral (i.e. a zero or a low weight). Loans partially collateralised by these assets will also attract the equivalent low weights on that part of the loan which is fully collateralised.

40. As regards loans or other exposures guaranteed by third parties, the Committee has agreed that loans guaranteed by OECD central governments, OECD public-sector entities, or OECD incorporated banks will attract the weight allocated to a direct claim on the guarantor (e.g. 20 per cent in the case of banks). Loans guaranteed by non-OECD incorporated banks will also be recognised by the application of a 20 per cent weight but only where the underlying transaction has a residual maturity not exceeding one year. The Committee intends to monitor the application of this latter arrangement to ensure that it does not give rise to inappropriate weighting of commercial loans. In the case of loans covered by partial guarantees, only that part of the loan which is covered by the guarantee will attract the reduced weight. The contingent liability assumed by banks in respect of guarantees will attract a credit conversion factor of 100 per cent (see sub-section (vi) below).

(v) Loans secured on residential property

41. Loans fully secured by mortgage on occupied residential property have a very low record of loss in most countries. The framework will recognise this by assigning a 50 per cent weight to loans fully secured by mortgage on residential property which is rented or is (or is intended to

be) occupied by the borrower. In applying the 50 per cent weight, the supervisory authorities will satisfy themselves, according to their national arrangements for the provision of housing finance, that this concessionary weight is applied restrictively for residential purposes and in accordance with strict prudential criteria. This may mean, for example, that in some member countries the 50 per cent weight will only apply to first mortgages, creating a first charge on the property; and that in other member countries it will only be applied where strict, legally-based, valuation rules ensure a substantial margin of additional security over the amount of the loan. The 50 per cent weight will specifically not be applied to loans to companies engaged in speculative residential building or property development. Other collateral will not be regarded as justifying the reduction of the weightings that would otherwise apply.[4]

(vi) Off-balance-sheet engagements

42. The Committee believes that it is of great importance that all off-balance-sheet activity should be caught within the capital adequacy framework. At the same time, it is recognised that there is only limited experience in assessing the risks in some of the activities; also that for some countries, a complex analytical approach and detailed and frequent reporting systems cannot easily be justified when the amounts of such business, particularly in the newer, more innovative instruments, are only small. The approach that has been agreed, which is on the same lines as that described in the Committee's report on the supervisory treatment of off-balance-sheet exposures issued to banks in March 1986,

---

[4]One member country feels strongly that the lower weight should also apply to other loans secured by mortgages on domestic property, provided that the amount of the loan does not exceed 60 per cent of the value of the property as calculated according to strict legal valuation criteria.

APPENDIX

is comprehensive in that all categories of off-balance-sheet engagements, including recent innovations, will be converted to credit risk equivalents by multiplying the nominal principal amounts by a credit conversion factor, the resulting amounts then being weighted according to the nature of the counterparty. The different instruments and techniques are divided into five broad categories (within which member countries will have some limited discretion to allocate particular instruments according to their individual characteristics in national markets):

(a) those which substitute for loans (e.g., general guarantees of indebtedness, bank acceptance guarantees and standby letters of credit serving as financial guarantees for loans and securities)—these will carry a 100 per cent credit risk conversion factor;

(b) certain transaction related contingencies (e.g., performance bonds, bid bonds, warranties and standby letters of credit related to particular transactions)—a 50 per cent credit risk conversion factor;

(c) short-term, self-liquidating trade-related contingent liabilities arising from the movement of goods (e.g., documentary credits collateralised by the underlying shipments) — a 20 per cent credit risk conversion factor;

(d) commitments with an original maturity[5] exceeding one year (the longer maturity serving broadly as a proxy for higher risk facilities) and all NIFs and RUFs —a 50 per cent credit risk conversion factor. Shorter-term commitments or commitments which can be

---

[5]In order to facilitate data collection, during the transitional period up to end-1992, but not beyond, national supervisory authorities will have discretion to apply residual maturity as a basis for measuring commitments.

unconditionally cancelled at any time, it is agreed, generally carry only low risk and a nil weight for these is considered to be justified on de minimis grounds:

(e) interest and exchange rate related (e.g., swaps, options, futures)—the credit risk equivalent amount for these contracts will be calculated in one of two ways (see below and Annex 3).

43. Special treatment is needed for the items in (e) above because banks are not exposed to credit risk for the full face value of their contracts, but only to the cost of replacing the cash flow if a counterparty defaults. Most members of the Committee accept that the correct method of assessing the credit risk on these items is to calculate the current replacement cost by marking to market and to add a factor to represent potential exposure during the remaining life of the contract. Some member countries, however, are concerned about the consistency of this method in relation to the rest of the system which only makes broad distinctions between relative risks for on-balance-sheet items, particularly for banks where these off-balance-sheet items currently constitute only a very small part of the total risks. They would prefer to apply an alternative approach consisting of conversion factors based on the nominal principal sum underlying each contract according to its type and maturity. The Committee has concluded that members will be allowed to choose either of the two methods. The details of the two alternative methods are set out in Annex 3.

III. A Target Standard Ratio

44. In the light of consultations and preliminary testing of the framework, the Committee is agreed that a minimum standard should be set now which international banks generally will be expected to achieve by the end of the transitional period. It is also agreed that this standard

should be set at a level that is consistent with the objective of securing over time soundly-based and consistent capital ratios for all international banks. Accordingly, the Committee confirms that the target standard ratio of capital to weighted risk assets should be set at 8 per cent (of which the core capital element will be at least 4 per cent). This is expressed as a common minimum standard which international banks in member countries will be expected to observe by the end of 1992, thus allowing a transitional period of some four-and-a-half years for any necessary adjustment by banks who need time to build up to those levels. The Committee fully recognises that the transition from existing, sometimes long-established, definitions of capital and methods of measurement towards a new internationally agreed standard will not necessarily be achieved easily or quickly. The full period to end-1992 is available to ensure progressive steps towards adjustment and banks whose ratios are presently below the 8 per cent standard will not be required to take immediate or precipitate action.

IV. Transitional and Implementing Arrangements

(i) Transition

45. Certain transitional arrangements have been agreed upon to ensure that there are sustained efforts during the transitional period to build up individual banks' ratios towards the ultimate target standard: and to facilitate smooth adjustment and phasing in of the new arrangements within a wide variety of existing supervisory systems.

46. The transitional period will be from the date of this paper to the end of 1992, by which latter date all banks undertaking significant cross-border business will be expected to meet the standard in full (see paragraph 50 below). In addition, there will be an interim standard to be met by the end of 1990 (see paragraph 49 below).

47. Initially no formal standard or minimum level will be set. It is the general view of the Committee, however, that every encouragement should be given to those banks whose capital levels are at the low end of the range to build up their capital as quickly as possible and the Committee expects there to be no erosion of existing capital standards in individual member countries' banks. Thus, during the transitional period, all banks which need to improve capital levels up to the interim and final standards should not diminish even temporarily their current capital levels (subject to the fluctuations which can occur around the time new capital is raised). A level of 5 per cent attained by application of the framework and transitional arrangements is considered by some countries to be a reasonable yardstick for the lower capitalised banks to seek to attain in the short term. Individual member countries will, of course, be free to set, and announce, at the outset of the transitional period the level from which they would expect all their banks to move towards the interim and final target standard. In order to assess and compare progress during the initial period of adjustment to end-1990 in a manner which takes account both of existing supervisory systems and the new arrangements, the Committee and individual supervisory authorities will initially apply the basis of measurement set out in paragraph 48 below.

48. In measuring the capital position of banks at the start of the transitional period, a proportion of the core capital may be made up of supplementary elements up to a maximum of 25 percent of core capital elements, reducing to 10 per cent by end-1990. In addition, throughout the transitional period up to end-1992, subject to more restrictive policies which individual authorities may wish to apply, term subordinated debt may be included without limit as a constituent of supplementary elements and the deduction from tier 1 capital elements in respect of goodwill may be waived.

APPENDIX

49. At end-1990 there will be an interim minimum standard of 7.25 per cent of which at least half should be core capital. However, between end-1990 and end-1992 up to 10 per cent of the required core elements may be made up of supplementary elements. This means, in round figures, a minimum core capital element of 3.6 per cent of which tier 1 elements should total at least 3.25 per cent, is to be achieved by the end of 1990. In addition, from end-1990, general loan loss reserves or general provisions which include amounts reflecting lower valuations of assets or latent but unidentified losses present in the balance sheet will be limited to 1.5 percentage points, or exceptionally up to 2.0[6] percentage points, of risk assets within supplementary elements.

50. At end-1992 the transitional period ends. The minimum standard will then be 8 per cent of which core capital (tier 1, equity and reserves) will be at least 4 per cent, supplementary elements no more than core capital and term subordinated debt within supplementary elements no more than 50 per cent of tier 1. In addition, general loan loss reserves or general provisions (having the characteristics described in paragraph 49) will be limited at end-1992 to 1.25 percentage points, or exceptionally and temporarily up to 2.0[6] percentage points, within supplementary elements.

For ease of reference, the arrangements described in paragraphs 45 to 50 are summarised in a table at Annex 4.

(ii) Implementation

51. The arrangements described in this document will be implemented at national level at the earliest possible oppor-

---

[6]These limits would only apply in the event that no agreement is reached on a consistent basis for including unencumbered provisions or reserves in capital (see paragraphs 20 and 21).

tunity. Each country will decide the way in which the supervisory authorities will introduce and apply these recommendations in the light of their different legal structures and existing supervisory arrangements. In some countries, changes in the capital régime may be introduced, after consultation, relatively speedily without the need for legislation. Other countries may employ more lengthy procedures, and in some cases these may require legislation. In due course the member states of the European Community will also need to ensure that their own domestic regulations are compatible with the Community's own legislative proposals in this field. None of these factors needs result in any inconsistency in the timing of implementation among member countries. For example, some countries may apply the framework in this report, formally or informally, in parallel with their existing system, certainly during the initial period of transition. In this way banks can be assisted to start the necessary process of adjustment in good time before substantive changes in national systems are formally introduced.

July 1988

Annex 1

Definition of Capital Included in the Capital Base
(To apply at end-1992—see Annex 4 for transitional arrangements)

A. Capital elements
    Tier 1 (a) Paid-up share capital/common stock
             (b) Disclosed reserves
    Tier 2 (a) Undisclosed reserves
            (b) Asset revaluation reserves
            (c) General provisions/general loan loss reserves
            (d) Hybrid (debt/equity) capital instruments
            (e) Subordinated term debt

The sum of Tier 1 and Tier 2 elements will be eligible for inclusion in the capital base, subject to the following limits.

B. Limits and restrictions

   (i) The total of Tier 2 (supplementary) elements will be limited to a maximum of 100 per cent of the total of Tier 1 elements;

  (ii) subordinated term debt will be limited to a maximum of 50 per cent of Tier 1 elements;

 (iii) where general provisions/general loan loss reserves include amounts reflecting lower valuations of asset or latent but unidentified losses present in the balance sheet, the amount of such provisions or reserves will be limited to a maximum of 1.25 percentage points, or exceptionally and temporarily up to 2.0 percentage points, of risk assets;[1]

 (iv) asset revaluation reserves which take the form of

---

[1] This limit would only apply in the event that no agreement is reached on a consistent basis for incuding unencumbered provisions or reserves in capital (see paragraphs 20 and 21).

latent gains on unrealised securities (see below) will be subject to a discount of 55 per cent.

C. Deductions from the capital base

From Tier 1: Goodwill

From total
capital: (i) Investments in unconsolidated banking and financial subsidiary companies

N.B. The presumption is that the framework would be applied on a consolidated basis to banking groups.

(ii) Investments in the capital of other banks and financial institutions (at the discretion of national authorities).

D. Definition of capital elements

(i) Tier 1: includes only *permanent shareholders' equity* (issued and fully paid ordinary shares common stock and perpetual non-cumulative preference shares) and *disclosed reserves* (created or increased by appropriations of retained earnings or other surplus, e.g. share premiums, retained profit,[2] general reserves and legal reserves). In the case of consolidated accounts, this also incudes minority interests in the equity of subsidiaries which are less than wholly owned. This basic definition of capital excludes revaluation reserves and cumulative preference shares.

(ii) Tier 2: (a) undisclosed reserves are eligible for inclusion within supplementary elements provided these reserves are accepted by the supervisor. Such reserves consist of that part of the accumulated after-tax surplus of retained profits which banks in

---

[2]Including, at national discretion, allocations to or from reserve during the course of the year from current year's retained profit.

ANNEX

some countries may be permitted to maintain as an undisclosed reserve. Apart from the fact that the reserve is not identified in the published balance sheet, it should have the same high quality and character as a disclosed capital reserve; as such, it should not be encumbered by any provision or other known liability but should be freely and immediately available to meet unforeseen future losses. This definition of undisclosed reserves excludes hidden values arising fron holdings of securities in the balance sheet at below current market prices (see below).

(b) Revaluation reserves arise in two ways. Firstly, in some countries, banks (and other commercial companies) are permitted to revalue fixed assets, normally their own premises, from time to time in line with the change in market values. In some of these countries the amount of such revaluations is determined by law. Revaluations of this kind are reflected on the face of the balance sheet as a revaluation reserve.

Secondly, hidden values or "latent" revaluation reserves may be present as a result of long-term holdings of equity securities valued in the balance sheet at the historic cost of acquisition.

Both types of revaluation reserve may be included in Tier 2 provided that the assets are prudently valued, fully reflecting the possibility of price fluctuation and forced sale. In the case of "latent" revaluation reserves a discount of 55 per cent, will be applied to the difference between historic cost book value and market value to reflect the potential volatility of this form of unrealised capital and the notional tax charge on it.

(c) General provisions/general loan loss reserves: provisions or loan loss reserves held against future, presently unidentified losses are freely available to meet losses which subsequently materialise and therefore qualify for inclusion within supplementary elements. Provisions ascribed to impairment of particular assets or known liabilities should be excluded. Furthermore, where general provisions/general loan loss reserves include amounts reflecting lower valuations of assets or latent but unidentified losses already present in the balance sheet, the amount of such provisions or reserves eligible for inclusion will be limited to a maximum of 1.25 percentage points, or exceptionally and temporarily up to 2.0 percentage points.[3]

(d) Hybrid (debt/equity) capital instruments. This heading includes a range of instruments which combine characteristics of equity capital and of debt. Their precise specifications differ from country to country, but they should meet the following requirements.:
- they are *unsecured, subordinated* and *fully paid-up;*
- they are *not redeemable* at the initiative of the holder or without the prior consent of the supervisory authority;
- they are *available to participate in losses* without the bank being obliged to cease trading (unlike conventional subordinated debt);
- although the capital instrument may carry an obligation to pay interest that cannot permanently be reduced or waived (unlike dividends

---

[3]This limit would apply in the event that no agreement is reached on a consistent basis for including unencumbered provisions or reserves in capital (see paragraphs 20 and 21).

ANNEX

on ordinary shareholders' equity), *it should allow service obligations to be deferred* (as with cumulative preference shares) where the profitability of the bank would not support payment.

Cumulative preference shares, having these characteristics, would be eligible for inclusion in this category. In addition, the following are examples of instruments that may be eligible for inclusion: long-term preferred shares in Canada, titres participatifs and titres subordonnés à durée indéterminée in France, Genussscheine in Germany, perpetual subordinated debt and preference shares in the United Kingdom and mandatory convertible debt instruments in the United States. Debt capital instruments which do not meet these criteria may be eligible for inclusion in item (e).

(e) Subordinated term debt: includes conventional unsecured subordinated debt capital instruments with a minimum original fixed term to maturity of over five years and limited life redeemable preference shares. During the last five years to maturity, a cumulative discount (or amortisation) factor of 20 per cent per year will be applied to reflect the diminishing value of these instruments as a continuing source of strength. Unlike instruments included in item (d), these instruments are not normally available to participate in the losses of a bank which continues trading. For this reason these instruments will be limited to a maximum of 50 per cent of Tier 1.

Annex 2

Risk Weights by Category of on-Balance-Sheet Asset

0%	(a) Cash[1]
	(b) Claims on central governments and central banks denominated in national currency and funded in that currency
	(c) Other claims on OECD[2] central governments[3] and central banks
	(d) Claims collateralised by cash or OECD central-government securities[3] or guaranteed by OECD central governments[4]
0, 10, 20 or 50% (at national discretion)	(a) Claims on domestic public-sector entities, excluding central government, and loans guaranteed[4] by such entities
20%	(a) Claims on multilateral development banks (IBRD, LADB, AsDB, AfDB, EIB)[5]

---

[1] Includes (at national discretion) gold bullion held in own vaults or on an allocated basis to the extent backed by bullion liabilities.

[2] The OECD comprises countries which are full members of the OECD or which have concluded special lending arrangements with the IMF associated with the Fund's General Arrangements to Borrow

[3] Some member countries intend to apply weights to securities issued by OECD central governments to take account of investment risk. These weights would, for example, be 10 per cent for all securities or 10 per cent for those maturing in up to one year and 20 per cent for those maturing in over one year.

[4] Commercial loans partially guaranteed by these bodies will attract equivalent low weights on that part of the loan which is fully covered. Similarly, loans partially collateralised by cash or securities issued by OECD central governments and multilateral development banks will attract low weights on that part of the loan which is fully covered.

[5] Claims on other multilateral development banks in which G-10 countries are shareholding members may, at national discretion, also attract a 20 per cent weight.

and claims guaranteed by, or collateralised by securities issued by such banks[4]
(b) Claims on banks incorporated in the OECD and loans guaranteed[4] by OECD incorporated banks
(c) Claims on banks incorporated in countries outside the OECD with a residual maturity of up to one year and loans with a residual maturity of up to one year guaranteed by banks incorporated in countries outside the OECD
(d) Claims on non-domestic OECD public-sector entities, excluding central government, and loans guaranteed[4] by such entities
(e) Cash items in process of collection

50% (a) Loans fully secured by mortgage on residential property that is or will be occupied by the borrower or that is rented

100% (a) Claims on the private sector
(b) Claims on banks incorporated outside the OECD with a residual maturity of over one year
(c) Claims on central governments outside the OECD (unless denominated in national currency—and funded in that currency —see above)
(d) Claims on commercial companies owned by the public sector
(e) Premises, plant and equipment and other fixed assets
(f) Real estate and other investments (including non-consolidated investment participations in other companies)

ANNEX

(g) Capital instruments issued by other banks (unless deducted from capital)
(h) All other assets

Annex 3

Credit Conversion Factors for Off-Balance-Sheet Items

The framework takes account of the credit risk on off-balance-sheet exposures by applying credit conversion factors to the different types of off-balance-sheet instrument or transaction. With the exception of foreign exchange and interest rate related contingencies, the credit conversion factors are set out in the table below. They are derived from the estimated size and likely occurrence of the credit exposure, as well as the relative degree of credit risk as identified in the Committee's paper "The management of banks' off-balance-sheet exposures: a supervisory perspective" issued in March 1986. The credit conversion factors would be multiplied by the weights applicable to the category of the counterparty for an on-balance-sheet transaction (see Annex 2).

Instruments	Credit conversion factors
1. Direct credit substitutes, e.g. general guarantees of indebtedness (including standby letters of credit serving as financial guarantees for loans and securities) and acceptances (including endorsements with the character of acceptances)	100%
2. Certain transaction-related contingent items (e.g. performance bonds, bid bonds, warranties and standby letters of credit related to particular transactions)	50%
3. Short-term self-liquidating trade-related contingencies (such as	

documentary credits collateralised by the underlying shipments) — 20%

4. Sale and repurchase agreements and asset sales with recourse,[1] where the credit risk remains with the bank — 100%

5. Forward asset purchases, forward forward deposits and partly-paid shares and securities,[1] which represent commitments with certain drawdown — 100%

6. Note issuance facilities and revolving underwriting facilities — 50%

7. Other commitments (e.g. formal standby facilities and credit lines) with an original[2] maturity of over one year — 50%

8. Similar commitments with an original[2] maturity of up to one year, or which can be unconditionally cancelled at any time — 0%

(N.B. Member countries will have some limited discretion to allocate particular instruments into items 1 to 8 above according to the characteristics of the instrument in the national market.)

---

[1] These items are to be weighted according to the type of asset and not according to the type of counterparty with whom the transaction has been entered into. Reverse repos (i.e. purchase and resale agreements—where the bank is the receiver of the asset) are to be treated as collateralised loans, reflecting the economic reality of the transaction. The risk is therefore to be measured as an exposure on the counterparty. Where the asset temporarily acquired is a security which attracts a preferential risk weighting, this would be recognised as collateral and the risk weighting would be reduced accordingly.

[2] But see footnote 5 in the main text.

ANNEX

Foreign exchange and interest rate related contingencies

The treatment of foreign exchange and interest rate related items needs special attention because banks are not exposed to credit risk for the full face falue of their contracts, but only to the potential cost of replacing the cash flow (on contracts showing positive value) if the counterparty defaults. The credit equivalent amounts will depend inter alia on the maturity of the contract and on the volatility of the rates underlying that type of instrument.

Despite the wide range of different instruments in the market, the theoretical basis for assessing the credit risk on all of them has been the same. It has consisted of an analysis of the behaviour of matched pairs of swaps under different volatility assumptions. Since exchange rate contracts involve an exchange of principal on maturity, as well as being generally more volatile, higher conversion factors are proposed for those instruments which feature exchange rate risk. Interest rate contracts[3] are defined to include single-currency interest rate swaps, basis swaps, forward rate agreements, interest rate futures, interest rate options purchased and similar instruments. Exchange rate contracts[3] include cross-currency interest rate swaps, forward foreign exchange contracts, currency futures, currency options purchased and similar instruments. Exchange rate contracts with an original maturity of 14 calendar days or less are excluded.

A majority of G-10 supervisory authorities are of the view that the best way to assess the credit risk on these items is to ask banks to calculate the current replacement cost by

---

[3]Instruments traded on exchanges may be excluded where they are subject to daily margining requirements. Options purchased over the counter are included with the same conversion factors as other instruments, but this decision might be reviewed in the light of future experience.

marking contracts to market, thus capturing the current exposure without any need for estimation, and then adding a factor (the "add-on") to reflect the potential future exposure over the remaining life of the contract. It has been agreed that, in order to calculate the credit equivalent amount of its off-balance-sheet interest rate and foreign exchange rate instruments under this current exposure method, a bank would sum:

—the total replacement cost (obtained by "marking to market") of all its contracts with positive value and

—an amount for potential future credit exposure calculated on the basis of the total notional principal amount of its book, split by residual maturity as follows:

Residual Maturity	Interest Rate Contracts	Exchange Rate Contracts
Less than one year	nil	1.0%
One year and over	0.5%	5.0%

No potential credit exposure would be calculated for single currency floating floating interest rate swaps; the credit exposure on these contracts would be evaluated solely on the basis of their mark-to-market value.

A few G-10 supervisors believe that this two-step approach, incorporating a "mark to market" element, is not consistent with the remainder of the capital framework. They favour a simpler method whereby the potential credit exposure is estimated against each type of contract and a notional capital weight allotted, no matter what the market vaue of the contract might be at a particular reporting date. It has therefore been agreed supervisory authorities should have discretion[4] to apply the alternative method of calcula-

---

[4]Some national authorities may permit individual banks to choose which method to adopt, it being understood that once a bank had chosen to apply the current exposure method, it would not be allowed to switch back to the original exposure method.

ANNEX

tion described below, in which credit conversion factors are derived without reference to the current market price of the instruments. In deciding on what those notional credit conversion factors should be, it has been agreed that a slightly more cautious bias is justified since the current exposure is not being calculated on a regular basis.

In order to arrive at the credit equivalent amount using this original exposure method, a bank would simply apply one of the following two sets of conversion factors to the notional principal amounts of each instrument according to the nature of the instrument and its maturity:

Maturity[5]	Interest Rate Contracts	Exchange Rate Contracts
Less than one year	0.5%	2.0%
One year and less than two years	1.0%	5.0% (i.e. 2% + 3%)
For each additional year	1.0%	3.0%

It is emphasised that the above conversion factors, as well as the "add-ons" for the current exposure method, should be regarded as provisional and may be subject to amendment as a result of changes in the volatility of exchange rates and interest rates.

Careful consideration has been given to the arguments put forward for recognising netting. i.e., for weighting the net rather than the gross claims arising out of swaps and similar contracts with the same counterparties. The criterion on which a decision has been based is the status of a netting contract under national bankruptcy regulations. If

---

[5] For interest rate contracts, there is national discretion as to whether the conversion factors are to be based on original or residual maturity. For exchange rate contracts, the conversion factors are to be calculated according to the original maturity of the instrument.

a liquidator of a failed counterparty has (or may have) the right to unbundle the netted contracts, demanding performance on those contracts favourable to his client and defaulting on unfavourable contracts, there is no reduction in counterparty risk. Accordingly, it has been agreed that:
— banks may net contracts subject to novation,[6] since it appears that counterparty risk is genuinely reduced by the substitution of a novated contract which legally extinguishes the previous obligation. However, since under some national bankruptcy laws liquidators may have the right to unbundle transactions undertaken within a given period under a charge of fraudulent preference, supervisory authorities will have national discretion to require a phase-in period before a novation agreement can be recognised in the weighting framework:
— banks may not for the time being net contracts subject to close-out clauses.[7] The effectiveness of such agreements in an insolvency has not yet been tested in the courts, nor has it been possible to obtain satisfactory legal opinion that liquidators would not be able to overturn them. However, the Committee does not wish to discourage market participants from employing clauses which might well afford protection in certain circumstances in some national jurisdictions and would be prepared to reverse its conclusion if subsequent

---

[6] Netting by novation as defined in this context is a bilateral contract between two counterparties under which any obligation to each other to deliver a given currency on a given date is automatically amalgamated with all other obligations for the same currency and value date, legally substituting one single net amount for the previous gross obligations.

[7] Close-out as defined in this context refers to a bilateral contract which provides that, if one of the counterparties is wound up, the outstanding obligations between the two are accelerated and netted to determine the counterparty's net exposure.

ANNEX

decisions in the courts support the integrity of close-out netting agreements.[8] In any event, the Committee will continue its work to assess the acceptability of various forms of netting.

Once the bank has calculated the credit equivalent amounts, whether according to the current or the original exposure method, they are to be weighted according to the category of counterparty in the same way as in the main framework, including concessionary weighting in respect of exposures backed by eligible guarantees and collateral. In addition, since most counterparties in these markets, particularly for long-term contracts, tend to be first-class names, it has been agreed that a 50 per cent weight will be applied in respect of counterparties which would otherwise attract a 100 per cent weight.[9] However, the Committee will keep a close eye on the credit quality of participants in these markets and reserves the right to raise the weights if average credit quality deteriorates or if loss experience increases.

---

[8] The other principal form of netting, payments netting, which is designed to reduce the counterparty risk arising out of daily settlements, will not be recognised in the capital framework since the counterparty's gross obligations are not in any way affected.

[9] Some member countries reserve the right to apply the full 100 per cent weight.

Transitional Arrangements

	Initial	End-1990	End-1992
1. Minimum standard	The level prevailing at end 1987.	7.25%	8.0%
2. Measurement formula	Core elements plus 100%	Core elements plus 100% (3.625% plus 3.625%)	Core elements plus 100% (4% plus 4%)
3. Supplementary elements included in core	Maximum 25% of total core	Maximum 10% of total core (i.e. 0.36%)	None
4. Limit on general loan loss reserves in supplementary elements*	No limit	1.5 percentage points, or exceptionally up to 2.0 percentage points	1.25 percentage points, or exceptionally and temporarily up to 2.0 percentage points
5. Limit on term subordinated debt in supplementary elements	No limit (at discretion)	No limit (at discretion)	Maximum of 50% of Tier 1
6. Deduction for goodwill	Deducted from Tier 1 (at discretion)	Deducted from Tier 1 (at discretion)	Deducted from Tier 1

Annex 4

*This limit would only apply in the event that no agreement is reached on a consistent basis for including unencumbered provisions or reserves in capital (see paragraphs 20 and 21).

Glossary

Adjustable-rate preferred stock. See "Floating-rate preferred stock."

Auction-rate preferred stock. A type of floating-rate preferred stock whose dividend rate is based on the issuer's current credit rating. This dividend rate is reset periodically.

Basis swap. A type of interest rate swap in which the contracting parties exchange obligations to make floating interest rate payments. These payments are tied to various interest rate indexes.

Basle Agreement. The agreement on risk-based capital adequacy standards for commercial banks reached by central banking authorities from the United States, Western Europe, and Japan. It was finalized in July 1988 at the Bank for International Settlements in Basle, Switzerland. The Federal Reserve Board's final risk-based capital regulations are based on this agreement. Regulations that have been (or will be) issued by other U.S. federal banking regulators and by banking regulators in Western Europe and Japan are based on the Basle Agreement.

Basle Committee. The Committee on Banking Regulation and Supervisory Practices of the Bank for International Settlements, located in Basle, Switzerland. The committee consists of representatives from the central banks of the United States, Japan, and most Western European countries. The Basle Committee was responsible for drafting the Basle Agreement. Also called the Cooke Committee after its chairman, Peter Cooke, of the Bank of England.

Capital. Most generally, the difference between total assets and total liabilities (also known in this sense as net worth). In the context of banking regulation, those items included in the numerator when the capital/asset ratio is calculated.

Capital/asset ratio. The amount of capital maintained, divided by the total assets owned. Also known as a leverage ratio or gearing ratio.

Capital/risk-weighted assets ratio. The amount of capital maintained, divided by the sum of 1) the total assets owned, where the value of each asset is assigned a risk weight and 2) the credit equivalent amount of all off-balance-sheet activities, where each credit equivalent amount is assigned a risk weight.

Collateralized mortgage obligation. A type of pay-through mortgage-backed security that gives the holder a security interest in, but not ownership of, the underlying assets. Returns on a CMO are tied directly to returns on the underlying assets. Each CMO issue is divided into different maturity classes, called tranches.

Common stock. Shares of ownership in the issuing corporation that entitle the holder to dividend distributions made by the issuer. Common stock counts as Tier One capital.

Core capital. See "Tier One capital."

Counterparty. The other or opposite party to a contract.

Credit conversion factor. A percentage amount (100, 50, 20, or 0 percent) applied to the full face value of off-balance-sheet activities other than interest or foreign exchange rate contracts (and thus other than swaps) to determine a credit equivalent amount.

Credit enhancements. A generic term for collateral, letters of credit, guarantees, and other contractual mechanisms aimed at reducing the credit risk to which a creditor is exposed.

Credit equivalent amount. The deemed actual credit exposure arising from an off-balance-sheet activity. A credit conversion factor is applied to the full face value of the activity. A risk weight is then applied to the credit equivalent amount to calculate the risk-weighted value for the activity.

Credit risk. The risk that the counterparty will fail to make good on its obligations. Stated differently, the risk of counterparty default.

Cross-currency interest rate swap. An exchange of obligations between two parties. The first party agrees to make payments on an obligation incurred by the counterparty, and vice versa. The payments made by each party are in different currencies, and one party's payments are tied to a floating interest rate index while the other party's payments are fixed.

Cumulative perpetual preferred stock. See "Perpetual preferred stock."

Currency risk. The risk of financial loss from an adverse foreign exchange rate movement. Also called foreign exchange rate risk.

Currency swap. An exchange of obligations between two parties. The first party agrees to make payments on an obligation incurred by the counterparty, and vice versa. The payments made by each party are in different currencies.

Current credit exposure. The mark-to-market value of a foreign exchange rate contract or interest rate contract.

Current exposure method. The method prescribed in the Basle Agreement to calculate the credit equivalent amount on foreign exchange and interest rate contracts (and thus on all swaps). It involves calculation of the current credit exposure and the potential future credit exposure. The sum of these is the replacement cost, which is taken to be the credit equivalent amount. A risk weight is then applied to this amount.

Disclosed reserves. Reserves that are created or increased by appropriations of retained earnings or other surplus disclosed on the balance sheet. Essentially, disclosed reserves consist of retained earnings and paid-in capital in excess of par value (or capital surplus if no-par stock is issued).

Equity capital. Under the Basle Agreement, equity capital consists of common stock, noncumulative perpetual preferred stock, and (for bank holding companies) cumulative perpetual preferred stock.

Floating-rate preferred stock. Preferred stock whose yield varies with a certain index. The index may be a market interest rate, the issuer's credit standing, or the issuer's financial condition. Also called adjustable-rate preferred stock. See also "auction-rate preferred stock."

Foreign exchange rate contracts. The generic term in the Basle Agreement for cross-currency interest rate swaps, forward foreign exchange contracts, currency futures, currency options, and similar instruments. Exchange rate contracts with an original maturity of 14 days or less are excluded.

Foreign exchange rate risk. See "Currency risk."

Gearing ratio. See "Capital/asset ratio."

General provisions and general loan loss reserves. Provisions and reserves that are held against future unidentified losses and are freely available to meet any subsequent losses. At present, general but not specific reserves and provisions can be included without limit in Tier Two capital. The Basle Committee is attempting to develop a standard for differentiating general from specific provisions and reserves. If no standard exists by the end of 1990, the amount of provisions and reserves that can be included in Tier Two will be limited to 1.25 percent of the value of risk-weighted assets.

Goodwill. An intangible asset reflecting the excess of the purchase price over the fair market value of net assets in an acquisition in which the purchase method of accounting is used.

Hedging. Reducing or eliminating the risk arising from 1) an asset, 2) an off-balance-sheet activity, or 3) the mismatch between the payment streams associated with an asset and an off-balance-sheet activity. A bank may achieve the reduction or elimination by purchasing or selling another asset or entering into another off-balance-sheet transaction. It occurs because 1) the prices of the two assets or off-balance-sheet items move in opposite directions or 2) the income stream from one off-balance-sheet item matches the stream of payments owed on a liability.

Hidden reserves. See "Undisclosed reserves."

Hybrid instrument. Financial instruments that combine features of debt and equity. An example is mandatory convertible debt. Hybrid instruments may be included in Tier Two capital.

Interest only/principal only. See "Stripped mortgage-backed security."

Interest rate contracts. The generic term in the Basle Agreement for single-currency interest rate swaps, basis swaps, forward rate agreements, interest rate futures, interest rate options (including caps, collars, and floors), and similar instruments.

Interest rate risk. The risk of financial loss from an adverse interest rate movement.

Interest rate swap. An exchange of obligations between two parties. The first party agrees to make payments on an obligation incurred by the counterparty, and vice versa. The payments made by each party are tied to different interest rates. One party's payments are tied to a floating interest rate index while the other party's payments are fixed. Also called a plain vanilla swap.

Leverage ratio. See "Capital/asset ratio."

Limited life preferred stock. Preferred stock with a stated maturity.

Loan loss provisions. See "General provisions and general loan loss reserves."

Loss absorption. The reduction in a capital account that corresponds with the reduction in an asset account.

Mark-to-market value. The current market value of an item.

Mortgage-backed security. Securities backed by an underlying pool of mortgages. There are three types of mortgage-backeds: pass-throughs, mortgage-backed bonds, and pay-throughs.

Netting. Treating several transactions between the same counterparties not individually but as a whole. That is, considering the net claim arising from all transactions between the same counterparties rather than the gross claims. There are two forms of netting. In payment netting, the parties keep track of the cumulative net balance owed, but each underlying obligation remains in force. Netting by novation involves a written bilateral contract under which any obligation to make payments to the other party is automatically amalgamated with all other obligations of the same type (e.g., same currency and interest rate index). One single net obligation (the novated contract) replaces (extinguishes), in fact and in law, the several previous gross obligations.

Netting by novation. See "Netting."

Noncumulative perpetual preferred stock. See "Perpetual preferred stock."

Obligor. The party obligated to perform on a contract.

Payment netting. See "Netting."

Perpetual preferred stock. Preferred stock that has no fixed maturity and cannot be redeemed at the holder's option. Perpetual preferred stock may be noncumulative, which means that dividends do not accrue (if they are not paid, they do not accumulate as arrearages). By contrast, unpaid dividends on cumulative perpetual preferred stock do accrue and must be paid off before any dividends on common stock are paid.

Plain vanilla swap. See "Interest rate swap."

Potential future credit exposure. An estimate of the credit exposure on a foreign exchange rate contract or interest rate contract over the remaining life of the contract.

Preferred stock. Stock that entitles the holder to a preference in dividend distributions and/or a liquidation distribution over common stockholders. See "Limited life preferred stock" and "Perpetual preferred stock."

Replacement cost. The cost to the nondefaulting party of replacing the cash flows that it was entitled to under a foreign exchange or interest rate contract (such as a swap) but that were lost because of counterparty default. The credit risk on swaps is operationalized as replacement cost in the Basle Agreement.

Revaluation reserves. Reserve accounts on the right-hand side of the balance sheet that are increased whenever an asset on the left-hand side is revalued to reflect its market value. A revaluation reserve thus reflects the unrealized appreciation in an asset. The full amount of unrealized appreciation of fixed assets may be included in Tier Two capital, as may 45 percent of the unrealized appreciation of common stock. (U.S. banks and bank holding companies are not permitted to revalue assets, but banking organizations in some other countries, such as Japan, are permitted to do so.)

GLOSSARY

Risk weight. A percentage amount (0, 10, 20, 50 or 100 percent) applied to the full value of each on-balance-sheet asset and the credit equivalent amount of each off-balance-sheet activity.

Risk-weighted assets. The denominator of the capital/risk-weighted assets ratio. This denominator consists of the sum of 1) the risk-weighted amounts of all on-balance-sheet assets and 2) the risk-weighted credit equivalent amounts of all off-balance sheet activities.

Stripped mortgage-backed security. A type of mortgage-backed security where payments of interest and principal are wholly or partially separated into two different parts. The holder of the interest rate portion will receive only or almost exclusively interest rate payments, while the holder of the principal portion will receive only or almost exclusively principal payments. Interest only/principal only securities are a type of stripped mortgage-backed security.

Subordinated term debt. Fixed-term debt obligations that are subordinated in some way to other securities of the issuer. Examples include subordinated debentures and limited life preferred stock. The amount of subordinated term debt that can be included in Tier Two is limited to 50 percent of the value of Tier One. Further, the amount of any particular subordinated term debt instrument that can be included diminishes as the instrument nears maturity. Specifically, during the final five years of any subordinated term debt instrument's life, a 20-percent discount is applied.

Supplementary capital. See "Tier Two capital."

Swap. An exchange of obligations between two parties. See "Cross-currency interest rate swap," "Currency swap," and "Interest rate swap."

Tier One capital. The sum of equity capital and disclosed reserves, as adjusted. The adjustments involve goodwill and cumulative perpetual preferred stock. Goodwill must be deducted from the sum of equity capital and disclosed reserves (although there is an exception for supervisory mergers and a grandfathering provision for goodwill acquired before March 12, 1988). Bank holding companies may include cumulative perpetual preferred stock in Tier One. Also known as core capital.

Tier Two capital. The sum of general provisions and general loan loss reserves, hybrid debt/equity instruments, revaluation reserves, subordinated term debt, and undisclosed reserves. Also known as supplementary capital.

Total capital. The numerator of the capital/risk-weighted assets ratio. This numerator consists of the sum of Tier One capital, as adjusted, the Tier Two capital, minus investments in certain unconsolidated subsidiaries.

Undisclosed reserves. Accumulated after-tax retained profits that are not disclosed on a balance sheet. The Federal Reserve Board does not permit U.S. banks or bank holding companies to maintain undisclosed reserves. Regulators in other countries, such as Japan, do allow their banking organizations to maintain Undisclosed Reserves. These may be included in Tier Two. Also known as hidden reserves.

Bibliography

Listed here are the sources that were used in the preparation of this book. While it is not a comprehensive list of all reference material on risk-based capital, it should be of help to those who wish to pursue further research in bank capital regulation.

Books

Altman, E. "Managing the Commercial Lending Process." In *Handbook for Banking Strategy*, edited by R. Aspinwall and R. Eisenbeis. New York: John Wiley, 1985.

Andersen, T. *Currency and Interest Rate Hedging*. New York: New York Institute of Finance, 1987.

Beidleman, C. *Financial Swaps*. New York: Dow Jones-Irwin, 1985.

Benston, G., and G. Kaufman. "Risks and Failures in Banking." In *Deregulating Financial Services*, edited by G. Kaufman and R. Kormendi. Cambridge, Mass.: Ballinger, 1986.

Bollenbacher, G. *U.S. Government Securities Markets*. New York: New York Institute of Finance, 1988.

Brealey, R., and S. Myers. *Principles of Corporate Finance*, 3d ed. New York: McGraw-Hill, 1988.

Brigham, E., and L. Gapenski. *Intermediate Financial Management*. Chicago: Dryden, 1985.

Brudney, V., and M. Chirelstein. *Corporate Finance*, 3d ed. Mineola, N.Y.: Foundation Press, 1987.

Calmari, J., and J. Perillo *Contracts*, 3d ed. St. Paul, Minn.: West, 1987.

Dauber, N., J. Siegel, and J. Shim. *The Vest-Pocket CPA*. Englewood Cliffs, N.J.: Prentice Hall, 1988.

Friesen, C. *International Bank Supervision*. London: Euromoney, 1986.

Golembe, C., and D. Holland. *Federal Regulation of Banking 1986-87*. Washington, D.C.: Golembe Associates, Inc., 1986.

Heggestad, A. "Fundamentals of Mergers and Acquisitions." In *Handbook for Banking Strategy*, edited by R. Aspinwall and R. Eisenbeis. New York: John Wiley, 1985.

Henderson, S., and J. Price. *Currency and Interest Rate Swaps*. London: Butterworths, 1984.

Jackson, T. *The Logic and Limits of Bankruptcy Law*. Cambridge, Mass.: Harvard University Press, 1986.

Jones, E., and D. Jones. *Hedging Foreign Exchange*. New York: John Wiley, 1987.

Kieso, D., and J. Weygandt. *Intermediate Accounting*, 5th ed. New York: John Wiley, 1986.

Koch, T. *Bank Management*. Chicago: Dryden, 1988.

Maisel, S. *Risk and Capital Adequacy in Commercial Banks*. Chicago: University of Chicago Press, 1981.

Manning, B. *Legal Capital*. Mineola, N.Y.: Foundation Press, 1981.

Merten's Law of Federal Income Taxation. Vol. 11. Deerfield, Ill.: Callaghan, 1987.

Mosich, A., and E. Larsen. *Intermediate Accounting*, 6th ed. New York: McGraw-Hill, 1986.

Nagel, R., and B. Petersen. "Capitalization Problems in Perspective." In *Handbook for Banking Strategy*, edited by R. Aspinwall and R. Eisenbeis. New York: John Wiley, 1985.

Rosenthal, J., and J. Ocampo. *Securitization of Credit*. New York: John Wiley, 1988.

Roussakis, E. *Commercial Banking in an Era of Deregulation*. New York: Praeger, 1984.

Ryan, R. "Interest Rate and Currency Swaps." In vol. 1, *The International Financial Markets Institute*. Practicing Law Institute, 1984.

Scott, H. "Securitization of Assets by Banks." In *Current Developments in International Banking and Corporate Financial Operation*, edited by National University of Singapore. 1989 (forthcoming).

Sinkey, J., Jr. "Regulatory Attitudes Toward Risk." In *Handbook for Banking Strategy*, edited by R. Aspinwall and R. Eisenbeis. New York: John Wiley, 1985.

Slighton, R. "International Risk Management." In *Handbook for Banking Strategy*, edited by R. Aspinwall and R. Eisenbeis. New York: John Wiley, 1985.

Sprague, I. *Bailout*. New York: Basic Books, 1986.

Wolkowitz, B. "Managing Interest Rate Risk." In *Handbook for Banking Strategy*, edited by R. Aspinwall and R. Eisenbeis. New York: John Wiley, 1985.

Journal Articles

Areskoug, K. "Common Bank Capital Standards: A Step Toward Global Financial Integration." *The Journal of International Securities Markets* **2** (Summer 1988): 147-150.

Arnold, T. "How to Do Interest Rate Swaps." *Harvard Business Review* **62** (Sept./Oct. 1984): 96-101.

Avery, R., and T. Belton. "A Comparison of Risk-Based Capital and Risk-Based Deposit Insurance." Federal Reserve Bank of Cleveland *Economic Review* (1987 Quarter 4): 20-30.

Baestaens, D. "A Critical Look at the Recent U.S.-U.K. Agreement on Bank Capital Requirements." *The Journal of International Securities Markets* **1** (Autumn 1987): 47-57.

Balkin, J. "Deconstructive Practice and Legal Theory." *Yale Law Journal* **96** (March 1987): 743-786.

Bardos, J. "The Risk-Based Capital Agreement: A Further Step Toward Policy Convergence." Federal Reserve Bank of New York *Quarterly Review* **12** (Winter 1987-88): 26-34.

Barker, B. "Hedging Techniques for Interest Rate and Currency Risks." *Banking and Finance Law Review* **3** (October 1988): 37-53.

Benston, G. "The Problems and Future of Commercial Banks." *Midland Corporate Finance Journal* **5** (Winter 1988): 6-13.

———. "Why Continue to Regulate Banks?: An Historical Assessment of Federal Banking Regulation." *Midland Corporate Finance Journal* **5** (Fall 1987): 67-82.

Bicksler, J., and A. Chen. "An Economic Analysis of Interest Rate Swaps." *The Journal of Finance* **41** (July 1986): 645-655.

"BIS Proposals for Capital Measurement and Capital Standards." *The World of Banking* **7** (Jan./Feb. 1988): 16-22.

Burgess, R. "Sterling Debt Securities in the Mid-1980s." *The Journal of Business Law* (July 1986): 268-275.

Cates, D. "Bank Analysis: Why Measures of Performance Don't Work." *Bank Accounting and Finance* **1** (Fall 1987): 26-33.

———. "Bank Risk and Predicting Bank Failure." *Issues in Bank Regulation* **9** (Autumn 1985): 16-20.

Celarier, M. "Capital Ideas." *Global Finance* (February 1988): 54-59.

Chandler, C. "Risk-Based Capital Guidelines: Issues and Implications." *Issues in Bank Regulation* **12** (Fall 1988): 5-7.

Chessen, J. "Market Perceptions of Bank Risk." *Issues in Bank Regulation* **9** (Autumn 1985): 3-15.

———. "Risk-Based Capital Comes to the Fore." *Issues in Bank Regulation* **10** (Spring 1987): 3-15.

Comiskey, E., C. Mulford, and D. Turner. "Bank Accounting and Reporting Practices for Interest Rate Swaps." *Bank Accounting and Finance* **1** (Winter 1987-88): 3-14.

"Convergence of Capital Adequacy in the U.K. and the U.S." Bank of England *Quarterly Bulletin* **27** (February 1987): 85-86.

Cooper, K. "Coming to Grips with Off-Balance-Sheet Risks." *The Bankers Magazine* **168** (Nov./Dec. 1985): 32-35.
Corrigan, E. "Are Banks Special?" Federal Reserve Bank of Minneapolis *Annual Report* 1982, 2-18.
———. "Bank Supervision in a Changing Financial Environment." Federal Reserve Bank of New York *Quarterly Review* **10** (Winter 1985-86): 1-5.
Countryman, V. "Executory Contracts in Bankruptcy." *Minnesota Law Review* **57** (1973): 439.
Cunningham, D. "Swaps: Codes, Problems and Regulation." *International Financial Law Review* **5** (August 1986): 26-35.
Danielsson, S. "A Supervisory View of the Role of Capital and Capital Adequacy." *Issues in Bank Regulation* **9** (Spring 1986): 11-15.
Dince, R., and J. Fortson. "Bank Examination, Capital Adequacy and Risk." *The Bankers Magazine* **163** (May/June 1980): 49-54.
Ehlen, J. "A Review of Bank Capital and its Adequacy." Federal Reserve Bank of Atlanta *Economic Review* **68** (November 1983): 54-61.
Elliot, J. "Capital Planning for Regulatory Purposes." *Issues in Bank Regulation* **9** (Spring 1986): 16-22.
Felgram, S. "Interest Rate Swaps: Use, Risk, and Prices." Federal Reserve Bank of Boston *New England Economic Review* (November-December 1987): 22-32.
Ferron, M., and G. Handjinicolaou. "Understanding Swap Credit Risk: The Simulation Approach." *The Journal of International Security Markets* **1** (Winter 1987): 135-148.
Fischel, D., A. Rosenfield, and R. Stillman. "The Regulation of Banks and Bank Holding Companies." *Virginia Law Review* **73** (March 1987): 301-338.
Flammia, M. "Bank Capital Requirements: Placebo or Cure?" *Annual Review of Banking Law* **7** (1988): 485-503.
Fried, Frank, Harris, Shriver and Jacobson Law Firm. "Financial Services Update: Capital Requirements of Financial Institutions." (October 1988).

Friesen, C. "Capital Guidelines and Global Markets." *The Review of Financial Services Regulation* **4** (July 1988): 123-132.

Furlong, F. "Changes in Bank Risk-Taking." Federal Reserve Bank of San Francisco *Economic Review* (Spring 1988): 45-56.

Furlong, F., and M. Keeley. "Bank Capital Regulation and Asset Risk." Federal Reserve Bank of San Francisco *Economic Review* (September 1987): 20-33.

Gardener, E. "A British View of Bank Capital Adequacy in Europe." *Issues in Bank Regulation* **9** (Spring 1986): 21-40.

———. "Securitization: The Challenge for World Banking." *The World of Banking* **7** (Jan./Feb. 1988): 3-6.

Gdanski, M. "French Interest Rate and Currency Swaps." *International Financial Law Review* **7** (September 1988): 23-26.

Gendreau, B. "Interest Rate and Currency Swaps." *Commercial Lending Review* **1** (Fall 1986): 47-54.

Gooch, A., and L. Klein. "Damage Provisions in Swap Agreements." *International Financial Law Review* **3** (October 1984): 36-40.

Graham, F., and J. Horner. "Bank Failure." *Issues in Bank Regulation* **12** (Fall 1988): 8-12.

Haberman, G. "Capital Requirements of Commercial and Investment Banks: Contrasts in Regulation." Federal Reserve Bank of New York *Quarterly Review* (Autumn 1987): 1-10.

Hammond, G. "Recent Developments in the Swap Market." Bank of England *Quarterly Bulletin* **27** (February 1987): 66-79.

Hedges, R., Jr. "The Loan Loss Reserve Decisions of 1987." *Bank Accounting and Finance* **1** (Winter 1987-88): 47-53.

Henderson, S. "Governmental Responses to Bank Risk in the International Capital Markets." *Butterworths Journal of International Banking Law* **1** (September 1986): 21.28.

———. "Has Credit Risk Increased or Decreased, and How Are Banks Reacting?" *Butterworths Journal of International Banking and Financial Law* **2** (April 1987): 15-16.

———. "Swap Credit Risk: A Multi-Perspective Analysis." Paper submitted to the Singapore Conference on Current Developments in International Banking and Corporate Financial Operations, 1988.

———. "Termination of Swaps Under U.S. Insolvency Laws." *International Financial Law Review* **3** (December 1984): 17-21.

———. "Termination Provisions of Swap Agreements." *International Financial Law Review* **2** (September 1983): 22-27.

Henderson, S., and L. Klein. "Glossary of Terms Used in Connection with Rate Swap, Currency Swap, Cap and Collar Agreements." *Butterworths Journal of International Banking Law* (June 1987 Supplement): 2.

———. "A User's Guide to ISDA Master Swap Agreements." *The Journal of International Securities Markets* **1** (Autumn 1987): 41-45.

Houghton, J. "Regulatory Provisions on Off-Balance-Sheet Capital Requirements: Netting Off Arrangements—The Legal Perspective." *Journal of International Banking Law* **2** (1987): 241-252.

Howcroft, J. "U.K. Bank Capital Adequacy and the Convergent Proposals." *Journal of International Banking Law* **2** (1987): 203-207.

Huertas, T., and R. Strauber. "Risk-Based Capital Requirements: Should They Apply to Bank Holding Companies?" *Issues in Bank Regulation* **12** (Summer 1988): 8-12.

Hull, J. "The Management of a Bank's Off-Balance-Sheet Exposures: The Case of Interest Rate Swaps." *Banking and Finance Law Review* **2** (1987-88): 47-60.

Humphrey, S., and D. Humphrey. "How Risk-Based Capital Will Affect Bank Operations." *The Bankers Magazine* **171** (March/April 1988): 22-27.

International Convergence of Capital Measurement and Capital Standards." *Issues in Bank Regulation* **12** (Fall 1988): 3-4.

Isaac, W. "Capital Adequacy and Deposit Insurance." *Annual Review of Banking Law* **1** (1982): 59-64.

Jenkins, J., and J. Binkly. "Accounting for Foreign Loan Swaps." *Bank Accounting and Finance* **1** (Winter 1987-88): 54-57.

Johnson, S., and A. Murphy. "Going Off the Balance Sheet." Federal Reserve Bank of Atlanta *Economic Review* **72** (Sept./Oct. 1987): 23-33.

Keeley, M. "Bank Capital Regulation in the 1980s: Effective or Ineffective?" Federal Reserve Bank of San Francisco *Economic Review* (Winter 1988): 3-20.

Kennedy, D. "Form and Substance in Private Law Adjudication." *Harvard Law Review* **89** (1976): 1685-1778.

Khoury, S., and K. Chan. "Hedging Foreign Exchange Risk: Selecting the Optimal Tool." *Midland Corporate Finance Journal* **5** (Winter 1988): 40-58.

Kim, D., and A. Santomero. "Risk in Banking and Capital Regulation." *The Journal of Finance* **43** (December 1988): 1219-1233.

Klein, W. "The Convertible Bond: A Peculiar Package." *University of Pennsylvania Law Review* **123** (1975): 547-573.

"Legal Doctrines Restricting the Secondary Market in Interest Rate Swaps." *Columbia Journal of Transnational Law* **26** (October 1988): 313-335.

Lereah, D. "The Growth of Interest Rate Swaps." *The Bankers Magazine* **169** (May/June 1986): 36-41.

Lichtenstein, C. "Introductory Note [to December 1987 Basle Proposal]." *International Legal Materials* **27** (1988): 524-529.

Macey, J., and G. Miller. "Bank Failures, Risk Monitoring, and the Market for Bank Control." *Columbia Law Review* **88** (October 1988): 1153-1226.

Malloy, M. "U.S. International Banking and the New Capital Adequacy Requirements: New, Old and Unexpected." *Annual Review of Banking Law* **7** (1988): 75-122.

Marino, J. "Comparison of Failed and Healthy Bank Capital Ratios: An Update." Federal Deposit Insurance Corporation *Economic Outlook* (November 1985): 26.

McGarry, S. "The Taxation of Exchange Gains and Losses: A Road Map." *The International Tax Journal* **14** (Winter 1988): 25-51.

McLaughlin, M., and M. Wolfson. "The Profitability of Insured Commercial Banks in 1987." *Federal Reserve Bulletin* (July 1988): 403-418.

McMahon, R. "Understanding Interest Rate Swaps." *The Bankers Magazine* **171** (Sept./Oct. 1988): 59-62.

Modigliani, F., and M. Miller. "The Cost of Capital, Corporation Finance and the Theory of Investment." *American Economic Review* (June 1958): 261.

Morris, C., and T. Merfeld. "New Methods for Savings and Loans to Hedge Interest Rate Risk." Federal Reserve Bank of Kansas City *Economic Review* **73** (March 1988): 3-15.

Moulton, J. "New Guidelines for Bank Capital: An Attempt to Reflect Risk." Federal Reserve Bank of Philadelphia *Business Review* (July/August 1987): 19-33.

Mullins, D. "Does the Capital Asset Pricing Model Work?" *Harvard Business Review* **60** (Jan./Feb. 1982): 105-114.

Murray, P., and B. Hadaway. "Mortgage-Backed Securities: An Investigation of Legal and Financial Issues." *The Journal of Corporate Law* **11** (Winter 1986): 203.

Neal, K., and K. Simons. "Interest Rate Swaps, Currency Swaps and Credit Risk." *Issues in Bank Regulation* **11** (Spring 1988): 26-29.

Nelson, J. "New Euromarket Products: RUFs, NIFs, and Eurocommercial Paper." *Commercial Lending Review* **1** (Summer 1986): 9-17.

Nicolaides, C. "Overview of the 1986 ISDA Rate Swap Code." *Butterworths Journal of International Banking and Financial Law* **1** (September 1986): 44-49.

Noonan, J., and S. Fetner. "Capital and Capital Standards." Federal Reserve Bank of Atlanta *Economic Review* **68** (November 1983): 50-53.

Orr, B. "The Fed Drops the Other Shoe." *ABA Banking Journal* **80** (October 1988): 124-131.

Parseghian, G. "Collateralised Mortgage Obligations: A Primer." *The Journal of International Securities Markets* **87** (Winter 1987): 87.

Peck, R. "Swap Programmes for Correspondent Banks." *International Financial Law Review* **4** (December 1985): 27-30.

Pemberton, L. "Convergence of Capital Standards and the Lessons of the Market Crash." Bank of England *Quarterly Bulletin* **28** (May 1988): 220-224.

Penn, G. "Sterling Commercial Paper." *Banking and Finance Law Review* **1** (1987-88): 195-209.

"Playing by the Same Rules." *Banking World* **6** (January 1988): 12.

Pollard, A. "Treatment of Swaps in Bankruptcy." *Butterworths Journal of International Banking and Financial Law* **3** (December 1988): 514-515.

"Proposals for International Convergence of Capital Measurement and Capital Standards." *Butterworths Journal of International Banking and Financial Law* **3** (April 1988): 343-346.

"Proposals for International Convergence of Capital Measurement and Capital Standards." *Issues in Bank Regulation* **11** (Winter 1988): 3-12.

"Proposed Risk-Based Capital System Developed by U.S. Regulators and the Bank of England." *Issues in Bank Regulation* **10** (Winter 1987): 3-4.

Putnam, B. "Concepts of Financial Monitoring." Federal Reserve Bank of Atlanta *Economic Review* **68** (November 1983): 6-12.

BIBLIOGRAPHY

Roberts, W., and R. Rosholt. "Risk-Adjusted Capital: How Can Banks Cope?" *Bank Accounting and Finance* **1** (Summer 1988): 29-40.

Robinson, C., and A. White. "Guaranteed Preferred Shares — Debt or Equity." *Banking and Finance Law Review* **1** (1987-88): 211-223.

Saunders, A., and I. Walter. "Are Banks Special?" *The Journal of International Security Markets* **1** (Winter 1987): 171-176.

Schimberg, A., J. Clark, and D. Williams. "Legislative and Judicial Developments in 1987: Part 1." *The Secured Lender* **44** (Jan./Feb. 1988): 20-32.

Schlag, P. "Rules and Standards." *UCLA Law Review* **33** (1985): 379-430.

Short, E. "Bank Problems and Financial Safety Nets." Federal Reserve Bank of Dallas *Economic Review* (March 1987): 17-28.

Silverberg, S. "Regulation of Bank Capital." *Issues in Bank Regulation* **9** (Spring 1986): 7-10.

Spencer, D. "Capital Adequacy: Towards a Level Playing Field." *International Financial Law Review* **7** (March 1988): 19-23.

Swegle, R. "Push-Down Accounting: Its Impact on Bank Capital." *Bank Accounting and Finance* **1** (Winter 1987-88): 28-31.

Taylor, B. "Swaps: A Creditor's Perspective on Rate Risk." *The Journal of International Securities Markets.* **1** (August 1987): 33-39.

———. "Swap Risk." *The Review of Financial Services Regulation* **4** (February 3, 1988): 17-28.

Topping, S. "Commercial Paper Markets: An International Survey." Bank of England *Quarterly Bulletin* **27** (February 1987): 46-53.

Wall, L. "Regulation of Banks' Equity Capital." Federal Reserve Bank of Atlanta *Economic Review* **70** (November 1985): 4-18.

Wall, L., and R. Eisenbeis. "Risk Considerations in Deregulating Bank Activities." *Federal Reserve Bank of Atlanta Economic Review* **69** (May 1984): 6-19.

Walter, I. "Country Risk and International Bank Lending." *University of Illinois Law Review* 1982: 71-88.

Weinrib, E. "Legal Formalism: On the Immanent Rationality of Law." *Yale Law Journal* **97** (May 1988): 949-1016.

Whittaker, J. "Interest Rate Swaps: Risk and Regulation." *Federal Reserve Bank of Kansas City Economic Review* **72** (March 1987): 3-13.

Wilson, J. "The Morality of Formalism." *UCLA Law Review* **33** (1985): 431-484.

Wood, P. "International Convertible Bond Issues." *Journal of International Banking Law* **1** (1986): 69-76.

Woolridge, J., and K. Shuey. "Floating Rate Preferred Stock —An Innovation in Bank Capital." *The Bankers Magazine* **166** (May/June 1983): 78-80.

Young, H. "Bank Capital Adequacy in the United States." *Issues in Bank Regulation* **9** (Spring 1986): 3-6.

———. "Bank Regulation Ain't Broke." *Harvard Business Review* **64** (Sept./Oct. 1986): 106-112.

Zavvos, G. "1992: One Market." *International Financial Law Review* **7** (March 1988): 7-11.

Official Documents

A. Accounting Principles Board (American Institute of Certified Public Accountants)

"Intangible Assets." Opinion Number 17, 1970.

B. Bank for International Settlements (Basle, Switzerland)

Committee on Banking Regulations and Supervisory Practices. "Proposals for International Convergence of Capital Measurement and Capital Standards." December 1987.

BIBLIOGRAPHY

———. "International Convergence of Capital Measurement and Capital Standards." July 1988.

C. Case Materials

Please refer to footnotes in the text for case law.

D. Federal Deposit Insurance Corporation

"Capital Maintenance; Final Statement of Policy on Risk-Based Capital." *Federal Register* **54** (final regulations, March 21, 1989): 11500-11517.

E. Federal Financial Institutions Examination Council (Washington, D.C.)

"Interest Rate Swap Reporting Standards." *Federal Register* **53** (November 9, 1988): 45386-45388.

F. Federal Home Loan Bank Board (Washington, D.C.)

"Loss Prevention Rules Considered for Federally Insured Thrifts." Federal Home Loan Bank Board News Release, November 28, 1988.

"Regulatory Capital Requirements for Insured Institutions." *Federal Register* **53** (December 23, 1988): 51800-51820.

"Required Capital Levels for Insured Institutions; Regulatory Intervention." *Federal Register* **54** (January 10, 1989): 826-830.

G. Federal Reserve System (Washington, D.C.)

"Bank Holding Companies and Change in Bank Control; Capital Maintenance; Supplemental Adjusted Capital Measure." *Federal Register* **51** (proposed January 31, 1986): 3976-3984.

"Bank Holding Companies and Change in Bank Control; Capital Maintenance; Supplemental Adjusted Capital Measure." *Federal Register* **51** (extension of comment period, April 16, 1986): 12865.

"Capital Maintenance; Revision to Capital Adequacy Guidelines." *Federal Register* **52** (proposed February 19, 1987): 5119-5139.

"Capital Maintenance; Revision to Capital Adequacy Guidelines." *Federal Register* **52** (proposed March 24, 1987): 9304-9312.

"Capital; Risk-Based Capital Guidelines." *Federal Register* **53** (proposed March 15, 1988): 8550-8587.

"Capital; Risk-Based Capital Guidelines." *Federal Register* **54** (final regulations, January 27, 1989): 4186-4221.

Memorandum Re: Risk-Based Capital (Taylor, Spillenkothen, Cornyn, O'Rourke, and Barger [Board]; and Spindler [New York]); (mimeo), August 1, 1988.

Memorandum Re: Risk-Based Capital Guidelines (Taylor, Spillenkothen, Cole, Pugh, O'Rourke, and Barger [Board]; and Spindler and Bardos [New York]); (mimeo), December 14, 1988.

"Potential Credit Exposure on Interest Rate and Foreign Exchange Rate Related Instruments," 1987.

H. International Swap Dealers Association (New York)

Code of Standard Wording, Assumptions and Provisions for Swaps, 1986.

de Saint-Aignan, Patrick, Chairman, ISDA. Letter to Brian Quinn, Head of Banking Supervision, Bank of England, and William Wiles, Secretary, Board of Governors of the Federal Reserve System, May 28, 1987.

"Interest Rate Swap Agreement," 1987.

"Interest Rate and Currency Exchange Agreement," 1987.

1987 Interest Rate and Currency Exchange Definitions, 1987.

User's Guide to the Standard Form Agreements, 1987.

I. Office of the Comptroller of the Currency

"Risk-Based Capital Guidelines." *Federal Register* **54** (final regulations, January 27, 1989): 4168-4184.

J. Securities and Exchange Commission (Washington, D.C.)

Rule 15(c)(3) (Net Equity Rule). Code of Federal Regulations, Title 17, Section 240.15c3-1.

K. State Statutes

Delaware General Corporation Law, Section 151(e).

New Jersey Statutes, Section 14A:7-9(1).
New York Business Corporation Law, Section 519(a)(1).
L. United States Statutes (United States Code)
Banking Statutes, Title 12, Sections 24, 335, 377, 378.
Bankruptcy Code, Title 11, Sections 101 *et seq.*
Internal Revenue Code, Title 26, Sections 368, 988.
M. United States Congress (Washington, D.C.)
(1) Bills
Senate Bill 2279, 100th Congress, 1st Session, 1988.
Senate Bill 1886, 100th Congress, 2d Session, 1988 (Financial Modernization Act of 1988).
(2) Reports
House Report No. 595, 95th Congress, 1st Session, 1977.
Senate Report No. 989, 95th Congress, 2nd Session, 1978.

Newspaper and Magazine Articles

"A Chill Over the Hot New Hybrids." *New York Times,* April 10, 1988.

"A Crisis Manager Takes on the Mechanics of the Market." *New York Times,* October 2, 1988.

"Agreement on Banks' Capital Set." *New York Times,* July 12, 1988, D1.

"Asset-Backed Securities." *International Financing Review,* June 18, 1988, 1921.

"Bank Capital Rule Expected to Slow the Pace of Lending." *New York Times,* July 13, 1988, D1.

"Banking System Will Be Safer with Higher Capital Requirements." *American Banker,* August 24, 1988, 4.

"Bank Loans for Buyouts to Be Placed Under Tighter Scrutiny by Regulators." *Wall Street Journal,* November 7, 1988, A3.

"Banks Given Deadline for Meeting Capital Standards Agreement." *Financial Times,* November 3, 1988, 12.

PERSPECTIVES ON RISK-BASED CAPITAL

"Banks May Suffer from LBO Loans, S&P Report Says." *Wall Street Journal,* December 5, 1988, C1.

"Banks' New Minimum Capital Rules Add to International Bankers' Worries." *Wall Street Journal,* July 12, 1988, 35.

"British Steel in the Bull's Eye." *Financial Times,* December 6, 1988, 27.

"Capital Ratio Is Set by Banks of 12 Nations." *Wall Street Journal,* July 12, 1988, 3.

"Central Bankers Approve Risk-Based Capital Plan." *American Banker,* July 12, 1988, 1.

"Central Banks Approve Risk-Based Capital Rules." *American Banker,* July 18, 1988, 9.

"Concern on 'Unbundled' Stock Units." *New York Times,* December 5, 1988, D1.

"Congress Is Moving Closer to Weighing Buyout Curbs," *New York Times,* December 5, 1988, D1.

"The Day the Nation's Cash Pipeline Almost Ran Dry." *New York Times,* October 2, 1988.

"Dow Rises by 31.48 to 2,123.76." *New York Times,* December 6, 1988, D1.

"'89 Will Bring Closer Scrutiny of Swap Products." *American Banker,* January 3, 1989.

"Fed Adopts Risk-Based Capital Guidelines; Will Also Propose Minimum Leverage Ratios." *BNA Banking Report,* January 2, 1989, 4.

"Fed Approves Rules Requiring More Capital at All Banks." *New York Times,* August 4, 1988, D2.

"Fed Clears Minimum Capital Standards, Forcing Some Banks to Raise $15 Billion." *Wall Street Journal,* July 12, 1988, 3.

"FFIEC May Require Banks to Recognize Interest Rate Swap Income Gradually." *BNA Banking Report,* November 14, 1988.

"Four Banks Ask Fed for Broad Powers to Underwrite, Deal in Corporate Issues." *Wall Street Journal,* October 26, 1988, A3.

BIBLIOGRAPHY

"Four Big Companies Set New Stock Unit Plans." *New York Times,* December 6, 1988, D6.

"Global Capital Adequacy." *International Financing Review,* May 7, 1988, 1438.

"Hard Times for Three Big Banks." *New York Times,* April 10, 1988, C1.

"Impact of Risk-Based Capital Rules to Be Eased." *American Banker,* October 28, 1988, 3.

"International Capital Markets: Just a Simple Idea." *Financial Times,* June 29, 1988, 5 (Survey Section).

"John McGillicuddy's Hot Seat." *Forbes,* April 25, 1988.

"John Reed's Bold Stroke." *Fortune,* June 22, 1987.

"Large U.S. Banks Should Easily Meet Fed's New Capital Rules, Analysts Say." *Wall Street Journal,* August 5, 1988, 20.

"ManHan's Answer to Reduce Risk Capital." *International Financing Review,* June 18, 1988, 1992.

"New Plan to Retire Companies' Equity." *Financial Times,* December 6, 1988, 27.

"New Tactic of Breaking Up Stocks Alters Landscape for Investors." *Wall Street Journal,* December 7, 1988, C2.

"New Wrinkle in Interest Swaps." *American Banker,* September 27, 1988.

"One Year After, the Market Lives but Matters Less." *New York Times,* October 2, 1988.

Osborn, N., and G. Evans. "Cooke's Medicine: Kill or Cure?" *Euromoney,* July 1988, 34.

"Risk-Based Capital Rules Will Not Require Capital Support for Ginnie Maes, Fed Official Says." *BNA Banking Report,* October 24, 1988.

"Shearson to Withdraw Unbundled Stock Plan." *Wall Street Journal,* March 29, 1989, C1.

"Some Big Firms to Break Up Stock Into New Securities." *Wall Street Journal,* December 5, 1988, C1.

"Stiffer Thrift Capital Rules Proposed by Bank Board." *Wall Street Journal,* December 20, 1988, A16.

"Stricter Thrift Capital Rules Are Proposed." *Wall Street Journal,* November 29, 1988, A4.

"Survey Shows Losses are Low in Swap Market." *American Banker,* July 20, 1988, 2.

"U.S. Banks Granted Concession in Basle." *Financial Times,* July 12, 1988.

Index

A
Asset/capital ratio, 99-101, 218
Asset growth, restraint by capital, 35-36

B
Bankruptcy, 152-163
Base-year bonds (BYBs), 70-76
Basic swaps, 105, 106, 120-124, 217. *See also* Swaps
Basle Agreement
  description, 5, 217
  regulations issued pursuant to, 6-12
  substance versus form, 12-15
  waps and, 133-142, 171-181
  text of, 193-216
Basle Committee, 217

C
Capital
  calculating total, 64-66, 245-249
  constituents of, under Basle Agreement, 197-203
  core or Tier One, 44-57, 64-66, 197-198
  definition, 218
  market determination of, 20-25
  regulatory-determined, 25-40
  supplementary or Tier Two, 57-66
Capital/asset ratio, 99-101, 218
Capital structure of bank, 17-40
Cherry picking, 157-160
Collateralized mortgage obligations (CMOs), 94-96, 218
Core capital, 44-57, 64-66, 197-198
Counterparty default, 147-163
Country risk, 82, 205-208
Credit enhancements, 171, 219
Credit risk, 31-32, 219
  mortgage-backed securities and, 88-94
  risked-weighting system and, 79-83
  swaps and, 147-171
  treasury securities and, 86-88
Cross-currency interest rate swaps, 106, 128-132, 219. *See also* Swaps
Cumulative perpetual preferred stock, 56-57, 223-224
Currency risk, 109-110, 144-147, 219
Currency swaps, 106, 124-128, 219. *See also* Swaps
Current exposure method (for valuing swaps), 173-178, 220

D
Debt/equity ratio, 17-20
Default, 147-163
Disclosed reserves as core capital, 49

E
Equity appreciation certificates (EACs), 70-76
Equity capital as core capital, 45-49

INDEX

F

Failures, prevention by capital, 32-34
FDIC, assistance by capital, 36-38
Federal Financial Institutions Examination Council (FFIEC) regulations, 138-142
Fixed/floating swaps, 103-105, 113-119, *See also* Swaps
Floating-rate preferred stock, 68
Floating/floating swaps, 105-106, 120-124. *See also* Swaps
Fraud risk, 31-32

G

Gearing (leverage) ratio, 99-101, 218
Goodwill, 49-56, 221
Guaranteed preferred shares, 67-68

H

Hostile takeovers, defense against, 73-74
Hybrid instruments, 61-63, 201, 221-222

I

Incremental dividend preferred shares (IDPs), 70-76
Interest rate risk
 definition, 222
 stripped mortgage-backed securities, 96-98, 225
 swaps as hedge against, 109-110, 144-147
 treasury securities, 86-88

Interest rate swaps, 103-105, 113-119, 222. *See also* Swaps
Internal Revenue Code Section 988, 142-144
International Swap Dealers Association (ISDA)
 Comment Letter of May 28, 1987, 181-186
 Master Agreements, 108-109, 163-168
 swap market and, 107-109
Investment risk, 31-32

L

Leverage
 ratio, 99-101, 218
 unbundled stock and, 74
Limited life preferred stock, 64
Liquidity risk, 31-32
Loan loss reserves as supplementary capital, 60-61, 199-201
Losses, absorption by capital, 43-66

M

Mandatory convertible debt instruments, 61-63
Market determination of capital, 20-25
Modigliani-Miller model, 17-20
Mortgage-backed securities, risk weights for, 88-94, 96-98

N

Netting, 168-171, 223
1986 Swaps Code, 108-109
Noncumulative perpetual preferred stock, 45-48, 223-224

267

O

Off-balance sheet items, risk weights for, 98-99
On-balance-sheet assets, risk categories, 83-86
Operating risk, 31-32
Original exposure method (for valuing swaps), 172-173

P

Pass-through certificates, 92-93
Pay-through bonds, 93
Payment netting, 168, 223
Perpetual preferred stock, 45-48, 56-57, 223-224

R

Regulatory-determined capital, 25-40
Revaluation reserves as supplementary capital, 59-60, 199
Risk. *See also particular risk type*
 categories under Basle Agreement, 204-205, 251-252
 effect of capital on, 31-32
Risk-weighting system
 Basle Agreement text, 204-212
 collateralized mortgage obligations, 94-96, 218
 definitions, 225
 gearing (leverage) ratio, 99-101, 218
 mortgage-backed securities, 88-94, 96-98
 off-balance-sheet items, 98-99, 255-261
 on-balance-sheet assets, 83-86

role of credit risk in, 79-83
stripped mortgage-backed securities, 96-98
treasury securities, 86-88

S

Status quo ante, 134-135, 149-151
Stock
 cumulative perpetual preferred, 56-57, 223-224
 floating-rate preferred, 68
 guaranteed preferred shares, 67-68
 limited life preferred, 64
 noncumulative perpetual preferred, 45-48, 223-224
 unbundled, 70-76
 upstream convertibles, 69-70
Stripped mortgage-backed securities, 96-98, 225
Subordinated term debt, 63-64, 201-202, 225
Supplementary capital, 57-64, 198-202, 226
Swaps
 bankruptcy and 152-153
 basis, 105-106, 120-124, 217
 brokerage, 111, 115, 117
 cherry picking, 157-160
 Code, 108-109
 cost reduction and, 110-111, 112-132
 counterparty default and, 147-163
 coverage under IRC Section 988, 142-144
 credit enhancements and, 171

INDEX

credit equivalent amount, 182-183, 219
credit risk, 147-181
cross-curency interest rate, 106, 128-132, 219
currency, 106, 124-128, 219
currency risk and, 109-110, 144, 147
definition and types, 103-107, 226
distinction from other off-balance-sheet items, 136
as executory contracts, 155-156
FFIEC regulations, 138-142
as financial accommodations, 157
hedging and, 109-110, 112-132
interest rate risk and, 109-110, 144-147
ISDA. *See* International Swap Dealers Association (ISDA)
netting, 168-171, 223
plain vanilla, 103-105, 113-119, 222
replacement cost, 171-177, 184-186, 224
required capital support, 177-181, 185
speculation and, 111-112
status quo ante and, 149-151
substantive functions, 109-132, 138-144
treatment by Basle Agreement, 133-142, 171-181
trustee's power to assume or reject, 157-160

T

Takeovers, defense against, 73-74
Tier One capital, 44-57, 64-66, 197-198
Tier Two capital, 57-64, 198-202, 226
Transitional arrangements, 263
Treasury securities, risk weights for, 86-88

U

Unbundled stock, 70-76
Undisclosed reserves as supplementary capital, 58-59, 226
Upstream convertibles, 69-70

269

About the Author

Raj Bhala will be joining the Legal Department of the Federal Reserve Bank of New York in the fall of 1989. He has held research positions at the World Bank, Harvard Law School, and Duke University. His professional interests include banking regulation, the regulation of financial markets, and commercial law.

Raj Bhala earned his bachelor's degree in economics summa cum laude from Duke University, where he was an Angier B. Duke Scholar and a member of Phi Beta Kappa. He won a Marshall Scholarship for graduate study in England. While there, he obtained a master's degree in economics from the London School of Economics and a master's degree in management from Oxford University. Raj Bhala recently received his J.D. from Harvard Law School.